ADVANCES IN
HUMAN ECOLOGY

Volume 1 • 1992

ADVANCES IN HUMAN ECOLOGY

A Research Annual

Editor: **LEE FREESE**
Department of Sociology
Washington State University

*PUBLISHED IN ASSOCIATION WITH THE
SOCIETY FOR HUMAN ECOLOGY*

VOLUME 1 • 1992

 **JAI PRESS INC.**

Greenwich, Connecticut   *London, England*

CONTENTS

LIST OF CONTRIBUTORS

William R. Catton, Jr.

Department of Sociology
Washington State University

C. Dyke

Department of Philosophy
Temple University

Richard Machalek

Department of Sociology
University of Wyoming

Alexandra Maryanski

Department of Sociology
University of California,
Riverside

Marvin E. Olsen

Department of Sociology
Michigan State University

David W. Pearce

Center for Social and Economic
Research on the Global Environment
University of East Anglia

R. Kerry Turner

Center for Social and Economic
Research on the Global Environment
University of East Anglia

Jeffrey S. Wicken

Behrend College
Pennsylvania State University
   Erie

Gerald L. Young

Program in Environmental Science
   and Regional Planning
Washington State University

PREFACE

EDITORIAL POLICY

This series publishes original theoretical, empirical, and review papers on scientific human ecology. Human ecology is interpreted to include structural and functional changes in human social organization and sociocultural systems as these changes may be affected by, interdependent with, or identical to changes in ecosystemic, evolutionary, or ethological processes, factors, or mechanisms. Three degrees of scope are included in this interpretation: (1) the adaptation of sociocultural forces to bioecological forces; (2) the interactions between sociocultural and bioecological forces; (3) and the integration of sociocultural with bioecological forces.

The goal of the series is to promote the growth of human ecology as a transdisciplinary problem-solving paradigm. Contributions are solicited without regard for particular theoretical, methodological, or disciplinary orthodoxies, and may range across ecological anthropology, socioecology, sociobiology, biosociology, environmental sociology, ecological economics, ecological demography, ecological geography, and other relevant fields of specialization. The editor will be especially receptive to contributions that promote the growth of general scientific theory in human ecology. Probably no single volume will represent the full range the series is intended to cover.

CONTENTS OF VOLUME 1

All the papers in this volume adopt a transdisciplinary attitude, and several contain explicit arguments on behalf of it. The first two papers illustrate their arguments by utilizing interspecific comparative methods that are employed for evolutionary analyses about forms of human sociality.

Alexandra Maryanski provides a detailed network analysis of data on the social bonds of contemporary Old World monkeys and apes, taking into account their patterns of dispersal (migration), so that she may infer social structural characters of the last ancestor common to apes and humans. Maryanski's conclusion is shocking for the received view in contemporary social science theory: Human beings are not as social as we think we are. Richard Machalek likewise makes evolutionary comparisons, but between two phylogenetically remote groups of social animals—humans and ants. Wanting to know why just these and the other social insects, but not social animals much closer to humans, have ever evolved large societies, Machalek analyzes the conditions that promote evolutionary selection for macrosocieties.

Evolution figures significantly into the next two papers also, but now as a ground and vital center for metatheoretical arguments about the inherent transdisciplinarity of basic ecological ideas. William R. Catton, Jr., whose grist is ecological communities and divisions of labor, argues forcefully against the long-standing tendency of sociological human ecology to divorce itself from general ecology. Jeffrey S. Wicken, by training a biochemist, ranges from Darwin, Kant, Marx, and Freud, and into thermodynamics, to trace the theme of ecological relationality and to situate it in perspective.

There follow two papers devoted, each in its turn, to a major concept often suggested to be essential for general human ecological theory. For Gerald L. Young the concept is hierarchy. Young surveys numerous connotations and interpretations the concept has come to have, reviews a variety of hierarchical organizational forms observed in nature, and illustrates the tendency to conceptually impose hierarchical forms in the organization of human experience. Young concludes that the understanding of hierarchies is, indeed, essential to human ecological theory. For C. Dyke the concept at issue is entropy. Thermodynamics has been seductive for the ecologically minded for a long time, and there have been many interpretations of the Second Law. Dyke charts through this minefield a path along which all must venture to find entropy (and themselves) intact. He does so with respect to economic systems, which he takes to be dependent upon ecosystems.

Economic systems and their connections to ecological systems take center stage in the paper by R. Kerry Turner and David W. Pearce. They suggest how the calculus of benefit-cost analysis can be modified to incorporate a rule that permits sustainable development and maintains intergenerational equity and environmental quality. The final paper, by Marvin E. Olsen, addresses one facet of the general relationship between sociophysical energy flows and the political economy and development of societies. Olsen analyzes comprehensive data for the industrialized nations in order to assess when energy consumption is and is not coupled with economic productivity and social well-being.

Lee Freese
Editor

THE LAST ANCESTOR:
AN ECOLOGICAL NETWORK MODEL
ON THE ORIGINS OF HUMAN SOCIALITY

Alexandra Maryanski

ABSTRACT

This paper employs an ecological network model and a historical comparative method to trace the social structural characteristics of the last common ancestor to apes and humans. By examining the nature of social relations among present-day Old World monkeys and apes, it is possible to reconstruct, in a general way, the social structure of the last common hominoid ancestor. What emerges from this analysis is that monkeys reveal comparatively high density in their network ties while apes reveal low density in their network ties. The last common hominoid ancestor is hypothesized to have possessed a rather loosely organized social structure, revolving around weak ties among adults and weakening ties between adult and older offspring. One implication of these inferences is that humans may not be as "social" as is often presumed in the social science literature. On the contrary, the data from Old World primates, as they provide glimpses of humans' distant ancestors, would suggest that low sociality and high individualism are derived hominoid characters and that humans are far more individualistic than is typically assumed.

Advances in Human Ecology, Volume 1, pages 1-32.

Little is known about the evolution of human social behavior. Peering into test tubes, even crystal ones, cannot provide unambiguous answers, since early hominid populations left few material traces of their patterns of social relations. For social forms do not fossilize, and as a result evidence about early hominid social behavior and ecology are limited (Potts 1987; see also Foley 1984; Tanner 1981; Isaac and McCown 1975; Kinzey 1987 for overviews). Yet human organization originated at some point in time, building upon a biologically based foundation. In lieu of trying to uncover or ever discover the details of humans' "ultimate social history," the purpose of this paper is to offer a suitable starting point for developing an alternative research strategy. This strategy makes use of the rich data now available from long-term field research on humans' closest living ape relatives. Like humans, apes are the end products of the hominoid lineage, a superfamily that according to the fossil record began to flourish in the early Miocene epoch (about 20 million years ago) (Fleagle 1986) and today can be conveniently divided into the families of the lesser apes (Hylobatidae), the great apes (Pongidae), and humans (Hominidae) (Andrews 1981; Napier and Napier 1985, p. 14). Hence, despite the absence of fossilized samples, reconstructing our early social history may still be possible, *if* we are willing to entertain the idea that the shared relational characters of present-day hominoids can be used as a looking glass in which images of the social structure of the last common hominoid ancestor of apes and humans are reflected.

The evidence to be cited draws from four sets of materials: (1) social relational data from humans' closest living hominoid relatives; (2) social relational data from Cercopithecoidea monkeys, the closest sister lineage to hominoidea; (3) social network analysis to provide a common comparative yardstick for organizing and interpreting the data; and (4) social/historical methodology for reconstruction by the comparative method using the relational features of the contemporary hominoids. The basic argument can be summarized as follows: Most primate species are social mammals because in their past (and present) history group living was beneficial for survival and reproductive success in a particular habitat. Humans and apes are Old World primates who once shared a common hominoid ancestor.[1] While we cannot hope to detail the evolutionary forces that shaped the social arrangements of this Last Common Ancestor species (LCA), we can examine the sociological end points of this process and assess the correspondences in social relationships among present-day hominoid descendants. Initial findings from this exploratory analysis suggest that (1) the adaptive potential of all extant hominoids (apes and humans) was probably limited by phyletically-based social predispositions that operated to constrain the forms of organizational structures to emerge; (2) the blueprint of the LCA structure strongly indicates that the hominoid stock was sprung from an ancestor that was predisposed toward low density networks and relatively low sociality, compared with that of monkeys; and (3) the major adaptive trend in hominoid social evolution was the building of social network ties, a trend that culminated in the human lineage. This paper is devoted to filling in the details of these conclusions. Before proceeding, however, some preliminary discussions of primate organization, network analysis and comparative methodologies are necessary.

SOCIAL ORGANIZATION OF OLD WORLD ANTHROPOIDS

The primate order has nearly two hundred species (made up of 70% monkeys, 25% prosimians (pre-monkeys), and 5% apes and humans), with male and female conspecifics normally organized into year-round social groups (Richard 1985, p. 334).[2] For highly intelligent animals with relatively long lifespans, such permanent arrangements require the integration of a variety of age and sex classes who, on the basis of particular social and physical characteristics, are classified into infants, juveniles, adolescents, and adults. Unlike most mammals, primate young are born one at a time, undergo a long period of maturation and are socialized mainly through observation and imitation (Napier and Napier 1985, p. 80; and for overviews see Chevalier-Skolnikoff, and Poirier 1977). While primate societies are flexible and adjust easily to changing environmental conditions, most species have a modal group size and a characteristic age and sex class ratio (for details see Eisenberg, Muckenhirn and Rudran 1972; Southwick and Siddiqi 1974; Jolly 1985, p. 115 and Clutton-Brock and Harvey 1977). Moreover, data on primate organization strongly suggest that both environmental conditions and phylogeny help restrict and regulate the movements of individuals (Hinde 1983; Cheney, et al. 1986; Clutton-Brock and Harvey 1977). For example, while group size and the spatial arrangements of primate species are strongly influenced by the nature and distribution of the food supply and predation pressures in a given habitat, each species brings a "different phyletic heritage into a particular ecological scene" (Struhsaker 1969, p. 113) that influences a structural tendency within a primate group, even when it must adjust to varying ecological conditions. Thus, in the words of Richard (1985, p. 349), in understanding primate organization "the phylogenetic history of each species is important in determining the responses of its living representatives to the environment."

With few exceptions, primate reproductive units are classified according to the number of breeding males within a reproductive unit and the endurance of the heterosexual bond (Gouzoules 1984). Among Old World anthropoids, three main breeding arrangements are recognized: (1) a rare "monogamous" pattern of one male and one female, along with their young; (2) a "harem" pattern of one male and two or more females, with their young; and (3) a "horde" pattern of multiple males and multiple females, as well as their young

(Napier and Napier 1985, p. 61; Jolly 1985, p. 115ff; Aldelman 1986). A primate having one of these mating arrangements will also exhibit a dispersal pattern in and out of a reproductive unit where males, females, or both sexes leave the natal unit after puberty. While these transfer patterns are not caused by the mating arrangements, a mating proclivity for a given species is associated with a stable transfer pattern (Greenwood 1980; Pusey and Packer 1987).[3]

In the Old World, monkeys (Cercopithecoidea) are distinguished from apes and humans (Hominoidea) by striking differences in anatomy, feeding, reproductive and developmental biology, and in locomotor morphology, leading researchers to conclude that the evolutionary divergence of monkeys and apes was marked by significant variations in their respective adaptive strategies (Temerin and Cant 1983; Tattersall, Delson, and Van Couvering 1988).[4] In social arrangements, cercopithecoids and hominoids also evidence marked organizational differences.[5] While monkeys vary in the particulars of social organization, most have remarkably stable social arrangements, where (1) members live in discrete, spatially bounded groups that either avoid or behave aggressively toward conspecifics in other monkey groups; (2) group members know each other well and have most of their positive interactions with each other; (3) members usually move in a synchronized fashion within a limited geographical or ranging area; and (4) with few exceptions, conspecifics follow either the "harem" reproductive pattern of one male and one or more females, or the "horde" pattern of multiple males and multiple females. Further, in most monkey groups the adult males are immigrants from other groups. In counterpose, monkey females are usually lifelong members of their natal groups and are organized into a number of strong-tie female cliques that often, as is the case in the well-studied monkey species to be discussed shortly, link up several generations of mothers, daughters, and sisters (for discussions of simian organization see Smuts, Cheney, Seyfarth, Wrangham, and Struhsaker 1987; Moore 1984; Fedigan 1982; Aldelman 1986; Napier and Napier 1985; Jolly 1985; Richard 1985).

In contrast to cercopithecoids (and most other primates), hominoid arrangements have defied classification, not only because of the variance relative to Old World monkeys but also because of the variance relative to each other. Yet, despite striking disparities in organization, a social network analysis of hominoid social structure reveals an intriguing pattern of shared network ties that will be used to sketch the social structure of the Last Common Ancestor (LCA). As will be argued, apes tend to form much more mobile, loosely coupled, and "individualistic" social networks than do monkeys. Before documenting this conclusion, however, a brief overview of the social network perspective is desirable.

THE SOCIAL NETWORK APPROACH

In the social science literature, a social structure can be described in terms of either (1) the attributes and behaviors of individuals, classes of individuals, and events or, (2) the patterns of relationships *among* individuals or classes of individuals. Traditionally the tendency in primate research, including humans, is to focus on the properties and qualities of individuals and their social behaviors. For example, personal attributes such as age, sex, and status are described for individuals; or aggregates of individuals are described in terms of social class, level of education, and occupational status. While the attributes vary, the overall emphasis is on individuals and behavior. In contrast, a network approach stresses the importance of relations among concrete social entities by focusing solely on the linkages among two or more individuals produced and reproduced by some of their social behaviors and on the forms or configurations of these linkages or ties (see Wellman and Berkowitz 1988; Knoke and Kuklinski 1982). For network analysis, a social behavior and a social relationship represent different foci. A social behavior is seen as a sequence of actions of individuals toward each other, whereas a social relation is viewed as an established and stable pattern of ties produced by some of these social behaviors. One goal of network analysis is to conceptualize how stable configurations of ties emerge from relevant subsets of social behaviors to constitute a separate level of analysis. While much is ignored with a focus on social structure alone, this perspective has the virtue of uncovering the underlying relational structure of a population, a configuration that is often difficult to detect with a focus on the attributes and social behaviors of individuals.

In this study, a network approach is used to compare one crucial property of hominoid social structure: the strength of social bonds and the effects of migration or dispersal patterns on these bonds. The historical comparative method will be used in conjunction with the social network approach to document these bonds and the effects of migration patterns.

THE HISTORICAL COMPARATIVE APPROACH

While historical data are the direct way to reconstruct past events, when the evolutionary process cannot be known from direct sources, the historical comparative method has become the standard tool for reconstruction in such fields as textual criticism, historical linguistics, and comparative biology (Andrews and Martin 1987; Jeffers and Lehiste 1979; Platnick and Cameron 1977). In these fields, the basic procedures involve an identification of a limited group of entities believed to be the end points or descendants of an evolutionary or developmental process and, then, an evaluation of the historical interrelationships of these descendants is undertaken with the idea that an "original" or common ancestor can be reconstructed through the detection of shared diagnostic characters, or as this is termed in biology "derived characters." While the implied genealogical relationships are not directly testable, this technique incorporates two fundamental assumptions that are considered testable: (1) the Relatedness Hypothesis that the similarities found in a class of objects are not due to chance but through a historical connection of descent from a common ancestor; and (2) the Regularity Hypothesis that modifications from the ancestral form to descendant forms are not randomly acquired but evince a systematic bias (Jeffers and Lehiste 1979). Thus, in textual criticism, the comparative method is used to evaluate the interrelationships of alternative forms of the same manuscript, with the ultimate goal of tracing or reconstructing the original text from which all subsequent ones were copied (Platwick and Cameron 1977; Maas 1958). In historical linguistics this approach is used to evaluate linguistic units showing similarities in form and meaning assumed to be descended from the same source with the goal of reconstructing the mother "speech forms" from which daughter languages were all evolved (Hass 1966; Jeffers and Lehiste 1979; Gaeng 1971; Hoenigswald 1950, 1960). In comparative biology, cladistic analysis (the biological version of this approach) is used to evaluate and classify taxa on the basis of diagnostic characters shared by two or more related forms (Hennig 1966). In comparative biology, a sister lineage or what is termed the "outgroup population," is often identified as a further basis for comparison. Similarities and differences between this "next-most-closely-related taxonomic group" (Andrews and Martin 1987) and those in the taxon of interest are considered an additional way to distinguish "evolutionary novelties" or sets of nested resemblances uniquely shared by genealogical taxon. The results of a cladistic analysis are then plotted on a genealogical tree or cladogram that depicts the relationships among the taxa under study.

Thus the great merit of the comparative method is its utility in allowing us to reconstruct ancestral patterns (Hass 1966), whether of an original text, a proto-language, an ancestral lineage or, an ancestral social structure.

MATERIALS AND METHODS

Research on the ontogeny of primate social relationships has affirmed that primates form attachments to particular individuals rather than to conspecifics in general, with a primate society largely held together by a network of relations. Moreover, primates socially groom, engage in alliances, and form support networks not only for immediate benefits but to establish and maintain particular social relationships (Cheney, Seyfarth, Smuts, and Wrangham 1987, p. 3). These bonds appear to be circumscribed by innate predispositions because each species has a characteristic profile of attachment—ranging from pronounced antagonism to strong attraction—for sex and age classes (for discussions see Cheney et al. 1986; Sade 1972; Hinde 1983). The relational data for this paper are drawn from the accumulated field studies on the present-day nonhuman hominoids—the gibbon (Hylobates), the orangutan (Pongo), the gorilla (Gorilla) and the common chimpanzee (Pan)—and from selected data of well studied Old World cercopithecoids, a sister lineage that for comparison will serve as the out-group population.

To analyze hominoid and cercopithecoid social networks, two simplifying procedures are required. First, the patterns of ape relations are assumed symmetrical and positive. That is, while negative and asymmetric relations are also characteristic of primates, affective ties are normally assessed on the basis of mutually reinforcing and affable interactions between dyads. Second, these attachments are described along a simple scale of tie strength: absent ties, weak ties, moderate ties, strong ties. An ordinal scale of tie strength is used because it accommodates the data of investigators without having to make undue inferences. Generally, investigators assess the strength of bonds between dyads on the basis of time spent together, social grooming, embracing (but often excluding sexual contact), food sharing, aiding and protecting, cooperative alliances and the endurance and intensity of a social relation.[6]

In assigning gradations to assess the degree of attachment among primate species, it was assumed that individuals who have unknown ties (e.g., father-daughter where paternity cannot be known) or those who seldom, if ever, interact, have absent ties; those who interact occasionally and in a positive friendly manner have weak ties; those who affiliate closely for a time, but without emotion or endurance over time (at least for adults), have moderate ties; and those who exhibit extensive physical contact accompanied by observable affect (e.g., reciprocal grooming), mutual support, high rates of interaction, and stable relations over time, have strong ties. Variation in tie strength ranges, therefore, from little or no interaction to binding intimacy. It should be mentioned that scaling strength of ties for well-studied primate species is a straightforward procedure since the clear-cut tendencies that age and sex conspecifics have for particular social relations are consistently observed by researchers.

While distinct bonding patterns exist for all age and sex conspecifics, only the key classes of social ties are arrayed here for illustrative purposes: (1) adult male-adult male ties, (2) adult female-adult female ties, (3) adult male-adult female ties, (4) mother-child daughter ties, (5) mother-child son ties, (6) father-child daughter ties, (7) father-child son ties, (8) mother-adult daughter ties, (9) mother-adult son ties; (10) father-adult daughter ties, and (11) father-adult son ties. The nature of these eleven classes of ties among hominoids and Old World monkeys is adequate for this comparative analysis of primate social structure, with social structure defined here as the network of patterned social relationships for a given primate species. In comparing nonhuman hominoid ties, a basic tenet of the comparative method will be adopted that if all or most apes possess the same social character, and if it is not normally present in the out-group population, the character was likely derived from the LCA population. An alternative position is to assume that each hominoid character was evolved independently, the null hypothesis. Once this ancestral structure is sketched, it can then serve as a blueprint for considering (1) in what ways the descendant social structures were modified from the ancestral structure and (2) in what ways human social structures were influenced from the ancestral hominoid social structure. Let us now turn to the hominoid family tree and a brief organizational profile of gibbons, orangutans, chimpanzees and gorillas.

ORGANIZATIONAL PROFILES OF
THE HOMINOID FAMILY TREE

In the Old World alone, more than sixty-five species of monkeys exist in a wide variety of arboreal and terrestrial habitats. In contrast, about twelve hominoid species (eight of them gibbons) exist in such specialized and restricted habitats that contemporary apes are often labeled "atypical relict forms" (Corruccini and Ciochon 1983, p. 14) and "evolutionary failures" (Andrews 1981, p. 25; Temerin and Cant 1983). It is important to emphasize, however, that when true apes first appear in the fossil record during the early Miocene epoch, they were far more abundant than monkeys and occupied a broader variety of ecological zones (Andrews 1981; Tattersall, Delson, and Van Couvering 1988). While the time and place of hominoid beginnings are still unclear,[7] it is a widely accepted hypothesis that gibbons, orangutans, chimpanzees, gorillas, and humans form a monophyletic grouping that when set forth on a cladogram denotes that all hominoids originally descended from a single ancestral population (Andrews and Martin 1987; Martin 1986). In drawing cladograms, branching points often vary depending on the derived characteristics which are best interpreted as ancestor-descendant sequences or as forming a clade. One well supported cladogram depicting hominoid phylogeny is shown in Figure 1, with the nodes simply reflecting the joint possession of more and more mutually exclusive and specialized derived characters within clades (Tattersall et al. 1988, p. 136; Martin 1986; Andrews and Martin 1987).

Both contemporary and fossil hominoid data are included on this cladogram and the time of divergence of the major branching points is based on molecular data and on the oldest fossil records contained within the respective clades. The LCA is an integral part of a cladogram because in any theory of biological evolution ancestor-descendant relationships are implied. Following the cladogram, the current consensus is that the gibbon line diverged first from

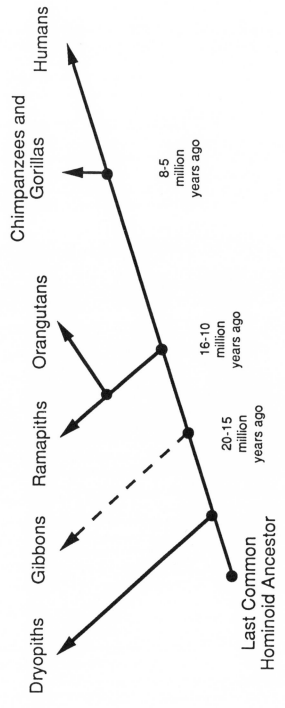

Figure 1. Family-Tree Cladogram

Note: A cladogram is a set of relationships. A cladistic analysis assumes that trait patterns are developed as a result of ancestor-descendant relationships. In this limited cladogram, Dyopithecus and Ramapithecus, two extinct Miocene genera known only through the fossil record, are included for illustration. Among the present-day hominoids, the gibbon line is believed to have branched off first although its placement vis-à-vis Ramapiths and Dryopiths is still conjectural (indicated by the broken line). Orangutans and Ramapiths are conjectured by a number of scholars to be sister genera on the basis of morphological characters. Chimpanzees, gorillas and humans are considered to have a close phyletic relationship on the basis of molecular and morphological characters. The branching points within Hominoidea are based on the dating of fossils and dating by the molecular clock (see Ciochon 1983, for a similar summary cladogram).

9

the ancestral stem between 20 and 15 million years ago (Cronin 1983; Boaz 1983; Tattersall et al. 1988, p. 251). Then, from 16 to 10 million years ago, the great apes diverged into Asian and African lines and the orangutan branched off (Tattersall et al. 1988; Zihlman and Lowenstein 1983; Cronin 1983; Boaz 1983). The African apes and humans were last to separate, with the molecular data (fossil evidence is lacking for the initial separation of this clade) suggesting that gorillas, chimpanzees, and humans shared an ancestor until between 8 and 5 million years ago (Cronin 1983; Zihlman and Lowenstein 1983; for discussions see the edited volume of Ciochon and Corruccini 1983; Ciochon and Fleagle 1987).

In addition, it should be mentioned that the primate order originated at least 60 million years ago, and, for this reason, present-day monkeys and apes are the recipients of many shared "primitive" characters derived from remote common ancestors. The historical comparative method is designed to focus only upon "evolutionary novelties" or the nested suite of derived features that are diagnostic for constructing and testing hypotheses about the interrelationships of taxa connected by ancestor-descendant sequences. Let us now turn to a brief overview of the organizational profiles of present-day nonhuman hominoids.

Contemporary Non-Human Hominoids

Gibbon (Hylobates)

Gibbons are fruit-eating lesser apes (weighing on average 18 pounds) who are dispersed throughout the rain forests of southeastern Asia.[8] Living high in the forest canopy, gibbons are isolated into rare monogamous "family" groups, with a modal size of about four individuals (Leighton 1987; Groves 1984; Ellefson 1974; Gittens 1980; Chivers 1984). Manifesting little or no sexual dimorphism, an adult male and female (and sometimes dependent offspring) fiercely protect their small stable territory from conspecifics and this conjugated alliance may facilitate the formation of the strong heterosexual pair bond, that seemingly comes close to the monogamous ideal of "mating for life" (MacKinnon and MacKinnon 1984, p. 291). Normally, adult gibbons have few social relations outside the nuclear family, leaving them dependent upon each other and on bonds with their offspring (Tilson 1981).[9] Gibbon partners typically interact in a relaxed, tolerant and well-coordinated manner (Leighton 1987), with most established pairs engaged in activities that include the singing of morning duets (Tuttle 1986, p. 251; Leighton 1987; MacKinnon and MacKinnon 1984) and in one well-studied species, regular family sunbathing in sparsely leafed trees. Unlike the vast majority of primates, gibbons are considered "co-dominant" in their daily activities with males and females equally involved in such leadership roles as guiding and coordinating daily foraging progressions (Leighton 1987). Gibbon fathers also lend a hand in child care by playing with and grooming their offspring (Chivers 1974; Leighton 1987), an adaptive strategy that culminated in the subgenus (Symphalangus) or siamang gibbon, where males and females share almost equally the burdens of child care. However, as gibbon young mature (at between 5 and 7 years old), bonds lessen between parents and young as adults become increasingly aggressive toward maturing offspring and actively exclude them from family activities (see Tuttle 1986, pp. 249-255 for a discussion). At puberty, sons and daughters depart their natal group to seek mates and to resettle in another territory. This one male-one female arrangement, with a strong heterosexual pair bond, paternal care, and offspring transfer at puberty, is an undeviating pattern among gibbons and is connected to the social network patterns outlined at the top of Table 1.

Orangutans (Pongo)

Orangutans are Asian great apes (females average about 80 pounds, males average about 150 pounds) who inhabit the northern forests of Borneo and Sumatra (Galdikas 1988; Rodman and Mitani 1987). Among apes, orangutans are as unique for their solitary habits as gibbons are for their monogamy (Tuttle 1986, p. 12). The orangutan or "red ape" is a slow-moving arboreal fruit-eater who forages daily, mostly alone or in small, subgroupings that average about 1.8 individuals (Rodman 1973; MacKinnon 1971, 1974, p. 257; Rodman and Mitani 1987). While many of the particulars of orangutan organization are still unclear,[10] most researchers agree that an orangutan population (or all conspecifics moving about in a single continuously inhabited block of forest up to 2 square miles), can be divided into "residents" (those present throughout the year) and "nonresidents" (those present only part of the year) (Rodman and Mitani 1987; Sugardjito, te Boekhorst and van Hooff 1987). Adult females are the most stable residents with each female occupying a ranging area that overlaps with the larger ranges of males (Rodman and Mitani 1987). Adult males are more transient, wandering in and out of a particular ranging area (Galdikas 1985). The widely dispersed and fragmented parts of an orangutan regional population are normally composed of (1) solitary adult males; (2) single adult females with immature offspring; (3) independent adolescent males and females; and (4) heterosexual consortships although, relative to gibbons, adult male and female orangutans are only occasionally observed together in the forest (Tuttle 1986, p. 255; Galdikas 1985). The most frequent and permanent daily grouping is that of a mother and her dependent offspring (Galdikas 1988); while the most gregarious social units in an orangutan population are adolescents who congregate and form temporary traveling-bands, seemingly for purely social reasons (Sugardjito et al. 1987; Rijksen 1975). When adolescents reach maturity, however, associations become less

Table 1.   Social Network Ties in Reproduction Units
Among Non-Human Hominoidea

	Adult Kinship or Voluntary Relations			Adult/Child Procreation Relations			
	Male/ Male	Female/ Female	Male/ Female	Mother/ Daughter	Mother/ Son	Father/ Daughter	Father/ Son
Gibbon (Hylobates)	Absent to Weak Ties	Absent to Weak Ties	Strong Ties	Strong Ties	Strong Ties	Strong Ties	Strong Ties
Orangutan (Pongo)	Absent to Weak Ties	Absent to Weak Ties	Weak Ties	Strong Ties	Strong Ties	Absent Ties	Absent Ties
Gorilla (Gorilla)	Weak Ties	Absent to Weak Ties	Moderate to Strong Ties Females with Dependents Weak Ties Females without Dependents	Strong Ties	Strong Ties	Unknown Ties Likely Absent Ties	Unknown Ties Likely Absent Ties
Chimpanzee (Pan)	Weak to Moderate Ties - Voluntary Strong Ties Between Siblings	Absent to Weak Ties	Weak Ties	Strong Ties	Strong Ties	Absent Ties	Absent Ties
Last Common Hominoid Ancestor	3/4 Absent to Weak Ties*	4/4 Absent to Weak Ties*	2/4 Weak Ties*	4/4 Strong Ties*	4/4 Strong Ties*	3/4 Absent Ties*	3/4 Absent Ties*

frequent (Rodman 1973). While adult males are very solitary, they become noticeably social during mating periods (Galdikas 1985; Rodman and Mitani 1987), and although orangutans are considered to mate promiscuously (that is, transitory mating) (Rodman and Mitani 1987; Schurmann 1982), females seemingly prefer adult males in residence within their ranging area (Galdikas 1979). Observed consortships last on average 8 days, with a mature male and female traveling together as a single foraging unit (Rodman and Mitani 1987). For mother and offspring, strong bonds are reported for the first 7 years. But, as males and females mature, social grooming ceases between mother and offspring along with the tendency to coordinate movements, with the result that an adolescent begins to lag behind the mother to forage at its own pace (see Tuttle 1986, p. 256ff). At puberty, both sexes depart from the mother to range on their own (Rodman and Mitani 1987). While adult daughters tend

Table 1.   (continued)

Adult/Adult Procreation Relations				Gender Dispersal from Mother at Puberty	Organizational Type	Residence Type For Offspring after Puberty
Mother/ Daughter	Mother/ Son	Father/ Daughter	Father/ Son			
Absent to Weak Ties	Absent to Weak Ties	Absent to Weak Ties	Absent to Weak Ties	Males and Females	Monogamous Group	Neo-Local Males and Females
Weak Ties	Absent to Weak Ties	Absent Ties	Absent Ties	Males and Females	Horde Group	Neo-Local Males and Females
Absent to Weak Ties	Absent to Weak Ties	Unknown Ties Most Likely Absent Ties	Unknown Ties Most Likely Absent Ties	Males and Females	Horde/ Harem Group	Neo-Local Males and Females
Absent to Weak Ties	Strong Ties	Absent Ties	Absent Ties	Females	Higher Level Horde/ Community Regional Population	Viri-Local Males Neo-Local Females
4/4 Absent to Weak Ties*	3/4 Absent to Weak Ties*	4/4 Absent Ties*	4/4 Absent Ties*	Males and Females*	Horde Group*	Neo-Local Residence Males and Females*

Note: * The strength of an attachment among and within any given mating system is usually determined by qualitative measures such as social grooming, spatial proximity, cooperation, mutual aid, formation of alliances, etc. These values are assumed to be positive and symmetrical.

to forage near the ranging area of their mother, social contact between them is infrequent (Galdikas 1988). Adult sons appear to lead a more nomadic life, often migrating to another ranging area. Among same sex adults, social interactions are infrequent. Normally, adult females avoid or act aggressively toward each other, although females do interact occasionally (Galdikas 1979 1984 1985 1988; Cohen 1975). Adult males are almost always intolerant of each other (Galdikas 1985).

The solitary ways of orangutans are considered by all researchers to be a striking exception to other higher primates (Rodman 1979; MacKinnon 1979; Galdikas 1979). Even when adult individuals are in spatial propinquity, they normally elicit no friendly greetings, while appearing to lack interest in socializing with each other (MacKinnon 1979). The extremely fragmented and dispersed nature of orangutan organization is reflected in the relational patterns shown at the top of Table 1.

Gorilla (Gorilla)

These apes are the largest hominoids (males average 335 pounds while females average 185 pounds). Gorillas are distinct among apes in their dietary habits of consuming more plants than fruits and in their terrestrial lifestyle of traveling, feeding, and day resting on the ground (Jones and Pi 1971; Fossey 1983; Fossey and Harcourt 1977). While gorillas are sometimes sympatric with chimpanzees, they normally inhabit secondary (i.e., regenerating) or montane rain forests in two widely separated areas, one in West Africa and the other in northeastern Central Africa (Tuttle 1986, pp. 18-19; Dixson 1981; Fossey and Harcourt 1977). In grouping arrangements, gorillas reveal two spatial patterns: (1) relatively stable heterosexual groups (with an average size of 10-12 animals), and (2) unattached adult males (Weber and Vedder 1983; Maryanski 1986; Fossey 1976). Although a third of gorilla groups have up to four adult males, a typical gorilla group is composed of one mature male, and two or more females with dependent offspring (Harcourt, Stewart, and Fossey 1981; Yamagiwa 1983; Schaller 1962; Weber and Vedder 1983). Typically, four or more gorilla groups and some single males share a home range (average 10 square miles), with resident groups occasionally meeting up, traveling and sometimes even bedding down together overnight (Fossey 1972; Yamagiwa 1983; Schaller 1962). Normally, each gorilla group is headed by a dominant "silverback male" who is typically the preferred sexual partner for the resident females. Females are always free, however, to mate with any resident male or to transfer to another group or to a lone male (Harcourt 1977, 1979c; Schaller 1962; Fossey 1976). Within groups, gorilla relations are normally fluid and casual (Yamagiwa 1983; Schaller 1962). Familiar adult males are highly tolerant of each other but, since they engage in few overt social interactions, ties are weak (Fossey 1976, 1983; Harcourt 1977; Schaller 1962). Adult females are also tolerant of each other, but ties are absent to weak since adult females actively avoid interactions with each other (Harcourt 1979b, 1979c; Stewart and Harcourt 1987; Yamagiwa 1983). The bonds between a dominant male and resident females vary dramatically, being crucially linked to the status of a male and the maternal responsibilities of a female (Stewart and Harcourt 1987; Harcourt 1977). During day-resting periods a female with dependent offspring is usually in close proximity to the leader silverback. In contrast, a female without a dependent (or with a sudden loss of her offspring) is typically found on the edge of her group; and such peripheral females are likely to transfer to another group or to a lone adult male. It is conjectured that a mother will form a stable, moderate tie with a leader male only when she is successful in raising her offspring (Harcourt 1977, 1979a, 1979c; Yamagiwa 1983). For this reason perhaps, leader males normally assist mothers with dependent offspring, by playing, grooming, and even "baby-sitting" immatures (Harcourt 1979c; Stewart 1981). Secondary adult males and resident females interact only occasionally (Fossey 1983; Harcourt 1977, 1979a). Some gorilla groups are transient, reflecting a shifting collection of individuals, since adult members may freely depart any group (Stewart and Harcourt 1987; Schaller 1962; Fossey 1976, 1983; Yamagiwa 1983). But most groups are stable units over many months (Yamagiwa 1983; Stewart 1981; Stewart and Harcourt 1987). Relations between a mother and her young offspring are intimate, but at puberty (at about 8 years) both males and females migrate out of their natal group after which males wander about alone for a time and females join another group or a lone male (Harcourt 1978; Stewart and Harcourt 1987; Weber and Vedder 1983; Harcourt et al. 1976, 1981). The gorilla organizational profile, where a leader silverback heads a relatively stable group composed of a female core and dependent offspring, where mothers form close ties with a leader silverback, seemingly in exchange for father-like infant care, and where both males and females leave their natal unit at puberty, is shown in the middle of Table 1.

Chimpanzees (Pan troglodytes)

Chimpanzees are African great apes (males average 100 pounds, while females average 85 pounds), with a distribution throughout the West, East and Central forest belts of tropical Africa (Jones and Pi 1971; Tuttle 1986). In line with Asian apes, common chimpanzees rely upon ripe fruits for much of their dietary needs, although chimpanzees are much less specialized in subsistence and habitat, being comfortable on the forest floor or in the trees and occupying both primary and secondary forests, along with open canopy woodlands and forest fringe habitats (Itani 1979; Tuttle 1986; Goodall 1986). Among nonhuman primates, chimpanzee organization is placed in a class by itself since it closely resembles human organization (Goodall-Lawick 1975). That is, chimpanzee organization is not composed of stable, discrete groups, but is centered around the wholly independent movement of adult individuals *within* a more inclusive regional population (which spatially varies from 8 square miles in the rainforest to 120 square miles in a mixed savannah-woodland habitat). Within a regional population or what is termed a "community," up to 100 familiar chimpanzees come and go about their daily activities either alone or, if they choose, in company with an "ever-changing" mixture of community residents who gather temporarily in social clusterings (or parties) that can last a few minutes, an hour or occasionally a few days, although the resident population itself (or all those who co-occupy a home range) remains relatively stable in composition over time (Halperin 1979; Tutin, McGrew, and Baldwin

1983; Nishida 1979; Nishida and Hiraiwa-Hasegawa 1987). Within a chimpanzee community, mating is promiscuous, with an adult female choosing a temporary partner for a single consortship or sequentially mating with multiple partners (referred to in the literature as "gang sex") (Tutin 1979; McGinnis 1973; Tuttle 1986). Ties between voluntary adult males range from weak to moderate with strong ties normally confined to brothers and occasionally to a voluntary "friendship" tie (Nishida and Hiraiwa-Hasegawa 1987; Goodall 1986, p. 276ff; Tuttle 1986, p. 266ff). In contrast, ties between adult females are absent to weak since most adult females are semi-solitary, spending 70% of their time traveling alone, accompanied only by their dependent offspring (Wrangham and Smuts 1980; Hayaki 1988; Nishida 1979; Tuttle 1986, p. 266ff). In part, the reclusive nature of females is due to their migration at 7 to 10 years old from their natal community and to the shyness of females toward each other (Pusey and Packer 1987, p. 252; Nishida and Hiraiwa-Hasegawa 1987; Wrangham and Smuts 1980). However, even when adult daughters occasionally return to their natal community, the bonds between mothers and daughters remain relatively weak because once a female reproduces she normally travels about alone accompanied only by dependent offspring (Goodall 1986, p. 168; Phooij 1984, p. 17). Male-female bonds are also weak, for unless a female is sexually receptive she normally refrains from interactions with adult males (Bauer 1976; Halperin 1979; Nishida 1979; Goodall-Lawick 1975). The exception is mother-son relations that normally remain strong even *after* puberty, in part because males are not burdened with dependents and remain in their natal community (Hayaki 1988; Pusey 1983; Pusey and Packer 1987). It is of consequence that adult males are independent social units after puberty. However, they often "visit" with their mothers for social reasons alone since a mother and son (in line with other well-studied Old World primates) very rarely have sexual intercourse with each other (Pusey 1983). Of course, father-offspring ties are absent in a society with transient sexual bonds. The kinds of social ties that exist in association with common chimpanzee mating and transfer are delineated at the bottom of Table 1.

In looking over the organizational profiles of the present-day apes, major differences exist. First, ape genera are widely scattered and adapted to diverse habitats, with the gibbon and orangutan in Asia and the chimpanzee and gorilla in Africa. Second, the apes utilize different kinds of space. The gibbon and orangutan are arboreal, the chimpanzee is both arboreal and terrestrial, and the gorilla is mostly terrestrial. Third, the apes have different reproductive strategies. The gibbon is monogamous; the gorilla is usually polygynous (although loosely so), and the chimpanzee and orangutan are overall promiscuous. Fourth, the apes evince some variation in dispersal patterns: Among all apes, daughters normally disperse after puberty and seldom interact with their mothers as adults. Among gibbons, orangutans, and gorillas, sons normally disperse after puberty and seldom interact with their mothers as adults; while among chimpanzees, sons frequently interact with their mothers as adults. These social differences and other major organizational differences that distinguish hominoids point to the operation of intense environmental pressures since extant hominoids shared a last common ancestor. Yet, we might ask why such idiosyncratic distinctions exist among such closely related genera? Old World monkeys are also the terminal products of an equally long evolutionary history, yet, within major phylogenetic groups they are likely to evince much more consistency in reproductive patterns (Jolly 1985, p. 129). Moreover, monkeys, with only a few exceptions, are organized into stable, discrete groups with a transfer pattern that almost without exception follows a male-biased dispersal system (Pusey and Packer 1987; Greenwood 1980; Aldelman 1986). What, then, do these network patterns, as summarized in Table 1, tell us about the social structure of the Last Common Ancestor?

THE SOCIAL STRUCTURE OF THE LAST COMMON ANCESTOR: THE RELATEDNESS HYPOTHESIS

In reconstructing the LCA social structure, no attempt is made to trace the social history of hominoids or to delineate the evolutionary process involved in this history. Instead, only the strict methodological procedures of the comparative method, as used in textual criticism, linguistics, and biology, will be employed. In line with the Relatedness Hypothesis, it is assumed that any relational pattern common to the gibbon, orangutan, gorilla, and chimpanzee was likely present in the LCA structure. Moreover, as noted earlier, only the patterned relations of contemporary hominoid descendants are used as building blocks for the ancestral structure. Finally, in line with the Regularity Hypothesis, the plausibility of the reconstructed structure is dependent upon a demonstration that the structural modifications that now distinguish the four ape genera conform to a clear systematic bias, thereby confirming the hypothesis that these social forms are historically connected. At the bottom of Table 1 this hypothesized LCA structure is delineated (an asterisk is traditionally used to indicate a reconstructed form).

If we begin our assemblage of this ancestral structure from left to right by tallying social ties that are *common to all hominoids*—that is, a correspondence of four out of four, or 4/4—we find the following regularities: *adult female/ adult female* = absent to weak ties (gibbon, orangutan, gorilla and chimpanzee); *mother/child daughter* = strong ties (gibbon, orangutan, gorilla, and chimpanzee); *mother/child son* = strong ties (gibbon, orangutan, gorilla, and chimpanzee); *mother/adult daughter* = absent to weak ties (gibbon, orangutan, gorilla, and chimpanzee); *father/adult daughter* = absent ties (gibbon, orangutan, gorilla, and chimpanzee) and *father/adult son* = absent ties (gibbon, orangutan, gorilla, and chimpanzee).

Second, in tallying social ties that are *common to most hominoids*—that is, a correspondence of three out of four, or 3/4—we find the following matches: *adult male-adult male* = absent to weak ties (gibbon, orangutan, and gorilla); *father/child daughter* = absent ties (orangutan, gorilla and chimpanzee); *father/ child son* = absent ties (orangutan, gorilla, and chimpanzee); and *mother/adult son* = absent to weak ties (gibbon, orangutan, and gorilla).

Third, in tallying ties that are split equally between the four genera—that is, a correspondence of two out of four or 2/4—we find the following regularities: *adult male-adult female* = moderate to strong ties (gibbon and gorilla); and *adult male-adult female* = weak ties (chimpanzee and orangutan). As the moderate to strong ties for gorilla males and females are linked to the reproductive status of a female with ties between the sexes otherwise weak, we can infer with reasonable confidence that, overall, weak ties between the sexes were probably present in the LCA population. In looking over the hypothesized social structure in Table 1, two questions must be addressed: first, is the reconstruction credible; and, second, is the reconstruction useful in increasing our understanding of the social foundations of human societies?

On the problem of plausibility, it is important to initially consider the null hypothesis that the shared hominoid tie patterns are independently derived *after* each genera branched off from the ancestral structure. While this hypothesis cannot be ruled out, several factors minimize this conclusion. In considering the tie patterns in Table 1, then, it is important to first place them in juxtaposition with the tie patterns of the outgroup monkey population in Table 2.

If we begin with adult male monkeys, most ties are absent to weak. This is a consistent relational pattern for most Old World monkeys and apes, and it is usually associated with male-biased dispersal. Other common monkey and ape ties include the strong mother-child daughter and son ties (common to all mammals); the absent to weak father-child daughter and son ties; and the absent to weak father-adult son and daughter ties (due in large part to the rarity of the monogamous mating pattern and the lack of male parental care). In comparing key relational differences between monkeys and apes, the adult female-adult female ties and the mother-adult daughter ties are reversed in monkey and ape social relations. Among adult hominoid females, absent to weak ties prevail; whereas, among adult cercopithecoid females (and most female primates) strong ties in reproductive groups prevail (Jolly 1985, p. 123). Further, hominoid mother and adult daughter ties are normally absent or weak after puberty, while among cercopithecoids (and most primates) mother-adult daughter ties are strong and remain so throughout the lifecycle. In light of the fact that the absent to weak ties among female hominoids are rare among primates (and mammals in general), and are associated with the equally rare female dispersal pattern, it seems unlikely that such exceptional traits were independently evolved for each hominoid. Instead, while the relationship between network structures and dispersal at puberty is complex and, as yet, little understood, what data are available suggest that ties between hominoid primary kin are already breaking down *before* offspring dispersal at puberty (see Tuttle 1986 for a review). And the innate mechanism that facilitates a breakdown in female bonds and female dispersal likely evolved as an evolutionary novelty in the common ancestor and was passed on to descendants. Additionally, since three ape genera also evince the widespread male dispersal pattern, it also seems likely that both sexes dispersed after puberty in the LCA population.

Another clear difference between monkeys and apes is the wide variance in group continuity. Among Old World monkeys (and most other primates), a male-biased dispersal pattern keeps the females spatially bound to and knitted into high density female networks. One consequence of keeping natal females together is *kinship based recruitment*, with the endurance of the mother-daughter bond assuring the perpetuation of the matrifocal group of mothers, sisters, and daughters over generations. For example, in patas, geladas, macaque, and baboons groups (and most primate groups), a core of females form a permanent group nucleus (Jolly 1985, p. 124ff; Napier and Napier 1985, p. 71). In contrast, in gibbons, orangutans, and gorillas, male and female dispersal cuts short kinship-based recruitment over generational time, while female dispersal in chimpanzees has much the same consequences. Thus, in gibbons the nuclear family dissolves upon the death of the mated pair; in orangutans, the matrifocal unit of mother and offspring dissolves upon the maturation of offspring; in gorillas, the group itself dissolves upon the death of the leader silverback (when females disperse to other mates), and, in chimpanzees, the matrifocal unit of mother and offspring dissolves upon the maturation of offspring. However, in chimpanzees, while both sexes leave the mother, each sex has a decidedly different dispersal pattern: Daughters usually migrate to another regional community, while males usually continue to live in their natal community, maintaining their ties with their mothers and with other natal males. Yet, unlike the "female-bonded" societies of monkeys shown in Table 2, equivalent *kin-based* "male-bonded" societies cannot exist without stable heterosexual relations and male investment in offspring. Chimpanzee males remain in their natal community, but as long as paternity is unknown, intergenerational recruitment on the basis of kinship ties must be limited to those between a mother and her son(s). Thus, among all nonhuman hominoids, regeneration of the natal group as a spatially bounded entity is lacking, although this pattern is somewhat modified in chimpanzee organization.

In looking over the data on the living hominoids, then, there appears to be a systematic bias for female dispersal that is associated with (1) the disruption

Table 2.   Social Network Ties in Reproduction Units
Among A Few Well-Studied Cercopithecoidea

	Adult Kinship or Voluntary Relations			Adult/Child Procreation Relations			
	Male/ Male	Female/ Female	Male/ Female	Mother/ Daughter	Mother/ Son	Father/ Daughter	Father/ Son
Gelada Monkeys (Theropithecus)	Absent to Weak Ties	Strong Ties	Weak Ties (To Most Harem Females)	Strong Ties	Strong Ties	Weak Ties	Weak Ties
Patas Monkeys (Erythrocebus)	Absent to Weak Ties	Strong Ties	Weak Ties (To Most Harem Females)	Strong Ties	Strong Ties	Weak Ties	Weak Ties
Most Species of Macaque Monkeys (Macaca)	Weak Ties	Strong Ties	Weak To Moderate Ties	Strong Ties	Strong Ties	Unknown Ties, Likely Absent	Unknown Ties, Likely Absent
Most Species of Baboons (Papio)	Weak Ties	Strong Ties	Weak To Moderate Ties	Strong Ties	Strong Ties	Unknown Ties, Likely Absent	Unknown Ties, Likely Absent
Last Common Cercopithecoidea Ancestor	4/4 Absent to Weak Ties *	4/4 Strong Ties*	4/4 Weak Ties*	4/4 Strong Ties*	4/4 Strong Ties*	4/4 Absent to Weak Ties*	4/4 Absent to Weak Ties*

of the mother-daughter bond and (2) the disruption of group recursiveness. All four ape genera are predisposed toward these rare organizational characteristics, lending credence to the hypothesis of a derived character from the LCA population.

A final consideration is reproductive patterns. While breeding arrangements are naturally tied to environmental factors, we can still consider the LCA breeding arrangement. First, we can probably dismiss the gibbon pattern of monogamy as unlikely to mirror the LCA because among primates (and most mammals), it is rare, highly specialized, and inflexible, being faithfully observed among all eight gibbon species. Instead, the most parsimonious arrangement for the LCA is a horde or multiple male-multiple female "open-mating" pattern for the following reasons: It is a flexible pattern that is common to both the *Asian* orangutan and the *African* chimpanzee. The *African* gorilla breeding

Table 2.   (continued)

Adult/Adult Procreation Relations				Gender Dispersal from Mother at Puberty	Organizational Type	Residence Type For Offspring after Puberty
Mother/ Daughter	Mother/ Son	Father/ Daughter	Father/ Son			
Strong Ties	Absent To Weak Ties	Absent To Weak Ties	Absent To Weak Ties	Males	Harem Group	Neo-Local Males Matri-Local Females
Strong Ties	Absent To Weak Ties	Absent To Weak Ties	Absent To Weak Ties	Males	Harem Group	Neo-Local Males Matri-Local Females
Strong Ties	Absent To Weak Ties	Unknown Ties, Likely Absent	Unknown Ties, Likely Absent	Males	Horde Group	Neo-Local Males Matri-Local Females
Strong Ties	Absent To Weak Ties	Unknown Ties, Likely Absent	Unknown Ties, Likely Absent	Males	Horde Group	Neo-Local Males Matri-Local Females
4/4 Strong Ties*	4/4 Absent to Weak Ties*	4/4 Absent to Weak Ties*	4/4 Absent to Weak Ties*	Males*	Horde Group*	Neo-Local Males Matri-Local Females*

Note: * The strength of an attachment among and within any given mating system is usually determined by qualitative measures such as social grooming, spatial proximity, cooperation, mutual aid, formation of alliances, etc. These values are assumed to be positive and symmetrical.

arrangement, while technically a one male-multiple female harem pattern, is still semi-promiscuous, since adult females may freely depart any gorilla group at will in search of a new sexual partner—a pattern *never* observed in harem monkey groups. A second reason is that a horde breeding strategy corresponds most to the conjectured fluid, low density networks of the LCA structure, and the dispersal of both sexes after puberty. Thus, it can be hypothesized that the LCA population was a loosely organized horde, with the mother/child tie being the only stable grouping.

TRENDS IN HOMINOID EVOLUTION:
THE REGULARITY HYPOTHESIS

In order to substantiate the ancestral reconstruction, it is important to examine the descendant structures with an eye toward explaining the modifications discussed in Table 1. As stated earlier, the fossil record indicates that after an initial wide-ranging hominoid radiation in the early Miocene, ape species declined dramatically in the middle Miocene, while monkey species multiplied, moving in to the former ape habitats (Andrews 1981). Why did apes decline and monkeys proliferate? While the ecological background for the replacement of apes by monkeys is too detailed to be reviewed here (but see Andrews 1981; Temerin and Cant 1983 for discussions), it is important to emphasize that during the Miocene many ecological zones were becoming less favorable for the reproductive success of the hominoid lineage. Assuming that the reconstructed LCA structure is somewhat representative of the original form, one hypothesis is that the trend in hominoid evolution for heightened sociality involved selection pressures that would favor the likelihood that hominoid genera would survive. Yet, in this drive for greater support networks, the ancestral female dispersal pattern was not modified to create a more monkey-like "female bonded" social structure. If we assume that the future course of hominoid evolution included a retention of female dispersal at puberty, the building of core ties would be contingent upon other tenable bonds and be evident in the social structures of the extant apes. In keeping with the Regularity Hypothesis, it can be hypothesized that one reason present-day apes evince such novel organizational structures is that selection operated to forge unconventional primate ties, while retaining the biologically-based constraint of female dispersal at puberty.

In profiling the social arrangements of the nonhuman hominoids, we find that all ape genera have elaborated their network ties in ways consistent with the retention of female dispersal at puberty. Among gibbons, the kernel network structure is the bonded pair in a nuclear family structure. With offspring dispersing at puberty, gibbon social structure pivots on a strong heterosexual bond that is seemingly reinforced by sexual equality in all social and domestic activities. Among gorillas, the core network structure is a male and resident mothers with dependents. But unlike monkey harems where natal females are closely linked together, this network structure is star shaped, with mothers only tied to the leader male and with negligible ties to each other. Among chimpanzees, the community structure hinges upon the relations among adult resident males, male siblings, and the continuance of the mother-son bond. Even adult orangutans, who otherwise have negligible bonds, have their structural ties in heterosexual relationships. Orangutan social structure which, because of the solitary nature of orangutans, is in striking contrast to all other higher primates appears to be the least modified from the ancestral social structure. That the "red ape" is also the least successful hominoid in terms of population numbers and distribution is probably not coincidental, confined as it is to the outlying islands of Borneo and Sumatra, while chimpanzees, gorillas, and gibbons are more widely distributed on the African and Asian mainlands. Thus, in every hominoid social structure, there are novel network linkages, and among present-day apes these relational distinctions are consistent with selection pressures working around a female dispersal pattern. Seemingly, ecological circumstances either favored a retention of female dispersal for each ape genera or the reproductive costs involved in the disruption of this ancestral process invoked phylogenetic constraints.

IMPLICATIONS FOR HUMAN SOCIAL STRUCTURE

What, then, can we conclude about the origins of human sociality from the data in Table 1 and Table 2 as well as the above discussion? In attempting to draw inferences from these data, we should initially consider the major implications for hominoids in general.

First, in comparing the social structures of Old World monkeys and apes with a focus on the most central, stable and pervasive adult ties, it is evident that monkeys are generally "female-bonded" societies (as they are called in the primate literature) (Wrangham 1980; Jolly 1985, p. 123ff); gibbons and gorillas are "male-female bonded" (with the orangutans leaning this way); and, common chimpanzees are "male-bonded" societies.[11] Thus, monkey and ape networks evince different structural ties.

Second, in looking over Old World monkey and ape networks, it can be seen that they vary in network density. In Table 2, almost all monkeys are organized into relatively closed and compact social groups where females *greatly outnumber* males. In most monkey groups, either a single harem male is present or, in horde arrangements, a number of males are present, arranging themselves in a hierarchy where strict dominant-subordinate relations prevail. Monkey females are organized into sets of tightly knit cliques, where adult mothers, daughters and sisters groom each other and, in so doing, provide social as well as emotional support (Wrangham 1980; Aldelman 1986). In network terms, a monkey group can be visualized as a high density network, since it is structured around strongly tied matrifocal cliques. The hypothesized LCA of Cercopithecoidea shown at the bottom of Table 2, while reconstructed from too few living monkey genera for serious consideration, does at least lend itself to the suggestion that the LCA of Old World monkeys was probably structured around the mother-daughter bond, matrilocal residence and a male-biased dispersal pattern. In contrast, all nonhuman hominoids are organized into relatively low density networks. For gibbons, the mated pair is strongly tied but otherwise spatially isolated from other adults. For orangutans, strong ties are almost unknown among adults. For gorillas, only the leader male is reported to have a moderate to strong tie with each resident mother with dependents. And, for common chimpanzees, strong ties are found between a mother and her son(s), between male siblings, and between adult males who occasionally have close "friendship" ties. Thus, set against Old World monkey ties, apes ties are highly individualized and built mostly on voluntary-based recruitment rather than kinship-based recruitment.

Does the above shed any light on the origins and evolution of human sociality? In approaching this question we should keep in mind that while humans have greatly excelled in their adaptive strategies over apes, they remain one of the "evolutionary leftovers" on the hominoid family tree. And, in line with other hominoids, humans have, to say the least, atypical social arrangements for a primate species. In looking over the ape ties in Table 1, imagining them simply as social fields of linked conspecifics, apes stand as an anomaly in an order renowned for its high sociability. In orangutans, mostly lone individuals are reported; in gibbons, heterosexual pairs who share domestic activities prevail; in gorillas, lone males are common, while groups members mostly keep to themselves; and in chimpanzees, adult males are gregarious, but are more frequently alone, while adult females are semi-solitary. Overall, apes are self-contained and highly individualistic. What, then, are the implications of these tendencies for understanding human organization?

One of the great assumptions of sociology and anthropology is that high sociality is part of human nature, leading humans to seek out high levels of group involvement and embeddedness. Sociology's most cherished concepts denoting human "pathologies"—for example, anomie, alienation, and egoism—assume that it is "natural" and, by implication, genetically programmed for humans to need social solidarities. If humans belonged to the cercopithecoid family where synchronized movements and close-knit, discrete groups prevail, this sociological presumption would be clearly justified. But humans are hominoids and, therefore, assumptions about their inherent gregariousness are questionable. At the very least, the data presented suggest that we should inquire into how strong humans' genetic social predisposition is. That natural selection pressures for greater sociality have enhanced human network ties relative to other hominoids cannot be denied. Yet, as shown in the cladogram in Figure 1, humans and the African apes recently shared a common ancestor, and at the molecular level the chimpanzee and human DNA differ by only 1.1%, which is far smaller than that between species within a genus of mice, frogs or flies (King and Wilson 1975). Is it possible that what appears to be intense group-bonding tendencies may, in fact, be largely culturally generated and socially transmitted needs that are not rooted in humans' genetic structure (except to the extent that a large brain makes culture possible)?

If we look at the first human societal type—that is, a simple hunting and gathering system—what we find is a flexible and fluid structure made up of 30 to 100 individuals. The core of a hunter-gatherer band is the nuclear family that includes a man, his wife or wives and dependent offspring (culturally created by marriage rules), and so we can assume that selection pressures worked to increase stable ties between parents and adult offspring and between males and females (probably facilitated by subsistence specialization in the sexual division of labor). In common with chimpanzees, weak to moderate tie formations exist among familiar adult males and strong ties exist especially between male siblings. Culturally defined incest taboos exist in all human societies, which probably represent a social elaboration of the mother-son sexual avoidance pattern found in both hominoids and cercopithecoids. Selection for greater bonding between familiar human females is clearly evident although, as with chimpanzees, hunting and gathering bands (as well as tribal societies), have overwhelmingly retained female-biased dispersal (although it is enforced through a cultural rule of exogamy)[12] (Ember 1978; Murdock 1967). At the band level (usually composed of several nuclear family units), there are only slight modifications from African ape ranging patterns. In chimpanzee "communities," members individually move and forage on a common ranging area; in gorillas, one-male groups and some lone males freely move and forage on a shared ranging area and, in hunting and gathering bands, members move and forage on a common ranging area as a loose collective unit, or they break down and disperse into nuclear families in times of scarce resources. Human societies have, in common with chimpanzees, overwhelmingly favored virilocal (or patrilocal) residence (Murdock 1967; Ember 1978). Moreover, band membership is fluid and flexible, since members can move from band to band, or create new bands from members of old bands—a pattern of organizational fluidity reminiscent of apes and the LCA structure. The lack of a dominant leader among hunters and gatherers (a headman without power usually exists) (Lenski and Lenski 1987, p. 115), deviates from the gorilla "silverback" males and the chimpanzee "alpha male" but is close to the reconstructed LCA, where male dominance probably was not prominent. Seemingly, African apes and humans originally evolved in different directions with respect to male dominance, but even here, the divergence is overall slight, when compared with many Old World monkeys who reveal much more rigid male hierarchies. Indeed, the lack of hierarchy in hunters and gatherers again signals humans' connection to the LCA (for general discussions of food collecting societies see Lee and DeVore 1968; Lenski and Lenski 1987; Service 1962, 1966; Bicchieri 1972).

At an even more speculative and philosophical level, the conclusions above might help us to understand the constant tension and vacillation in humans over constraint versus freedom, individualism versus collectivism, freedom of choice versus the collective good, and so on. At a biological level, humans may be far more solitary and individualistic than the collectivist-communal biases of sociology and anthropology would admit; and the constant tension between the individual and the collective may be the result of enduring degrees of humans' derived heritage from the LCA and humans' capacity to create secondary "cortical" bonds largely generated by cultural and social representations. In briefly touching upon the secondary mechanisms for human tie-building at the sociocultural level, it would seem that the evolution of the rich panhuman capacity for linguistically-based communication greatly enhanced the human potential for affective as well as "cortical" bonds, thereby increasing opportunities for successful adaptation to new ecological zones when opportunities for successful pursuit of the basic ape strategy were becoming more and more limited.

Does all this mean that humans are less than social? By no means. It does suggest, however, that the inherent hominoid nature of high individuality and detachment may still be pretty much intact in humans despite all later modifications. Yet, in the *hominid* trend of building network ties, individuality was interweaved with greater sociality. For despite lingering traits of individualism from the LCA, much of what gives humans the identifying feelings of self and individualism are, curiously enough, culturally generated through such social rewards as status, equality and, above all, a sense of membership in primary and secondary groups. Thus, in our search for insights into human social behavior, we might consider a more broadly-based evolutionary framework, since our social history involves a series of events that essentially transformed an ape into a human. While no single factor is responsible for this change, a comparative focus on hominoid social structure and ecology may, if nothing else, lend itself to the asking of new questions while making us aware that things are not always what they appear to be.

NOTES

1.   The ancestor concept is used here to denote genealogical descent through ancestor-descendant relationships. An "ancestor" refers, of course, to a species or population ancestor and *not* to a single organism as ancestor.

2.   The primates are distributed in South and Central America (New World primates), and in Asia and Africa (Old World primates). The fossil evidence strongly points to Africa as the home of the first hominids or human-like primates.

3.   The primates follow most higher vertebrates in the dispersal of one or both sexes around puberty (see Greenwood 1980, for a discussion).

4.   Primate taxonomy rests on organismal, biomolecular, and behavioral evidence. These data arrange primates in a linear sequence of prosimians, New World monkeys, Old World monkeys and hominoids. Two characteristic features of Old World monkeys (Cercopithecoidea) are a generalized skeletal adaptation for a form of locomotion known as arboreal quadrupedalism, where both forelimbs and hindlimbs are relatively short and similar in length, with a tail for balance, and bilophodont dentition. In contrast, apes and humans (Hominoidea) evidence a complex of

adaptations that emphasize forelimb flexibility and suspension, where limbs are long and of unequal length, with the absence of a tail, joints that permit wide mobility in all directions, less specialized teeth and a trend toward larger brains and body size. Anatomical features are often used to infer foraging patterns and, in turn, foraging patterns are seen to interact with morphology and social systems in a complex pattern of cause and effect relations (for discussions see Napier and Napier 1985; Rodman and Cant 1984; Tattersall et al. 1988).

5.   Social organization is used throughout this paper in the broadest sense to refer to any organizational pattern, whether spatial or behavioral, for any discussed primate species.

6.   These measures are independent of each other but are usually intercorrelated. For example, grooming dyads help each other in the removal of ectoparasites, and these same individuals also support each other in antagonistic encounters.

7.   While the earliest basal hominoid fossils come from deposits of Oligocene age in the fayum depressions near Egypt, they lack any derived morphological features linking them with Miocene hominoid taxa (Ciochon 1983). The issue of how these primitive Oligocene hominoids and Miocene apes are linked remains complex and controversial (see Kay and Simons 1980).

8.   Gibbons are the most numerous apes in absolute numbers and species. Taxonomic classifications vary and this paper follows Groves' (1984) and Tuttle's (1986) assessment of eight species and three subgeneria.

9.   Gibbon pairs on average have six offspring over a 10 to 20 year reproductive cycle (Tilson 1981).

10.   Despite years of observing the mating and reproductive behaviors of free-ranging orangutans, research has been hampered by the orangutans long life spans, long birth intervals, and the relatively short field studies relative to birth intervals (Rodman and Mitani 1987).

11.   The Bonobo chimpanzee (Pan paniscus) is a small isolated population limited to Zaire. Relational data on this pygmy species of chimpanzee was not complete enough for a reliable network analysis. However, unlike common chimpanzees, the strongest ties are believed to be between adult males and females (see Wrangham 1986 for a discussion).

12.   Female-biased dispersal is not only the prevalent rule in band, tribal and in Eastern civilizations, like India and China, but is also at the foundation of Western civilization. An example of regulating relations on dispersal is the following Biblical text:

then will we give our daughters unto you, and we will take your daughters to us, and we will dwell with you, and we will become one people (Genesis 34:16—quoted in Fox 1967).

REFERENCES

Aldelman, S. 1986. "Ecological and Social Determinants of Cercopithecine Mating Patterns." Pp. 201-216 in *Ecological Aspects of Social Evolution*, edited by D. Rubenstein and R. Wrangham. Princeton, NJ: Princeton University Press.

Andrews, P. 1981. "Species Diversity and Diet in Monkeys and Apes during the Miocene." Pp. 25-61 in *Aspects of Human Evolution*, edited by C. B. Stringer. London: Taylor and Francis.

Andrews, P., and L. Martin. 1987. "Cladistic Relationships of Extant and Fossil Hominoids." *Journal of Human Evolution* 16:101-118.

Bauer, H. 1976. *Ethological Aspects of Gombe Chimpanzee Aggregations with Implications for Hominisation*. Dissertation, Stanford University.

Bicchieri, M. 1972. *Hunters and Gatherers Today: A Socioeconomic Study of Eleven Such Cultures in the Twentieth Century*. New York: Holt, Rinehart and Winston.

Boaz, N. T. 1983. "Morphological Trends and Phyletic Relationships from Middle Miocene Hominoids to Late Pliocene Hominids." Pp. 705-720 in *New Interpretations of Ape and Human Ancestry*, edited by R. Ciochon and R. Corruccini. New York: Plenum Press.

Cheney, D., R. Seyfarth, and B. Smuts. 1986. "Social Relationships and Social Cognition in Nonhuman Primates." *Science* 234:1361-1366.

Cheney, D., R. Seyfarth, B. Smuts, and R. Wrangham. 1987. "The Study of Primate Societies." Pp. 1-8 in *Primate Societies*, edited by B. Smuts, D. Cheney, R. Seyfarth, R. Wrangham and T. Struhsaker. Chicago: University of Chicago Press.

Chevalier-Skolnikoff, C., and F.E. Poirier. 1977. *Primate Bio-Social Development: Biological, Social and Ecological Determinants*. New York: Garland.

Chivers, D. 1974. "The Siamang in Malaya." *Contributions to Primatology* Vol. 40. New York: S. Karger.

_____. 1984. "Feeding and Ranging in Gibbons: A Summary." Pp. 267-281 in *The Lesser Apes*, edited by H. Prevschoft, D. Chivers, W. Brockelman and N. Creel. Great Britain: Edinburgh University Press.

Ciochon, R. 1983. "Hominoid Cladistics and the Ancestry of Modern Apes and Humans: A Summary Statement." Pp. 781-843 in *New Interpretations of Ape and Human Ancestry*, edited by R. Ciochon and R. Corruccini. New York: Plenum Press.

Ciochon, R., and R. Corruccini. eds. 1983. *New Interpretations of Ape and Human Ancestry*. New York: Plenum Press.

Ciochon, R. and J. Fleagle. 1987. *Primate Evolution and Human Origins*. New York: Aldine De Gruyter.

Clutton-Brock, T., and P. Harvey. 1977. "Primate Ecology and Social Organization." *Journal of Zoology London* 183:1-39.

Cohen, J. 1975. "The Size and Demographic Composition of Social Groups of Wild Orangutans." *Animal Behaviour* 23:543-550.

Corruccini, R. S., and R. L. Ciochon. 1983. "Overview of Ape and Human Ancestry: Phyletic Relationships of Miocene and Later Hominoidea." Pp. 3-15 in *New Interpretations of Ape and Human Ancestry*, edited by R. L. Ciochon and R. S. Corruccini. New York: Plenum.

Cronin, J. E. 1983. "Apes, Humans, and Molecular Clocks: A Reappraisal." Pp. 115-135 in *New Interpretations of Ape and Human Ancestry*, edited by R. Ciochon and R. Corruccini. New York: Plenum Press.

Dixson, A. F. 1981. *The Natural History of the Gorilla*. New York: Columbia University.

Eisenberg, J., N. Muckenhirn, and R. Rudran. 1972. "The Relations between Ecology and Social Structure in Primates." *Science* 176:863-874.

Ellefson, S. O. 1974. "A Natural History of White-Handed Gibbons in the Malaysian Peninsula." Pp. 1-136 in *Gibbons and Siamang*, Vol. 3, edited by D. Rumbaugh. Basel: Karger.

Ember, C. 1978. "Myths about Hunter-Gatherers." *Ethnology* 17:439-448.

Fedigan, L. 1982. *Primate Paradigms: Sex Roles and Social Bonds*. Montreal, Canada: Eden Press.

Fleagle, J. 1986. "The Fossil Record of Early Catarrhine Evolution." Pp. 131-156 in *Major Topics in Primate and Human Evolution*, edited by B. Wood, L. Martin, and P. Andrews. London: Cambridge University Press.

Foley, R. 1984. *Hominid Evolution and Community Ecology*. London: Academic Press.

Fossey, D. 1972. *Living with Mountain Gorillas*. Washington, DC: National Geographic Society.

_____. 1976. *The Behaviour of the Mountain Gorilla*. Dissertation, University of Cambridge.

_____. 1983. *Gorillas in the Mist*. Boston: Houghton Mifflin Company.

Fossey, D., and A. Harcourt. 1977. "Feeding Ecology of Free-Ranging Mountain Gorilla (Gorilla gorilla beringei)." Pp. 415-447 in *Studies of Feeding and Ranging Behaviours in Lemurs, Monkeys and Apes*, edited by T. H. Clutton-Brock. London: Academic Press.

Fox, R. 1967. *Kinship and Marriage*. Middlesex, England: C. Nicholls & Company.

Gaeng, P. 1971. *Introduction to the Principles of Language*. New York: Harper and Row.

Galdikas, B. 1979. "Orangutan Adaptation at Tanjung Puting Reserve: Mating and Ecology." Pp. 194-233 in *The Great Apes*, edited by D. Hamburg and E. McCown. Menlo Park: Benjamin/Cummings.

————. 1984. "Adult Female Sociality Among Wild Orangutans at Tanjung Puting Reserve." Pp. 217-235 in *Female Primates: Studies by Women Primatologists*, edited by M. Small. New York: Alan Liss.

————. 1985. "Adult Male Sociality and Reproductive Tactics Among Orangutans at Tanjung Puting." *Folia Primatologica* 45:9-24.

————. 1988. "Orangutan Diet, Range, and Activity at Tanjung Puting, Central Borneo." *International Journal of Primatology* 9:1-35.

Gittens, S. P. 1980. "Territorial Behavior in the Agile Gibbon." *International Journal of Primatology* 1:381-99.

Goodall-Lawick, J. 1975. "The Behavior of the Chimpanzee." Pp. 74-134 in *Hominisation and Behavior*, edited by G. Kurth and I. Eibl-Eibesfeldt. Stuttgart: Gustav Fischer Verlag.

Goodall, J. 1986. *The Chimpanzees of Gombe: Patterns of Behavior*. Massachusetts: Harvard University Press.

Gouzoules, S. 1984. "Primate Mating Systems, Kin Associations, and Cooperative Behavior: Evidence for Kin Recognition?" *Yearbook of Physical Anthropology*, 27:99-134.

Greenwood, P. J. 1980. "Mating Systems, Philopatry, and Dispersal in Birds and Mammals." *Animal Behaviour* 28: 1140-62.

Groves, C. 1984. "A New Look at the Taxonomy of the Gibbons." Pp. 542-561 in *The Lesser Apes: Evolutionary and Behavioural Biology*, edited by H. Prevschoft, D. Chivers, W. Brockelman, and N. Creel. Edinburgh, Scotland: Edinburgh University Press.

Halperin, S. O. 1979. "Temporary Association Patterns in Free-Ranging Chimpanzees: An Assessment of Individual Grouping Preferences." Pp. 491-499 in *The Great Apes*, edited by D. Hamburg and E. McCown. Menlo Park, CA: Benjamin/Cummings.

Harcourt, A. 1977. *Social Relationships of Wild Mountain Gorillas*. Dissertation, University of Cambridge.

————. 1978. "Strategies of Emigration and Transfer by Primates, with Particular Reference to Gorillas." *Tierpsychologie* 48-401-420.

————. 1979a. "Social Relationships Between Adult Male and Female Gorillas in the Wild." *Animal Behaviour* 27:325-342.

————. 1979b. "Social Relationships Among Adult Female Mountain Gorillas." *Animal Behaviour* 27:251-264.

————. 1979c. "The Social Relations and Group Structure of Wild Mountain Gorillas." Pp. 187-194 in *The Great Apes*, edited by D. Hamburg and E. McCown. Menlo Park, CA: Benjamin/Cummings.

Harcourt, A., K. Stewart, and D. Fossey. 1976. "Male Emigration and Female Transfer in Wild Mountain Gorilla." *Nature* 263:226-227.

————. 1981. "Gorilla Reproduction in the Wild." Pp. 265-279 in *Reproductive Biology of the Great Apes*. New York: Academic Press.

Hass, M. 1966. "Historical Linguistics and the Genetic Relationship of Languages." *Current Trends in Linguistics* 3:113-153.

Hayaki, H. 1988. "Association Partners of Young Chimpanzees in the Mahale Mountains National Park, Tanzania." *Primates* 29:147-161.

Hennig, W. 1966. *Phylogenetic Systematics*. Urbana: University of Illinois Press.

Hinde, R. 1983. *Primate Social Relationships*. Oxford: Blackwell.

Hoenigswald, H. 1950. "The Principal Step in Comparative Grammar." *Language* 26:357-364.

————. 1960. *Language Change and Linguistic Reconstruction*. Chicago: University of Chicago Press.

Isaac, G., and E. McCown. 1975. *Human Origins: Louis Leakey and the East African Evidence.* Menlo Park, CA: Benjamin/Cummings.

Itani, J. 1979. "Distribution and Adaptation of Chimpanzees in an Arid Area." Pp. 55-72 in *The Great Apes*, edited by D. Hamburg and E. McCown. Menlo Park, CA: Benjamin/Cummings.

Jeffers, R., and I. Lehiste. 1979. *Principles and Methods for Historical Linguistics.* Cambridge, MA: MIT Press.

Jolly, A. 1985. *The Evolution of Primate Behavior.* New York: MacMillan.

Jones, C., and J. Sabeter Pi. 1971. *Comparative Ecology of Gorilla gorilla [Savage and Wyman] and Pan troglodytes [Blumenbach] in Rio Muni, West Africa.* New York: S. Karger.

Kay, R. F., and E. L. Simons. 1980. "The Ecology of Oligocene African Anthropoidea." *International Journal of Primatology* 1:21-37.

King, M., and A. Wilson. 1975. "Evolution at Two Levels in Humans and Chimpanzees." *Science* 188:107-116.

Kinzey, W. 1987. *The Evolution of Human Behavior: Primate Models.* Albany: State University of New York Press.

Knoke, D., and J. Kuklinski. 1982. *Network Analysis.* Beverly Hills: Sage.

Lee, R., and I. DeVore. 1968. *Man the Hunter.* Chicago: Aldine.

Leighton, D. 1987. "Gibbons: Territoriality and Monogamy." Pp. 135-145 in *Primate Societies*, edited by B. Smuts, D. Cheney, R. Seyfarth, R. Wrangham, and T. Struhsaker. Chicago: University of Chicago Press.

Lenski, G., and J. Lenski. 1987. *Human Societies.* New York: MacGraw Hill.

Maas, P. 1958. *Textual Criticism.* Oxford: Oxford University Press.

MacKinnon, J. 1971. "The Orang-utan in Sabah Today." *Oryx* 11:141-191.

———. 1974. "The Behaviour and Ecology of Wild Orang-utans." *Animal Behaviour* 22:3-74.

———. 1979. "Reproductive Behavior in Wild Orangutan Populations." Pp. 256-273 in *The Great Apes*, edited by D. Hamburg and E. McCown. Menlo Park, CA: Benjamin/Cummings.

MacKinnon, J. R., and K. S. MacKinnon. 1984. "Territoriality, Monogamy, and Song in Gibbons and Tarsiers." Pp. 267-281 in *The Lesser Apes*, edited by D. Chivers, W. Brockelman, and N. Creel. Edinburgh, Scotland: Edinburgh University Press.

Martin, L. 1986. "Relationships Among Extant and Extinct Great Apes and Humans." Pp. 161-187 in *Major Topics in Primate and Human Evolution*, edited by B. Wood, L. Martin, and P. Andrews. Cambridge: Cambridge University Press.

Maryanski, A. 1986. *African Ape Social Structure: A Comparative Analysis.* Dissertation, University of California, Irvine.

McGinnis, P. R. 1973. *Patterns of Sexual Behaviour in a Community of Free-Living Chimpanzees.* Dissertation, Cambridge University.

Moore, J. 1984. "Female Transfer in Primates." *International Journal of Primatology* 5:537-589.

Murdock, G. 1967. *Ethnographical Altas.* Pittsburgh, PA: University of Pittsburgh Press.

Napier, J. R., and P. H. Napier. 1985. *The Natural History of the Primates.* Cambridge, MA: MIT Press.

Nishida, T. 1979. "The Social Structure of Chimpanzees of the Mahale Mountains." Pp. 73-121 in *The Great Apes*, edited by D. Hamburg and E. McCown. Menlo Park, CA: Benjamin/Cummings.

Nishida, T., and M. Hiraiwa-Hasegawa. 1987. "Chimpanzees and Bonabas: Cooperative Relationships among Males." Pp. 165-180 in *Primate Societies*, edited by B. Smuts, D. Cheney, R. Seyfarth, R. Wrangham, and T. Struhsaker. Chicago: University of Chicago Press.

Phooij, F. 1984. *The Behavioural Development of Free-Living Chimpanzee Babies and Infants.* Norwood, NJ: Ablex Publishing.

Platnick, N., and H.D. Cameron. 1977. "Cladistic Methods in Textual, Linguistic, and Phylogenetic Analysis." *Systematic Zoology* 26:380-385.

Potts, R. 1987. "Reconstructions of Early Hominid Socioecology: A Critique of Primate Models." Pp. 28-47 in *The Evolution of Human Behavior: Primate Models*, edited by W. Kinzey. Albany: State University of New York.

Pusey, A. 1983. "Mother-Offspring Relationships in Chimpanzees After Weaning." *Animal Behaviour* 31:363-77.

Pusey, A. and Packer, C. 1987. "Dispersal and Philopatry." Pp. 250-266 in *Primate Societies*, edited by B. Smuts, D. Cheney, R. Seyfarth, R. Wrangham, and T. Struhsaker. Chicago: University of Chicago Press.

Richard, A. 1985. *Primates in Nature*. New York: W. H. Freeman.

Rijksen, H. 1975. "Social Structure in a Wild Orangutan Population in Sumatra." Pp. 373-379 in *Contemporary Primatology*, edited by S. Kordo, M. Kawai, and A. E. Hara. Basel: Karger.

Rodman, P. 1973. "Population Composition and Adaptive Organization Among Orangutans of the Kutai Reserve." Pp. 171-209 in *Comparative Ecology and Behaviour of Primates*, edited by R. P. Michael and J. H. Crook. London: Academic Press.

————. 1979. "Individual Activity Patterns and the Solitary Nature of Orangutans." Pp. 235-255 in *The Great Apes*, edited by D. Hamburg and E. McCown. Menlo Park, CA: Benjamin/Cummings.

Rodman, P., and J. Cant. 1984. *Adaptations for Foraging in Nonhuman Primates*. New York: Columbia University Press.

Rodman, P., and J. Mitani. 1987. "Orangutans: Sexual Dimorphism in a Solitary Species." Pp. 146-154 in *Primate Societies*, edited by B. Smuts, D. Cheney, R. Seyfarth, R. Wrangham and T. Struhsaker. Chicago: University of Chicago Press.

Sade, D. 1972. "Sociometrics of Macaca Mulatta: Linkages and Cliques in Grooming Matrices." *Folia Primatologila* 18:196-223.

Schaller, G. 1962. *The Ecology and Behavior of the Mountain Gorilla*. Dissertation, University of Wisconsin.

Schurmann, C. 1982. "Mating Behaviour of Wild Orangutans." In *The Orangutan: Its Biology and Conservation*, edited by L. de Boer. The Hague: W. Junk.

Service, E. 1962. *Primitive Social Organization*. New York: Random House.

————. 1966. *The Hunters*. Englewood Cliffs, NJ: Prentice-Hall.

Smuts, B., D. Cheney, R. Seyfarth, R. Wrangham, and T. Struhsaker. 1987. *Primate Societies*. Chicago: University of Chicago Press.

Southwick, C., and M. Siddiqi. 1974. "Contrasts in Primate Social Behavior." *Bio-Science* 24:398-406.

Stewart, K. 1981. *Social Development of Wild Mountain Gorillas*. Dissertation, University of Cambridge.

Stewart, K., and A. Harcourt. 1987. "Gorillas: Variation in Female Relationships." Pp. 155-164 in *Primate Societies*, edited by B. Smuts, D. Cheney, R. Seyfarth, R. Wrangham and T. Struhsaker. Chicago: University of Chicago Press.

Struhsaker, T. 1969. "Correlates of Ecology and Social Organization Among African Cercopithecines." *Folia Primatologica* 11:80-118.

Sugardjito, J., I.J.A. te Boekhorst, and J.H.R.A.M. Rvan Hooff 1987. "Ecological Constraints on the Grouping of Wild Orangutans (Pongo Pygmaeus) in the Gunung Leuser National Park, Sumatra, Indonesia." *International Journal of Primatology* 8:17-41.

Tanner, N. 1981. *On Becoming Human*. Cambridge: Cambridge University Press.

Tattersall, I., E. Delson, and J. Van Couvering. 1988. *Encyclopedia of Human Evolution*. New York: Garland Publishing.

Temerin, J., and J. Cant. 1983. "The Evolutionary Divergence of Old World Monkeys and Apes." *The American Naturalist* 122:335-351.

Tilson, R. L. 1981. "Family Formation Strategies of Kloss's Gibbons." *Folia Primatologica* 35:259-87.

Tutin, C. 1979. "Mating Patterns and Reproductive Strategies in a Community of Wild Chimpanzees (Pan troglodytes schwein furthii)." *Behavioral Ecology and Sociobiology* 6:29-38.

Tutin, C. E. G., McGrew, W. O, and Baldwin, P. J. 1983. "Social Organization of Savannah-Dwelling Chimpanzees, Pan Troglodytes Verus, at Mt. Asserik, Senegal." *Primates* 24:154-173.

Tuttle, R. 1986. *Apes of the World: Their Social Behavior, Communication, Mortality, and Ecology.* Park Ridge, NJ: Noyes.

Weber, A. W., and A. Vedder. 1983. "Population Dynamics of the Gorillas: 1959-1978." *Biological Conservation* 26:341-366.

Wellman, B., and S.O. Berkowitz. 1988. *Social Structures: A Network Approach.* New York: Cambridge University Press.

Wrangham, R. 1980. "An Ecological Model of Female-Bonded Primate Groups." *Behaviour* 74 262-299.

————. 1986. "Ecology and Social Relationships in Two Species of Chimpanzee." Pp. 352-378 in *Ecological Aspects of Social Evolution*, edited by D. Rubenstein and R. Wrangham. Princeton, NJ: Princeton University Press.

Wrangham, R. W., and B. Smuts. 1980. "Sex Differences in Behavioural Ecology of Chimpanzees in Gombe Natural Park, Tanzania." *Journal Reproductive Fertility* (Supplement), 28:13-31.

Yamagiwa, J. 1983. "Diachronic Changes in Two Eastern Lowland Gorilla Groups (Gorilla gorilla graueri) in the Mt. Kahuzi Region, Zaire." *Primates* 25:174-183.

Zihlman, A. L., and J.M. Lowenstein. 1983. "Ramapithecus and Pan paniscus: Significance for Human Origins." Pp. 677-694 in *New Interpretations of Ape and Human Ancestry*, edited by R. L. Ciochon and R. S. Corruccini. New York: Plenum.

THE EVOLUTION OF MACROSOCIETY:

WHY ARE LARGE SOCIETIES RARE?

Richard Machalek

ABSTRACT

A macrosociety features a very large population (hundreds to millions of individuals) that is organized into a complex division of labor executed by members of distinct social categories. Besides modern humans, the only other groups of organisms to have evolved macrosocieties are the social insects (ants, bees, wasps, and termites). This paper explains why macrosocieties have been extremely rare during the evolutionary history of social species. The evolution of macrosociality is inhibited by organismic, ecological, cost-benefit, and sociological constraints. The primary focus of this article is to identify the fundamental sociological constraints and explain how they impinge upon the evolution of macrosociality among organisms ranging from insects to humans.

A *macrosociety* features a very large population (hundreds to millions of individuals) that is organized into a complex division of labor executed by members of distinct social categories. Among humans, macrosociality first appeared with the rise of advanced horticultural societies (circa 4000 B.C.) and,

Advances in Human Ecology, Volume 1, pages 33-64.
Copyright © 1992 by JAI Press Inc.
All rights of reproduction in any form reserved.
ISBN: 1-55938-091-8

therefore, has been relatively recent in the human experience. Later, the Agrarian and Industrial Revolutions ushered in what might be called appropriately the Age of Macrosocieties. Today, the People's Republic of China, with a population in excess of one billion people, is the largest macrosocial nation-state, while the modern world-system may very well represent the largest macrosocial system ever to have evolved (Wallerstein 1974).

The rise of modern macrosocieties stimulated a reflectiveness about society that eventually culminated in the development of modern academic sociology (Ashley and Orenstein 1990). Although industrial macrosocieties represent the dominant preoccupation of most modern sociologists, macrosociality itself predates its earliest human expression by about 200 million years. Besides modern humans, the only other groups of organisms to have evolved the macrosocial mode of life are the social insects (ants, bees, wasps, and termites). This raises a fundamental question for a truly "comparative" sociology, one that crosses species lines: Why have macrosocieties been extremely rare during the evolutionary history of social species?

In nature, the sizes of the groups within which animals live range from dyads to aggregations composed of hundreds of millions of individuals (see Tables 1 and 2). For example, various species of invertebrates, fish, birds, and mammals live in large aggregations such as colonies, schools, flocks, and assorted motion and nesting groups. Although these groups typically lack a complex social structure, they are properly regarded as societies, because they involve cooperative behavior among members of the same species (Wilson 1975, p. 7). For example, species such as the blue wildebeest live in very large herds and cooperate by detecting and communicating the presence of predators. Yet, such groups lack an organized division of labor among categories of behavioral specialists, thereby disqualifying them from status as macrosocieties.

It is particularly curious that macrosociality has appeared only in two groups of organisms (social insects and humans) that are phylogenetically very distant from each other and do not share a recent common ancestor. Social insects and humans are separated from each other by about 600 million years of divergent evolution and five or six orders of magnitude in brain size. Consequently, there is little about the strictly biological characteristics of humans and ants, for example, that invites a comparsion of their systems of social organization and behavior. Somewhat ironically, however, the near biological and psychological incomparability between humans and insects may present a unique, if previously unappreciated, opportunity to conduct a new kind of comparative sociological analysis. Simply put, broad but fundamental similarities between the social organization of human and insect societies may represent comparable solutions to common problems of social structural design. Whatever the species, all social organisms confront the same basic

Table 1. Selected Mammals, by Group Size*

Group Size	Representative Mammals
1-10	orangutans, chinchillas, white-handed gibbons, porpoises, Hamadryas baboons
10-25	gray whales, hippopotamuses, zebras, wild pigs, elephants, white rhinoceroses, ring-tailed lemurs
25-50	eastern mountain gorillas, capybaras, mantled howler monkeys, wolves and wild dogs, lions, black-tailed prarie dogs, giraffes, pecarries, wallabies
30-80	chimpanzees
50-100's +	ungulates
1000	sperm whale, rough-toothed dolphins, ridge-backed dolphins
1000's	blue wildebeests, other ungulate "superherds"
100,000	ocean dolphins
30,000,000	Mexican free-tail bats

Note: *Derived from Wilson (1975).

Table 2. Selected Social Insects, by Group Size*

Group Size	Representative social insects
10-20	Bombinae (orchid bees)
100's-1000's	Vespinae (hornets, yellow jackets, wasps), Myrmeciinae (bulldog ants), Formicini (carpenter ants)
10's of 1000's	Apinae (stingless bees, stingless honeybees)
100's of 1000's	Dorylinae (driver and Old World army ants)
1,000,000	Rhinotermitidae (termites)
20,000,000	*Dorylus* (driver ants)
306,000,000	*Formica yessensis* (1,080,000 queens in 45,000 interconnected nests)

Note: *Derived from Wilson (1971, 1975, 1985).

problems of organizational design and regulation if they are to succeed in evolving macrosocieties. Understood in these terms, the occurrence of a common social form in two biologically remote taxa presents us with a unique opportunity to pose new kinds of questions of a purely sociological nature.

This paper is a case study in what biologists call convergent evolution and what sociologists could describe as comparative sociology, in the broadest sense of the term, involving sociological comparisons and analysis across phylogenetic lines. The analytical approach developed in this paper involves the application of common sociological concepts and principles to an uncommonly wide range of social phenomena. In order to describe the fundamental properties and processes constituting macrosociality, we abandon the nearly universal practice of restricting sociological inquiry to human social behavior. A concern with human sociality alone would be unacceptably restrictive for examining a topic as fundamental and broad as the evolution of macrosociality. Comparative analysis suggests that macrosocieties are rare, because they require the improbable coincidence of several sets of organismic, ecological, economic, and sociological factors. Accordingly, we shall explain why only humans and social insects have managed to overcome the formidible array of constraints which have inhibited the evolution of macrosociality among all other species.

MACROSOCIETIES LARGE AND SMALL

Among humans, macrosocieties began to appear in the advanced horticultural period and then became the characteristic social form of agrarian and industrial societies. In the view of most social scientists, however, the prototypical macrosociety is the industrial society. Industrial societies have extremely large populations, and they feature the most extensive and complex systems of divided labor. A convenient and significant indicator of the scale of macrosociality within industrial societies is the degree of occupational specialization found therein. For example, the *Dictionary of Occupational Titles* (U.S. Department of Labor 1977) lists 20,000 occupations within the United States, a figure that dramatizes the extensiveness of the division of labor within industrial macrosocieties. Since its inception, academic sociology has devoted itself largely to the study of the origins and nature of modern industrial society. This was the common theme pervading the analyses of most of the classical founding fathers of modern sociology (e.g., Spencer 1898; Durkheim 1893; Weber 1904-1905, 1925; Marx 1867; Tönnies 1887; Simmel 1900, 1950; Veblen 1914, 1915). Having had its agenda thus established very early in its disciplinary history, sociology proceeded to develop with an almost singular devotion to the study of human macrosocieties in their industrial and, less often, their agrarian forms. Despite this 100 year history dedicated to the analysis of macrosociality among humans, sociologists have yet to recognize the incidence of macrosociality among other taxa. By taking a less biologically provincial view and by looking beyond the narrow phylogenetic horizons of human societies alone, sociologists could capitalize on a valuable opportunity to gain a more fundamental understanding of the nature of macrosociality and the various sociological constraints which impinge on its evolution.

It is crucial to emphasize that a comparison between human and insect macrosociality is *not* the same activity as comparing humans and insects *as organisms*. As individuals, humans are of course enormously more complex than insects. Ant workers, for example, are usually limited to repertories of 25 to 60 largely instinctive acts, depending on the species (Oster and Wilson 1978). Thus, whatever similarities prevail between human and ant societies cannot be attributed to characteristics shared by the individuals comprising them. Instead, such common social traits represent *convergent evolution,* "the independent evolution of structural or functional similarity in two or more unrelated or distantly related lineages or forms that is not based on genotypic similarity" (Lincoln, Boxshall, and Clark 1982, p. 57).

Among both humans and social insects, then, macrosocieties share the same basic structural features: large populations of individuals organized into a complex division of labor executed by members of distinct social categories. Since few social scientists, including sociologists, are familiar with the subtle organization, the rich complexity, and the dynamism of insect societies, a brief description of insect sociality is required for us to proceed. While selecting ant societies as my preferred example, many of the organizational and behavioral traits described herein also typify bee, wasp, and termite societies as well.

Population Size

While the populations of ant colonies commonly include hundreds of individuals, single colonies of African driver ants may have over 20,000,000 members (Wilson 1985, p. 1489). Even more striking is a "supercolony" of ants reported by Higashi and Yamauchi (1979) that contained 306,000,000 workers and 1,080,000 queens. These societies are not merely aggregations of individuals sharing a tightly circumscribed territory. Rather, they are complex social systems which display intricate patterns of structural differentiation and functional integration. In fact, they give Durkheim's concept of organic solidarity a new richness of meaning that he would likely have found appealing (1893). While other animal societies display subtle and dynamic patterns of divided labor, none have attained the extensive patterns of complex cooperation at the level of very large populations. For example, cooperative predators such as lions, wolves, or African hunting dogs execute very sophisticated and highly coordinated hunting maneuvers, but these groups almost never involve more than twenty or so individuals (Wilson 1975, pp. 504-513). In short, humans excepted, vertebrates simply have not evolved or developed macrosocieties.

Division of Labor

Within colonies (nests), ants feature a highly coordinated division of labor, which biologists call polyethism, involving at least five kinds of tasks: foraging for and distributing food, mutual grooming, nest maintenance, nest and territorial defense, and brood care (Wilson 1971 1975 1985). By bringing these activities into even sharper focus for one ant species, Wilson identifies fifteen distinct tasks assumed by individual workers that shift according to their age (1985, pp. 1493-1494). Ant castes may be organized on the basis of morphological differences (especially size) among individuals (Wilson 1975, p. 299; 1971; Oster and Wilson 1978). The division of labor among ant castes is typically highly specialized and variable from species to species. In fact, the proportion of individuals within each caste can vary as a colony ages and increases (or decreases) in population size (Wilson 1985). Furthermore, some ant castes specialize in activities as diverse as guarding and defense, reproduction, storing food in their bodies as living "casks," nest construction and maintenance, leaf cutting, fungi harvesting, tending aphid "livestock," nursemaiding brood (eggs, pupae, and larvae), grooming queens, and so on.

Communication

Relatively simple organisms can behave, in aggregate, so as to create remarkably complex social systems. A key to this paradox lies in their system of communication: "The individual social insect, in comparison with the individual solitary insect, displays behavioral patterns that are neither exceptionally ingenious nor exceptionally complex. The remarkable qualities of social life are mass phenomena that emerge from the meshing of these simple individual patterns by means of communication" (Wilson 1971, p. 224).

Unlike humans, social insects rely predominantly upon chemical rather than visual or auditory signals to communicate. Theirs is an olfactory world. Odors are supplemented, to a lesser extent, by tactile signals such as tappings, strokings, and graspings, as well as by sounds created by rubbing specialized body parts together (stridulation). Ants possess up to a dozen or more glands that emit these communication chemicals (pheromones), but their chemical alphabet may be limited to as few as ten pheromones (Wilson 1962). And while individual ants are capable of limited learning and possess special memory capacities of spatial orientation, their behavioral ensemble is rather tightly circumscribed. All the same, they have evolved the capacity for a rather long list of communicative acts. This communication system greatly facilitates the rise of macrosociety among these creatures.

Predation is a serious threat for organisms as small as ants. As a result, they rely heavily upon a variety of chemical alarm systems to signal threat. Many of these are aerosols of sorts, and the degree to which the chemicals are concentrated helps determine the recepient's response. Among the most interesting aspects of chemical communication among social insects are their techniques for recruiting their colony members to join them in activities such as migration, nest building, nest defense, and food retrieval. Insect social life depends upon each individual's ability to recognize nestmates and caste members. Again, chemicals mediate these processes of social recognition and interaction (Wilson 1971).

This brief sketch is intended to introduce the basic characteristics of the deceptively complex insect societies. In order to answer the key question posed in this paper, we now identify and discuss four sets of constraints on the evolution of macrosociality.

CONSTRAINTS ON THE EVOLUTION OF MACROSOCIALITY

Macrosocieties are rare in nature, because their evolution requires the highly improbable coincidence of a number of complex factors. These factors first coalesced about 200 million years ago with the evolutionary emergence of the first social insects. Only very recently (about 6000-10,000 years ago) have these factors once again coincided to produce macrosociality among humans, a species which is phylogenetically remote from the social insects. These factors may be envisioned as sets of constraints which inhibit the evolution of macrosociality. Alternatively, they may be construed as "design problems," solutions to which have evolved only among modern humans and the social insects. Inasmuch as the social insects and humans have evolved extremely different, but analogous, devices by means of which to overcome these constraints and to organize themselves into macrosocieties, a comparison between these two remotely related social organisms presents a fertile topic for a comparative sociological study of convergent evolution. Constraints on the evolution of macrosociality may be classified into four general categories: (1) organismic (genetic, morphological, and physiological) constraints, (2) ecological constraints, (3) cost-benefit (economic) constraints, and (4) sociological constraints. The first three will be discussed briefly, but closest attention will be devoted to sociological constraints.

Organismic Constraints

The logic of classical Darwinian evolutionary theory rests upon a key premise: individual organisms are designed by natural selection to acquire traits, including behavior patterns, which maximize an individual's chances of reproductive success or "fitness" (the production of offspring which survive to reproductive age). This has come to be known commonly within evolutionary theory as the "maximization principle" (Barash 1982; Lopreato 1984; Trivers 1985; Wilson 1975). The maximization principle yields the Darwinian prediction that individual organisms should rarely forego opportunities to maximize personal (Darwinian) reproductive fitness. Perplexingly (even to Darwin) however, one major group of organisms, the social insects, has evolved a mode of social life that appears to violate dramatically the maximization principle.

Within a colony of ants, for example, it is not uncommon for all but one of the hundreds to thousands of females to refrain from laying eggs, opting instead to "comply" with an evolutionary arrangement whereby a single female monopolizes egg production, while all of the rest of the females labor in support of the reproductive efforts of this "queen" and her reproductive activity. It was not until the British evolutionary biologist W.D. Hamilton (1964) solved this Darwinian riddle that the genetic foundation of eusociality among ants, bees, and wasps was understood. The key to the puzzle resides in an unusual genetic phenomenon labeled haplodiploidy by biologists. A haplodiploid organism is one in which males have only one set of chromosomes (haploidy) and are the product of unfertilized eggs, while females derive from fertilized eggs and therefore have both sets of chromosomes (diploidy), one complement from each parent. Another relevant feature of haplodiploidy is that females are more highly related, on average, to their sisters ($r = .75$) than they are to either parent ($r = .50$). Consequently, haplodiploidy creates an unusual circumstance whereby a population of nonreproducing sisters may achieve higher fitness by foregoing individual reproduction and, instead, devoting themselves to the support of the reproductive success of a single (or a few) female which has been "assigned" the role of "reproductive organ" for the entire colony of females. Underwriting this entire, somewhat strange arrangement is the explanation that natural selection is ultimately driven by the replicative activity of genes, not simply the reproductive success of whole organisms (Dawkins 1976 1982 1989). Thus, under special circumstances, individuals may transmit more copies of their genes to subsequent generations by refraining from personal reproduction and supporting instead the reproductive efforts of close kin. Since close kin are likely to share genes, the *reproductive* success of one individual is likely to mean *genetic* replicative success for its close kin. The process has come to be known as kin-selection and is said to maximize inclusive fitness, not simply individual (Darwinian) fitness. Consequently, by using the calculus of kin-selection theory, Hamilton and his successors have explained, at least to the satisfaction of most contemporary evolutionary scientists, the existence of large populations of nonreproductive individuals within colonies of social insects.[1]

Unfortunately, however, the very success of Hamilton's explanation of eusociality has probably precluded evolutionary biology's recognition of the important sociological problem identified as the theme of this analysis. When faced with the evolutionary question, "why are large societies rare?" most evolutionary biologists would likely respond, "because haplodiploidy is rare." While haplodiploidy clearly creates a genetic "incentive" for natural selection to favor the emergence of macrosociality among certain genetically extraordinary species, it does not account fully for the evolution of macrosociality whatever the species in which it occurs. In short, despite the extraordinary inducement for the evolution of macrosociality that is presented by the genetics of haplodiploidy, genes in and of themselves are simply insufficient to generate macrosocieties. Instead, other requirements must be met as well. In fact, as the incidence of macrosociety among humans attests, an unusual degree of genetic relatedness is unnecessary for the emergence of macrosociality.

A brief look at one additional case of unusual genetics in the nonhuman animal world will help to underscore the argument that the evolution of macrosociality requires much more than an extraordinary degree of genetic relatedness among individuals. If a high degree of genetic relatedness among individuals were sufficient to promote a high degree of complex sociality among animals, then macrosociality should be prominent among nine-banded armadillos. Armadillos possess an unusual genetic trait whereby their litters are always comprised of identical quadruplets (Dawkins 1989, p. 93). Consequently, one might think that armadillo biology provides a strong genetic inducement for the evolution of highly cooperative, even sacrificial (altruistic) patterns of behavior among these curious mammals. Instead, armadillos are a solitary species with social behavior restricted to a limited period of maternal solicitude which is typical of many mammals. Given their unusually high degree of genetic relatedness, why are armadillo siblings not highly cooperative, as are the social insects?

A deceptively simple answer to this question is that armadillos have little to gain by living group lives, thus, natural selection would not have favored the evolution of cooperative behavior among these creatures. Unlike predators, armadillos forage by digging up and eating various invertebrates such as worms and insect larvae. This mode of foraging is unlikely to be enhanced by collective cooperation, as it is among canid packs. Nor does it appear that group life would offer much to the armadillo in defending itself against predators. Instead, the armadillo is equipped with a very tough, hard leathery shell that successfully thwarts the efforts of its more common predators such as coyotes and wildcats. Furthermore, it is equipped with very strong hind legs with which it can dig itself to safety into a burrow, further enhancing its success at avoiding predation. In short, the unique morphology and foraging strategies of armadillos means that they have very little to gain by assuming patterns of cooperative living. The armadillo's mode of foraging, self-defense, and reproduction have apparently made it a poor candidate for the evolution of highly cooperative group life, despite its strong, built-in genetic incentive for cooperation and perhaps, even altruism.

Other species, some with very high degrees of individual intelligence, also fail to evolve systems of social cooperation. As with armadillos, morphology may inhibit the evolution of sociality. This is seen most clearly with regard to what may be called production morphologies and defense morphologies. Production morphology refers to those physical traits which decree how an animal makes its living, that is, how it meets its needs for food and shelter. Ungulates, such as deer and antelope, provide a good case in point of how an animal's production morphology may limit its potential to evolve complex forms of cooperation. Biologists describe such animals as browsers and grazers, and there is little that group life can do to enhance browsing and grazing efficiency, short of providing more surveillance for predators. This holds true even for aquatic browsers and grazers, such as baleen whales which live off microorganisms ingested by filter feeding. However, herd animals such as deer and antelope do rely on concealment, early detection, and flight for defense against predators. This is, in fact, conducive to the evolution of living in aggregations and thereby "sharing" sense organs used to detect and communicate threat. In addition, by joining a sufficiently large aggregation of other antelope, a given individual reduces the probability that it will be singled out for attack by a marauding predator. Biologists refer to this as the selfish herd phenomenon (Hamilton 1971). Beyond this, there is little else that group life bestows upon antelope for protection against predators.

Consequently, it is clear that the production and defense morphologies of various species set basic limits on the extent to which complex forms of cooperative behavior can evolve. Some animals, such a whales, which are extremely intelligent and even appear to "enjoy" social life, are severely limited by their "body plans" in their capacities for patterns of complex cooperation. The evolution of a division of labor cannot occur among species in which individuals are incapable of engaging in diverse forms of productive behavior. When morphology constrains the range of diverse behaviors of which organisms are capable, it also constrains the evolution of a complex and extensive division of labor.

This discussion of organismic constraints on the evolution of macrosociality has been necessarily rather long because of the prior emphasis placed by biologists on the genetics of haplodiploidy in explaining macrosociety among the social insects. By considering how production and defense morphologies can limit (or facilitate) the nature and extent of cooperation among animals, we have added balance to previous biological discussions of organismic constraints on the evolution of social behavior.

Ecological Constraints

In addition to organismic constraints, the *ecological context* within which organisms live sets limits on group size and complexity. Ecosystems inhibit the evolution of macrosocieties most directly by limiting population size. Macrosocieties require resources (food, shelter, raw materials) in sufficient abundance to sustain their unusually large populations. In part, social insects have been very successful in evolving macrosocieties because insects are very small organisms, and they have little difficulty in finding environments with ample resources to sustain their very large populations. Similarly, some ecosystems inhibit the growth of large populations, because they contain greater varieties and denser populations of predators. Other environments generate higher mortality rates due to disease, thereby limiting population growth. The physical properties of the habitat in which a species lives may also set limits on population size. While some habitats, such as oceans and plains, are highly conducive to the assembly of very large aggregations, other types of habitat, for example, dense jungles, may severely limit group size. For arboreal animals, such as many primate species, tree-dwelling itself may erect insurmountable physical obstacles which preclude the evolution of viable macrosocieties. Finally, some species confront intense levels of competition with other species, thereby placing even further limits on population size. Although this brief enumeration of ecological factors hardly begins to identify the full range of ecological constraints which operate in nature, it serves to illustrate the manner in which ecological factors may inhibit the evolution of macrosociality.

Cost-Benefit Constraints

In addition to organismic and ecological factors, the evolution of macrosociality is also constrained by economic factors or various "costs and benefits" that accompany this societal form. The benefits of organizing large populations into a complex division of labor have long been recognized by social scientists (Durkheim 1893; Smith 1776). More recently,

> entomologists have come to recognize . . . [that] coordinated groups conduct parallel as opposed to serial operations and hence make fewer mistakes, especially when labor is divided among specialists. [Also,] groups can concentrate more energy and force at critical points than can single competitors, using sheer numbers to construct nests in otherwise daunting terrain, as well as to defend the young, and to retrieve food more effectively (Wilson 1985, p. 1489).

In the views of both sociologists and behavioral biologists, large societies with a high degree of division of labor typically are productively superior to smaller societies composed of behavioral generalists. Given its organizational superiority, it is curious that macrosociality is surprisingly rare.

Important insights into this problem can be gained by guidance from a relatively new form of cost-benefit analysis that recently has become commonplace in behavioral biology. Behavioral biologists interpret patterns of social behavior in terms of their contribution to the fitness of the individuals which enact them, and "every trait has both negative and positive effects on individual fitness" (Alcock 1984, p. 200). For example, male birds which display brightly colored feathers to attract mates (an evolutionary "benefit") also increase their chances of falling victim to a predator (an evolutionary "cost") because they sacrifice cryptic coloration for sexual attractiveness. Insights such as this have led to the development of optimality theory in behavioral biology (Wilson 1968; Oster and Wilson 1978). Optimality theory suggests that every evolved trait, including behavior, can be analyzed for the ratio of costs to benefits that it yields. This implies that there is an optimal state for every adaptive trait.

Consider, for example, the optimal size for a school of fish. Assume that the major benefit derived from schooling is predator detection and avoidance. The school should be large enough to provide maximum surveillance for predators and a minimum probability that any particular fish will be singled out and attacked if a predator approaches. Again, this is an example of Hamilton's (1971) selfish herd principle. By associating itself with a school, an individual fish receives at least two benefits denied it by a solitary life-style: (1) by surrounding itself with other fish, it reduces the probability that it will be singled-out by an approaching predator, and (2) it increases the chances that it will detect an approaching predator, because it can benefit from the detection of predators by other fish in the school. Nevertheless, such an arrangement is not without serious potential costs. If the size of the school becomes too large, it may attract more predators. Also, larger schools intensify competition among individuals and promote disease transmission within the school. In principle, optimality theory allows us to identify the optimal size of the fish school, the size at which the ratio of benefits to costs is the highest.

The logic of cost-benefit analysis can be applied to the organizational trait of the division of labor as well as to the trait of population size. As discussed earlier, by evolving societies with a complex division of labor among specialized castes, the social insects have used social organization to compensate for their small size as individuals and thus increase their ergonomic efficiency and effectiveness. This division of labor involves cooperation among individuals who recognize each other as members of castes, but not as individuals. Castes specialize in various tasks such as foraging, defense, brood-tending, nest-repair, and so on. Accordingly, an ant colony can be described as a system of cooperation which is so complex and highly integrated as to be described as a superorganism, a characterization originally introduced by the ant biologist W. M. Wheeler and developed more recently by E.O. Wilson (1971 1984). Yet, the very complexity and extensiveness of cooperation within these social systems make them particularly vulnerable to certain types of costs. Specifically, some ant societies fall victim to other organisms which have evolved to exploit the very division of labor evolved by the ants. This is called social parasitism, and it involves processes whereby alien invaders expropriate labor or food from unsuspecting ants. For example, the staphylinid beetle (*Atemeles pubicollis*) uses chemical signals to deceive ants and insinuate itself into the ant colony. After having gained entrance into the nest, the beetle then uses the same tactile stimulus that ants use to solicit food regurgitations from their nestmates. Consequently, the beetle is able to "break the code" of communication used by ants to share food, and it is thus able to exploit (parasitize) the system of cooperative food-sharing evolved by ants (Wilson

1975, pp. 375-377). The costs that ants pay for having evolved cooperative food production and sharing are vividly evident.

Ant macrosocieties are vulnerable not only to food parasites, but to labor parasites as well. Certain species of ants have evolved to raid the nests of other ants of a different but closely related species to steal their pupae. The raiders then return to their own nest with stolen pupae which eventually develop into workers. These captured workers then make a chemical error in kin-recognition and proceed to work cooperatively for their captors and against their own biological interests (Wilson 1975, p. 368-373). Once again, the "slave-makers" have evolved the capacity to deceive the "slaves" and thus exploit the labor power of the workers of another species. Since the highly cooperative division of labor among ants is mediated by a system of chemical and tactile communication which is susceptible to invasion by other species, this type of macrosociality carries with it a threat of serious potential costs in the form of social parasitism. In such cases, the benefits of macrosocial organization are at least partially offset by the costs imposed by various forms of social parasitism. Despite being one of the most productive forms of social organization ever to have evolved, macrosociality also creates a context of extremely rich opportunities for the evolution of social exploitation.

Sociological Constraints

Sociological constraints comprise the fourth set of constraints impinging on the evolution of macrosociality. Even when the three previously discussed sets of constraints are overcome, it is still highly unlikely that macrosociality will evolve among a particular species. A macrosociety requires a unique form of social interaction that is rare in nature, and requires the solution of formidable problems of social organization that are beyond the capacities of most organisms. The sociological constraints pertinent to the evolution of macrosociality involve three general problems:

1. individuals must be capable of impersonal cooperation;
2. labor must be divided and allocated among members of distinct social categories;
3. specialized patterns of labor must be coordinated and integrated.

These three sets of sociological constraints may be envisioned as "design problems" inherent in the evolution of macrosociality. Since only the social insects and modern humans have generated solutions to all three sets of design problems and thereby have succeeded in evolving macrosocieties, we shall compare insect to human macrosociality in order to elucidate the social evolutionary processes responsible for producing this rare and complex form of social organization.

The Problem of Impersonal Cooperation

Almost without exception, animal societies are essentially kinship groups. As Hamilton (1964) made clear in his explanation of the evolution of social behavior, genetic relatedness is *the* fundamental mechanism underwriting social organization and social behavior in the animal world. Consequently, this severely restricts the number of individuals that can be organized into a cooperative group. Among diploid organisms, at least, the average degree of relatedness among individuals tends to decline sharply as group size increases. For example, while full siblings have 5 chances in 10 of sharing the same allele (specific gene), second cousins have only 3 chances in 100 of carrying a common allele. This means that large, extended kinship groups will contain many individuals who are no more closely related to many of their "kin" than they are to nonkin within the population. The genetic forces which promote the evolution of cooperative sociality among animals quickly lose their potency as the degree of kinship among individuals within a population declines. Among diploid organisms, such as mammals, kinship therefore inhibits the evolution of macrosociality, because large groups rarely are comprised strictly of close kin.

Since kinship is the dominant organizing principle governing social behavior among animals, it is imperative that individuals have the basic capacity to distinguish kin from nonkin. Biologists call this capacity kin recognition, and a quarter century of sociobiological research has generated a large body of literature on this topic (see Fletcher and Michener 1987 for a current and comprehensive review of that literature). The general principle that links kinship to social behavior among animals may be stated as follows: The greater the degree of genetic relatedness among individuals, the higher the probability that they will interact cooperatively.

The social insects are able to distinguish kin from nonkin largely by means of chemical communication. However, there is no evidence that social insects have the capacity to recognize each other as individuals. On the other hand, individual recognition is well-developed among many vertebrates, especially mammals. Chimpanzees, and other primates as well, appear to rely heavily on facial characteristics to recognize individuals, both kin and nonkin (Goodall 1986). Consequently, chimpanzee social life is organized not only by general status attributes such as sex and age, but by the recognition of personal traits as well. As is true of all other social species, the *ultimate* (evolutionary) force organizing chimpanzee socialty is kin selection. However, the *proximate* mechanisms regulating patterns of social interaction include highly individualized, personal relationships, the construction and maintenance of which are based upon chimanzees' highly evolved capacity for individual recognition.

Research on interpersonal interaction among chimpanzees reveals social behavior that is subtle, flexible, and very complex (Goodall 1986; Van de Waal 1982). No doubt, the complexity of group life among chimpanzees owes largely to the high degree of individual intelligence among these animals. Nevertheless, chimpanzees do not assemble themselves into macrosocieties, but ants do. Why have chimpanzees, which are almost incalculably more intelligent than insects, failed to evolve macrosocieties, while their very near cousin, *Homo sapiens*, has achieved this insectan feat? Intelligence alone cannot account for this discrepancy, because social insects, which are possessed of negligible individual intelligence compared to any vertebrate, pioneered the evolution of macrosocieties hundreds of millions of years before humans.

It is quite possible that the limiting constraints on the evolution of macrosociality among chimpanzees may involve organismic, ecological, or cost-benefit factors of the sort that were discussed earlier. However, in direct relation to the thesis at hand, it is clear that chimpanzees, unlike humans and ants, are unable to come to grips with a fundamental sociological constraint which inhibits the evolution of macrosociety: the capacity for impersonal cooperation. Organisms with a highly evolved capacity for individual recognition form cooperative social relationships with others, typically close kin, which are highly personalized. It is very difficult for a social system that limits membership to close kin and organizes interaction on the basis of individual recognition to evolve into a macrosociety. Human macrosocieties have evolved because humans, unlike chimpanzees, have escaped the limiting influences of kinship and personal relationships as the basis of cooperative social behavior. Stated differently, a great many intelligent social species, such as chimpanzees, are confronted by a paradox that may render them incapable of macrosocial life. Because they possess a very high degree of individual intelligence and a highly-evolved capacity for individual recognition, such animals are virtually compelled to interact with conspecifics *as individuals*, in a highly personalized, nearly anthropomorphic manner. Consequently, however, they are apparently *incapable* of the patterns of impersonal interaction which are definitive of macrosociality among species such as ants and humans. Inasmuch as the social insects are apparently incapable of individual recognition, they escape the primate restriction of having to enter into a personal relationship in order to behave cooperatively. On the other hand, humans have evolved macrosocieties because they are empowered by culture to form highly cooperative patterns of behavior with "anonymous others." Thus, for the social insects, a state of permanent personal anonymity enables them to form large, complex societies comprised of purely impersonal cooperation among members of different castes. Humans, on the other hand, are capable of forming cooperative social systems based *either* upon personal relationships or impersonal status-role attributes.

Macrosociality requires that individuals interact cooperatively not as individuals, but as personal strangers. Since animal sociality has been organized almost exclusively upon the basis of close kinship, a society built out of patterns of impersonal cooperation among strangers appears unattainable by means of the normal evolutionary processes which organize social behavior. Yet, it is impersonal cooperation that lies at the very foundation of macrosociality. What are the advantages of impersonal cooperation, and how have the social insects and humans used different but functionally analogous strategies to achieve the capacity for close cooperation among anonymous others, thereby facilitating the evolution of macrosociety?

Generally, the number of conspecifics with which an animal may cooperate is strictly limited by kinship. The evolutionary biologist Robert Trivers (1971), however, explained how cooperative patterns of exchange may evolve among nonkin as well. The expansion of forms of cooperation to include individuals who are nonkin has been discussed at length recently by Axelrod (1984). By expanding patterns of cooperation beyond kin lines, individuals may gain access to a much wider range of resources and services than those made available only by close kin. If an individual is able to cooperate with nonkin in the larger population of which he or she is a member, then the range of potential cooperators is limited only by population size. This increases the potential rewards of sociality several-fold for any given individual within the population. One need only compare the potential economic "yield" from a system of exchange within a tribal, kin-based society to that of a modern, industrial, market economy in order to appreciate the significance of the evolution of nonkin based systems of reciprocity.

In macrosocieties, cooperation occurs not among individuals who interact *as individuals*, but instead as representatives of social categories. Under these circumstances, patterns of close cooperation are executed by individuals who typically are total personal strangers to each other. Again, consider the ants. A colony of several million fungus growing ants (*Atta colombica*) may include 1-2.5 million workers (Wilson 1971, p. 47). These ants are organized into extremely productive macrosocieties in which they participate in highly cooperative systems of fungus "gardening." Despite their highly cooperative patterns of interaction, fungus growing ants are not capable of forming several million social relationships on which to base cooperation. Indeed, it is highly unlikely that any species, humans included, would ever be capable of forming and sustaining even a few hundred personal social relationships, much less millions. Instead, macrosocial organization enables individuals to enter into cooperative relations with an almost infinite number of others.

The simple fact is that individual members of macrosocieties are not required to form a large number of social relationships in order to participate in societies with populations numbering into thousands or millions of individuals. Ants, for example, need only be capable of interacting with only 5 or 6 *types* of ants, not millions of *individual* ants. When ants cooperate, they do not interact as individuals, instead, they engage each other as members of socially distinct categories called castes. Thus, a colony of several million individuals is transformed, by the caste system, into a set of 5 or 6 social types (castes), a range of variation which is entirely manageable, even by ants. The caste system thus reduces drastically the number of types of social relationships which organisms are required to negotiate. At the same time, the caste system expands greatly the number of potential cooperators within the population. Such systems allow individuals in macrosocieties to cooperate with virtually an infinite number of other individuals if they can be recognized as members of a finite number of social types.

What are the specific mechanisms by means of which a population of 1 million individual ants are transformed into 5-6 types of individuals? Basically, ants use a system of tactile and chemical communication to "typify" other ants as members of a small number of castes. Each ant possesses up to a dozen glands that generate chemicals, called pheromones, which are used to communicate. Ants release as few as 10 pheromones to comprise the "alphabet" of their chemical system of communication. In addition, ants may use their antennae and forelimbs to "read" the body forms of other ants, much as a blind person uses Braille, in order to ascertain caste membership of other ants that it encounters. As a result, ants quickly determine the caste of any other ant which they encounter and then execute the appropriate sequence of behaviors which result in patterns of cooperation. Because it is almost mechanical, this system is virtually the embodiment of the idea of the sort of impersonal cooperation upon which macrosocieties are built.

Among humans, the production of impersonal cooperation is considerably more problematic than among ants. Arguably, humans evolved as a species wherein social relationships were organized along highly personal, individual lines. In fact, it is commonly reported that the only impersonal attributes which help organize patterns of social interaction among hunters and gatherers are age and sex. Beyond these two ascribed status attributes, social interaction among hunter-gatherers is determined largely by the individual traits and personal relationships of the actors involved. Since the mean population size of hunter and gatherer bands was about 40 people, it is not surprising that hunter-gatherer social structure was basically a network of interrelated personal relationships. Consequently, it is plausible to speculate that humans may have evolved as a species particularly well-adapted to a microsocial form of life. How, then, have humans managed to transcend their apparent microsocial evolutionary legacy to emerge as the species featuring the largest macrosocieties ever to have appeared on Earth?

As among any other social species, human macrosociality requires a device for converting individuals into social types. Among social insects, this is accomplished by means of chemical communication. Among humans, it is achieved by means of cognitive culture. By exploiting the cognitive process that phenomenological social theorists call typification, humans are able to classify each other into various social categories and interact primarily on the basis of the "scripts" implied therein (Berger and Luckmann 1967; Schutz 1967). The cultural device by means of which this is accomplished is the status-role complex. Although the idea of status-role is so familiar and basic to most sociologists as to be taken-for-granted, its evolutionary significance would be difficult to overstate. Status-role constructs are the evolutionarily convergent human analogue to the chemical and tactile typification processes among social insects upon which caste systems are built. Status-role typifications enable humans to ignore precisely the individual qualities of another actor, thereby increasing economy of cooperative interaction. Ants cannot apprehend each other as individuals; they can only employ olfactory and tactile cues to perceive other ants as members of a caste (e.g., major worker, minor worker, soldier, queen, drone, etc.). Humans, however, have an option unavailable to the social insects. They can *alternate* between using personal and impersonal attributes in organizing their social lives.

Systems of cooperation among humans that are organized in terms of impersonal status-role attributes are the very infrastructure upon which human macrosociety is erected. Impersonal cooperation in human macrosocieties allows total strangers who have never before met to engage in cooperative patterns of behavior, such as trade, without having the slightest personal knowledge or experience of each other. Such a system is mediated by tacit agreements to interact on the basis of shared understandings embodied in cognitive and normative culture. By employing status-role typifications not restricted to kinship, humans have expanded the range of potential cooperators to include the entire global human population. Consequently, the development of status-role constructs must be regarded as one of the greatest innovations to have occured in the history of cultural evolution.

This line of reasoning suggests an historical hypothesis that deserves mention. When humans lived almost exclusively in extended kin groups, we would expect that kinship terminology would dominate the status-role constructs used to organize and regulate social life. At some point in our evolutionary history, however, a class of new, *nonkin* status-role constructs would likely emerge. For example, these nonkin status-role complexes might designate occupation or craft, social class position, or region of origin. The proliferation of nonkin status-role constructs should be associated with the rise of macrosociality among humans, and it could be explained in positive feedback terms, as both a contributing cause and product of the rise of human macrosociety.

Finally, we close this discussion of the problem of impersonal cooperation with another look at the question posed earlier in this section: Why have not chimpanzees, humanity's very close cousins, evolved macrosociality? If the capacity for impersonal cooperation helps determine a species' prospects for evolving macrosociality, chimpanzees find themselves, as do many other mammals, at a double disadvantage in relation to insects and humans. Chimpanzees seem not to have evolved sufficiently complex systems of symbolic communication to enable them to transform individuals into social types. This may simply reflect a difference between humans and the great apes in terms of brain size or structure. Clearly, chimpanzee *microsocieties* feature very subtle, complex, and dynamic systems of cooperation (Goodall 1986; Van de Waal 1982). However, chimpanzee sociality does not feature large populations of individuals organized into social categories of behavioral specialists engaged in a complex division of labor. This is because chimpanzees apparently lack a sufficiently complex cognitive culture which could provide status-role typifications in terms of which these animals could regard each other not as individuals, but as workers, soldiers, reproductive specialists, and so on.[2] Perhaps only because we humans have evolved cognitive culture, which has enabled us to generate nonkin based status-role typifications, have we been able to achieve macrosociality, while chimpanzees, with whom we share over 99% of our genetic material, have not.

In summary, macrosociality entails the capacity for very large numbers of individuals to organize themselves into complex systems of cooperation with anonymous others. While individual anonymity is biologically ordained for the social insects, among humans it must be achieved. This has become possible only because of the evolution of complex cognitive culture. Both the social insects and modern humans employ strategies for typifying individuals as members of social categories, thereby escaping the overwhelming inefficiency and complexity which would characterize a social system organized on the basis of purely personal relationships. From the analytical perspective developed herein, it matters little if the typification medium is chemical or cultural. Either path solves the problems of promoting cooperation among strangers in very large populations, thereby overcoming a major hurdle toward the evolution of macrosociality.

Macrosocieties are based upon the capacity for large numbers of individuals to interact cooperatively as anonymous others. By escaping the common evolutionary limitation whereby cooperation is most often based upon either close kinship or individual recognition (reciprocal altruism/favoritism), macrosociality entails the existence of patterns of close cooperation among an indeterminate number of individuals, all of whom may be nonkin and total personal strangers to each other. The caste system among ants and status-role relationships among humans reduces the number of social relationships which an individual must negotiate while, at the same time, expanding vastly the number of potential cooperators in a population. Finally, systems of impersonal cooperation introduce efficiency and economy into a society, because impersonality specifies and delimits the range of mutual obligations among the parties to the interaction.

The Division of Labor

Labor can be divided among the members of a population in two ways. First, all the members of a population may simply share responsibility for performing the same tasks. For example, all of the birds in a flock may keep watch for predators and sound alarms when one is detected. Second, labor may be divided by allocating different types of tasks to different individuals or categories of individuals within a population. Stated differently, labor may be divided either among *generalists*, all of whom perform the same tasks or sets of tasks, or it may be divided among various types of *specialists* which assume responsibility for different types of tasks. Macrosociality entails a division of labor among task specialists.

Social scientists have long recognized the advantages that inhere in the division of labor (e.g., Durkheim, 1893; Perrow 1986). Basically, the division of labor is said to contribute to increased efficiency and effectiveness in task performance and productivity. As an organizational innovation, the division of labor ranks alongside various technological innovations such as the invention of the plow and the steam engine in its significance for human societal evolution.

It is common for sociologists to link the emergence of a complex division of labor directly to human intelligence and the evolution of cognitive culture, especially technological advancement (e.g., Lenski and Lenski 1987). Without doubt, cultural evolution and technological advancement, especially with regard to subsistence technology, promoted the emergence of macrosociality among humans. However, macrosociality has flourished among the social insects for millions of years before *Homo sapiens* even appeared on Earth, so intelligence, technology, and culture are clearly not prerequistes for the evolution of this societal form. Furthermore, to dismiss the important sociological questions raised by the division of labor among social insects by saying that they are "biologically determined" to live in macrosocieties simply begs the question and offers nothing by way of explanation. The self-assembly of societies organized into a complex division of labor among specialists presents a fundamental problem for sociological analysis, whatever the species at hand.

The basic problem of organizing a division of labor within a population involves transforming individuals from behavioral generalists into behavioral specialists. This is accomplished fundamentally by the *progressive restriction of developmental potential*, be it among ants or among humans. Recently, Wilson (1985) introduced the concept of sociogenesis in order to help explain the emergence of a complex division of labor within insect colonies. The idea of sociogenesis in evolutionary biology is based upon an analogy to morphogenesis in developmental biology. Morphogenesis refers to the "set of procedures by which individual cells or cell populations undergo changes in shape or position incident to organismic development... The definitive process at the level of the (insect) colony is sociogenesis, the procedures by which individuals undergo changes in caste, behavior, and physical location incident to colonial development" (Wilson 1985, pp. 1489-1490). In both morphogenesis and sociogenesis, then, biological units (cells and individuals) are molded into specialized structures through a variety of processes which yield differentiation.

To those ignorant of current behavioral biological literature, including many social scientists, the nature and causes of sociogenesis among insect colonies are easily misunderstood. A common reason for failing to recognize the sociological relevance of such a topic lies in the assumption that the organization and regulation of social behavior among nonhuman animals, and especially insects, is "merely biological or instinctive." This is a casual way of stating the assumption that variation in social organization and behavior is to be attributed solely to variation in genetic material. In the case of sociogenesis, this assumption turns out to be not only crude, but erroneous as well. Even among the social insects, the physical environment and the demographic and social context of the colony play major roles in organizing and regulating the division of labor.

How does the physical, demographic, and social interactive environment of an ant society help shape its system of the division of labor? Ant societies typically are organized into the following castes: one or more queens, male and other female reproductives, workers, and soldiers. In addition, workers are sometimes differentiated into "majors," "medias," and "minors." In some cases, these castes display pronounced morphological differences. For example, among species such as leafcutter ants (*Atta cehpalotes*) a major worker may be as large as 200x-300x the weight of a minor, gardener worker (Wilson 1985, p. 1492). It is tempting, therefore, to reduce the division of labor within ant colonies to strictly biological factors, especially where castes are morphologically distinct. Even in such cases, however, myrmecologists have concluded that the proximate causes of caste differentiation are environmental, not genetic.

Among social insects such as ants, caste differentiation assumes two forms: physical and temporal. Physical castes are those which display clear morphological differences (caste polymorphism) such as body size and weight or mandible shape. Temporal castes, on the other hand, are organized simply on the basis of the age of their members. As workers age, they assume different work roles within the colony. In either case, genes alone do not specify caste destiny. Rather, a certain flexibility is built into the organization and allocation of labor within an ant colony. While the number and types of castes are, in fact, genetically determined for an insect species, the proportion of individuals within each caste is not. This means that a colony can "apportion" its labor force, in varying proportions and in response to local conditions, among the various castes typical of its species.

Oster and Wilson (1978) discuss the adaptive demography evident among colonies of social insects and explain that the age-frequency distributions of social insect colonies represent adaptations that are responsive to the specific demographic, environmental, and social characteristics of a given colony. For example, as a colony grows older and larger in population size, the ratio of major to minor workers may change as an adaptive response to the increased labor resources represented by an increasing population. Since, in the case of social insects, natural selection operates on colonies, the overall division of labor within the colony is itself a trait that is subject to selection. This means that natural selection has "programmed" a certain flexibility into the division of labor which can accomodate the highly variable local conditions to which insect colonies are subjected. This organizational flexibility represents an evolved sociological dynamism that is far removed from a vulgar biological conception of insect sociality which views the social organization of insect societies as rigidly determined by genes alone.

At the egg stage, individual ants are available for development into any of several different castes. Their eventual caste destiny is shaped by six basic factors: larval nutrition, stimuli (such as pheromones) provided by castes within the colony, egg size (a function of nutrients available during its development), winter chilling, environmental temperature, and the age of the queen that produced the egg (Wilson 1985, p. 1490). The combination of these various environmental factors to which the egg is exposed will determine how the genetic potential represented by the eggs of an insect colony is realized, developmentally, in the allocation of individuals to various castes. This flexibility represents a colony-level adaptation to needs for different types of labor as caused by different environmental conditions. In short, social insects have evolved systems of dividing labor into distinct castes in response to the changing conditions of their environments and colony characteristics.

One final aspect of the mechanisms of caste assignment among the social insects sheds light on the adaptive demography of the division of labor. As social insect workers age, they occupy different temporal castes throughout the life cycle. Wilson observes that the pattern of this succession of caste statuses is usually centrifugal (1985, p. 1492). While they are young, the labor of these workers is allocated to tasks such as tending the queen or brood, and then they shift to tasks such as nest construction or repair and finally, during old age, they assume the hazardous assignment of foraging outside the nest. This life course of changing caste assignments is interpreted as an adaptive succession which maximizes the labor value of the insect to the colony at various stages of its life. In passing, it is worth noting that only when they are old and biologically spent do social insects typically assume increasingly hazardous roles. In fact, these old foragers and soldiers among harvester ants have been labeled a disposable caste by Porter and Jorgensen (1981).

With perhaps only slight biological differences among them, humans also begin life as basically equipotential organisms whose genes do not preordain them to one versus another work role in adulthood. As with the social insects, environmental, demographic, and social factors play a major role in allocating labor within the population. In addition to these factors, culture plays a role that is unimaginable in insect societies. Nevertheless, the basic "problem" faced by human macrosocieties in creating a division of labor among specialists is the same as that confronting the social insects: the progressive restriction of developmental potential among individuals in the population. But even among humans, biology plays a relevant, if limited, role in shaping adult work opportunities, especially in early life. As far back as the hunter-gatherer period, gender has been a basic criterion for allocating status assignments among humans. Today, patterns of neonatal care and nutritional regimens are recognized as having significant influences on the development of individual capacities such as learning, which later translate into different educational and occupational opportunities.

On the other hand, most social scientists attribute much greater significance to various cultural and social processes which function as mechanisms of restriction among humans. For example, various processes of status ascription have assumed great significance in excluding categories of people from certain social statuses, especially occupational roles. Sex, age, race, and ethnicity have been crucial social attributes in limiting access to certain social statuses in countless human societies. With the rise of advanced horticultural and agrarian societies, new types of status attributes, such as social class and religion, became major factors which either facilitated or inhibited the attainment of various adult work roles. Among industrial societies, entire institutional complexes (e.g., education and the state) function as mechanisms of allocation whereby individuals eventually occupy one or another social status within the society-wide division of labor. The most commonly identified by sociologists include family of birth, stratification systems, education, the economy, and the state. Of course, such institutional categories are but a notational convenience used by sociologists to summarize a wide-range of very complex and subtle sociocultural processes, and these terms often conceal as much as they reveal. Nevertheless, it is not my intention here to review or synthesize what sociologists have learned about the division of labor within human societies and the processes by means of which task specialization and task allocation occur. Instead, it is sufficient to acknowledge the general nature of mechanisms of restriction in human societies, such as the socialization process, in order to contrast the human to the social insect strategy for achieving a division of labor in macrosocieties.

Before concluding this section on the division of labor within macrosocieties, it is worth making a few general observations about the role of technology in the evolution of human macrosociality. As discussed earlier, morphological differences among individual insects, especially among the ants, occasionally tell us a great deal about the caste position and work responsibility of a particular individual. For instance, the mandibles of soldiers clearly may be adapted for distinct activities such as piercing, shearing, or crushing the bodies of enemy soldiers, while the mandibles of a minor worker may give evidence of a degree of dexterity and finesse that is obviously suited for technical tasks such as brood tending or nest construction. Some ants, such as *Camponotus truncatus*, have evolved heads that function as "living doors" which are used by members of the soldier caste to block tunnel entrances to their nests (Wilson 1971, p. 160). Such distinctive morphological adaptations provide vivid evidence of morphological differentiation as a basis for the evolution of physical caste systems upon which systems of divisions of labor can be erected.

Humans, on the other hand, almost never display the sorts of pronounced morphological differences among individuals which have given rise to the evolution of physical caste among ants. Nevertheless, human culture has given rise to an evolutionary trait that converges upon the system of physical caste found among ants. Among humans, technological development represents a clear instance of convergent evolution whereby human societies have converged upon the social insects to approximate their system of physical caste as a foundation for establishing a complex division of labor. This is not to say that technology has promoted morphological differences among humans; in fact, it might be more reasonable to argue, on evolutionary grounds, that technology has had the reverse effect. After all, humans barely display any noticeable sexual dimorphisms, much less any patterns of physical differences that could be intepreted as analogous to the striking caste polymorphism that is found among some social insect species. Nonetheless, it is consistent with the logic of convergent evolutionary reasoning to interpret human technology as the close analogue to polymorphism among the social insects. In lieu of specially evolved heads and mandibles, humans have acquired, through cultural evolution, specialized morphological extensions of the human body that range from bows and arrows and plows to laser-guided weapons systems and computers. In fact, the extraordinarily complex systems of modern work and production technologies effectively put to shame the morphological adaptations of the ants, however impressive they are in their own right as examples of the creativity of organic evolution.[3]

In summary, while insect polymorphism represents a powerful physical basis which clearly underwrites the division of labor within these invertebrate macrosocieties, human technologies of work and production are no less important as devices which greatly enable humans to approximate the more archaic, insectan form of sociality that we have labeled macrosociety.

Coordination and Integration

The evolution of a division of labor implies a new set of organizational problems: coordinating and integrating the diverse activities expressed by various categories of specialists. Having evolved the capacity to generate considerable behavioral diversity among social units such as castes, macrosocieties face the threat of organizational chaos in the absence of mechanisms of coordination and integration. This represents perhaps the most challenging and least understood of the three design problems inherent in the evolution of macrosociality.

Among humans, bureaucracy, a cultural innovation of major significance for social evolution, facilitated the rise of macrosocieties during the advanced horticultural and agrarian periods. The key feature of bureaucracy relevant to the problems of coordination and integration is the social structural trait of administrative hierarchy. The advanced horticultural and agrarian periods featured both the emergence of systems of stratification and the rise of the state. Both of these social institutions entailed the development of powerful and complex administrative hierarchies which eventually enabled the evolution of empires, nation-states, and the modern world-system. In addition to the social innovation of bureaucracy, the rapid development of both subsistence and military technologies fostered the rise of macrosocieties. Among humans, the social structural trait of administrative hierarchy has evolved as the key device enabling the coordination and integration of social interaction within macrosocieties.

Ironically, this process may be better understood with reference to human than to insect societies, because insect macrosocieties lack an administrative hierarchy of the sort found in human societies. Dominance hierarchies, common in animal societies, are not to be confused with administrative hiearchies, present only in human societies. A dominance hierarchy is a ranking of individuals in terms of their abilities to gain access to reproductive or somatic resources. However, dominance hierarchies in insect macrosocieties have not evolved as mechanisms of "supervision" and should not be confused with human administrative hierarchies. Contrary to the connotations of her regal title, the insect "queen" is not a high-level colony decisionmaker, supervisor, or administrator.

In the absence of administrative hierarchies, how then do the social insects achieve colony-wide coordination and integration? According to Wilson, coordination and integration within insect societies is the result of purely statistical outcomes which derive from strictly local interactions among colony members (1971, pp. 224-232, 1985). As Wilson puts it, "This circumstance leads to frequent near-chaotic states and the dependence on colony decision making by *force majeure*, a statistical preponderance of certain actions over others that lead to a dynamic equilibrium rather than clear binary choices" (1985, p. 1493).

Wilson goes on to explain that population level coordination and integration is achieved in much the same way that a highly integrated organism is assembled out of the local interactions of cells multiplying in response to the activities of their immediate neighbors. This process often involves activities within the colony which oppose each other. For example, "some honeybee workers build royal cells while a smaller number of workers set out to dismantle them. The final result is an equilibrial number of cells sufficient for the rearing of new queens" (Wilson 1985, p. 1493). This sociogenic process is analogous to morphogenic processes such as the development of the nervous system wherein neural "paths" assemble themselves only to die eventually and to be replaced by other neural paths. The important point illustrated by such phenomena is that the development and regulation of extremely complex structures does not require mechanisms of "central administration" (such as a brain or a Politburo) but instead, can result entirely from the statistical outcomes of innumerable local interactions. Therefore, macrosociality can evolve among organisms that are entirely incapable of administrating or supervising the behavior of others.

The social insects rely on two broad sets of mechanisms for coordinating and integrating the activities of caste members. For convenience, these may be called "mechanisms of inhibition" and "mechanisms of initiation." Mechanisms of inhibition direct behavior by suppressing certain types of activties, such as egg-laying or brood-tending, and allowing the expression only of other activities such as foraging or nest-repair. This may be achieved by a queen who physically dominates other females and prevents them from laying eggs, thereby diverting their energy to other forms of labor. It should be emphasized, of course, that this is not the queen's "intention." The queen produces such acts of behavioral suppression by ritualized dominance interactions (head-swinging) or the release of inhibitory pheromones. In fact, Wilson explains that, in the absence of the mother queen and the odor she generates, chaos will ensue among a colony of carpenter ant workers (1985, p. 1492). It is important to stress that such processes which coordinate and integrate behaviors within the colony should not be interpreted anthropomorphically as evidence of a naturalistic imperative toward colony "harmony." In fact, such mechanisms are better understood as the result of intense competition and struggle among females within colonies for reproductive "privilege" (Wilson 1985, pp. 1493-1494).

In contrast to mechanisms of inhibition, mechanisms of initiation activite rather than suppress behaviors. As is true of much insect behavior in general, chemical (pheromone) communication plays a major role in regulating behaviors within the colony. For example, ant larvae are instrumental in stimulating foraging and nest construction. Similarly, when individual ants need assistance in transporting food or in fighting, they will release "recruitment pheromones" to enlist the support of their sisters. Sometimes, behaviors are activitated by the cumulative effects of previous behaviors. For example, this is illustrated among termites by a process called stimergy (Wilson 1971, pp. 228-231). Termites construct nest arches by adding pellets of soil and excrement to those pellets already deposited by others. This begins when a few termites randomly deposit pellets until, by accident, some pellets are dropped upon and adhere to each other. This incipient column acts as a stimulus which attracts other termites and compels them to add more pellets to the growing structure. Thus, the product of previous labor serves to activate additional labor toward the construction of a termite mound.

Finally, coordination is enhanced by processes such as "modulatory communication"(Wilson 1985, p. 1493). This entails a form of signalling, such as the scraping together of body parts, whereby one individual alerts its nestmates to prepare to release chemical signals which, in turn, activate overt behaviors. As such, modulatory communication is a powerful process for coordinating patterns of mass behavior among extremely large numbers of individuals.

By using tactile, auditory, and olfactory media, the social insects have evolved complex and effective systems of communication upon which their macrosocieties are built. Natural selection has operated upon deceptively simple patterns of individual behavior among insects to create astoundingly complex systems of social behavior. The key to understanding the evolution of macrosociality is to realize that natural selection can create very large-scale, complex patterns of sociality out of the raw material of *either* complex or simple forms of individual behavior. As individuals, the social insects display rather simple and highly limited repertories of behavior. Humans, on the other hand, are probably without rival in their capacity for exhibiting complexity in individual behavior. Despite these enormous differences among individuals, however, macrosociality has evolved only among insects and humans. It is clear that natural selection has "solved" the design problems inherent in the evolution of macrosociality by acting on elementary social processes as well as the characteristics of individuals per se. Having evolved but a few, key behavioral capacities, such as the ability to interact cooperatively with anonymous others, a species may evolve macrosocial life despite the behavioral simplicity or complexity of its individuals. Among both insects and humans, then, macrosociality has evolved as a consequence of selection acting upon social processes as well as individual traits.

CONCLUSION: A NEW COMPARATIVE SOCIOLOGY

The evolution of macrosociality requires the solution of at least three fundamental design problems, whatever the species in question. Even though social behavior may be mediated by chemicals in one species and culture in another, the basic design problems inherent in the evolution of macrosocial structure remain the same. Among all known social species, only the social insects and modern humans have devised viable solutions to these design problems, thereby enabling the evolution of macrosocieties among these species. Other design problems inherent in the evolution of macrosociality may, as yet, remain unidentified. This essay represents a first approximation of the type of new sociolgical analysis required to understand the evolution of social behavior across species lines.

This analysis is based upon the premise that new insights can be gained by subordinating, at least occasionally, the study of social *beings* to the study of *sociality*. This implies a willingness on the part of the social scientist, especially the sociologist, to part with a long-standing tradition of attending exclusively to human societies and human social behavior. Instead, a primary focus on sociality invites the development of a truly comparative sociology which places an interest in social organization and social behavior ahead of an interest in any specific social organism, humans included. Until very recently, this approach has been seriously underdeveloped within the social sciences and is almost completely absent from sociology. This is slightly ironic, because a very influential tradition within the positivist strain of Western sociology has long maintained that sociology can be a science of "social facts" and "forms of sociation," independent of any particular content (e.g., Durkheim 1893; Simmel 1971; Parsons 1951; Merton 1968). Unfortunately, practitioners of this same tradition have almost always behaved as if the fundamental and exclusive content of sociology should be *human* social behavior. This has produced consequences that are phylogenetically provincial. Recent developments within behavioral biology in general and in evolutionary and ecological theory in particular have made anthropocentrism within sociology unnecessary, if not obsolete. Without having to sacrifice any fundamental, hard-earned insights about *human* nature and *human* behavior, sociologists are now in a position to raise entirely new kinds of questions about social organization and social behavior across species lines. Instead of suffering the fate of being subsumed under a branch of behavioral biology, sociology is now presented with an opportunity to expand its range of social inquiry to thousands of nonhuman social species as well.

Not surprisingly, obstacles remain in the path of such developments, most of which are rooted in fundamental misunderstandings of social evolution and sheer ignornance of recent developments in fields such as behavioral ecology and sociobiology. For example, social scientists' fears of biological reductionism and genetic determinism have commonly inhibited their serious consideration of advances in biology that might inspire and enrich social science research. As this paper has made clear, a naive biological reductionism is inadequate in providing an understanding of social organization and conduct even among ants. Accordingly, there is even less reason to fear that an ecological evolutionary approach to human sociality will be any more reductionistic. Similarly, a sophisticated evolutionary ecological approach to social behavior does not lead to vulgar genetic determinism in the study of either human or insect societies. While genes do, in fact, guide the self-assembly of the "machinery" of behavior (nervous systems, endocrine systems, and motor systems), including social behavior, this does not lead to the conclusion that experience, learning, communication, interpretation, cognition, and reflection are somehow strictly prescribed by DNA. In fact, as this analysis has shown, a purely sociological analysis need not be concerned primarily with the various media (such as thought, symbolic communication, or chemical communication) by means of which social patterns are organized and executed. An evolutionary analysis of sociality must acknowledge, a priori, that different organisms use different sensory, communicative, and interactive modes. Bats echolocate, porpoises employ biosonar, ants spray aerosols, and humans speak and write. And clearly, these various modes of communication and the different types of brains which regulate them result in unique types of social behavior, with human sociality representing one variant of uniqueness. An evolutionary ecological approach to social analysis, however, demands explicit recognition of the unique behavioral properties and capacities featured in turn by each and every social species. This includes an explicit acknowledgement of the complexities introduced to social systems by a culture-bearing species.

The logic developed within this analysis calls for explicit attention to sociological problems of societal design and social conduct. This sort of sociological analysis leaves room for patterns of behavior that are tightly biologically constrained and largely unaffected by diverse experience or variable circumstance, as well as patterns of behavior that are extremely sensitive to the slightest change in context or the subtlest twist of interpretation. An evolutionary ecological analysis of sociality seeks to understand the evolution and development of societal traits whether they are mediated by chemicals or culture.

Although interspecific comparisons are largely alien to the social science tradition, especially to sociology, comparing insect to human societies is fundamentally more sociological than comparing human societies to each other. This is because none of the similarities between human and insect societies can be taken to reflect biological, much less psychological or individual, traits common to both insects and people. Thus, any social organizational similarities between the societies of these two taxa can be understood only in sociological and ecological terms. Only by assuming an uncharacteristically broad view of sociality can sociologists notice and appreciate the striking fact that, among the thousands of other social species in the biosphere, only the social insects share with humans the propensity for macrosociality. Finally, this broad view promises to enliven social theory and research by raising entirely new types of sociological questions about the evolution of social behavior across species lines.

ACKNOWLEDGMENTS

I am very grateful to Edward O. Wilson for his encouragement and incisive comments about an early draft of this paper. In addition, I am thankful to the Social Insects Group at the Museum of Comparative Zoology at Harvard University for their hospitality and assistance during my sabbatical work in 1986. Lawrence Cohen and Joseph Lopreato provided important insights during the early stages of writing, and additional keen observations and useful criticisms were contributed by Kenneth Boulding, Norman Carlin, Napoleon Chagnon, Ivan Chase, Timothy Crippen, James A. Davis, Mark Moffett, Daniel Rigney, Paul Robertson, Robin Stuart, and Daniel Wegner. An earlier version of this paper was presented at the 1989 meetings of the Human Behavior and Evolution Society at Northwestern University, Evanston, Illinois.

NOTES

1. Malte Andersson's essay (1984), "The Evolution of Eusociality," constitutes an excellent review and criticism of the role of haplodiploidy in the evolution of eusociality.
2. Recently, the biologist J.T. Bonner has expanded the study of culture and its evolution to nonhuman species (1980). Bonner defines culure as "the transfer of information by behavioral means, most particularly by the process of teaching and learning" (1980, p. 10). Bonner demonstrates convincingly that the nonhuman natural world abounds with cultural phenomena which merit evolutionary analysis. Nonetheless, it is apparent that cultural information must be highly evolved and constituted, at least in part, by symbols if it is to facilitate the evolution of macrosociality.
3. See Dawkins' *The Blind Watchmaker* (1986) for an eloquent and highly accessible treatise on the complex creativity inherent in the absolutely impersonal processes constituting natural selection.

REFERENCES

Alcock, J. 1984. *Animal Behavior: An Evolutionary Approach* (3rd ed.). Sunderland, MA: Sinauer Associates, Inc.
Andersson, M. 1984. "The Evolution of Eusociality." *Annual Review of Ecology and Systematics* 15:165-189.
Ashley, D., and D. M. Orenstein. 1990. *Sociological Theory: Classical Statements* (2nd ed.). Boston: Allyn and Bacon.
Axelrod, R. 1984. *The Evolution of Cooperation.* New York: Basic Books.
Barash, D.P. 1982. *Sociobiology and Behavior* (2nd ed.). New York: Elsevier.
Berger, P.L., and T. Luckmann. 1967. *The Social Construction of Reality: A Treatise in the Sociology of Knowledge.* New York: Anchor Books.
Bonner, J.T. 1980. *The Evolution of Culture in Animals.* Princeton, NJ: Princeton University Press.
Dawkins, R. 1976 (1989). *The Selfish Gene.* Oxford: Oxford University Press.
_____. 1982. *The Extended Phenotype: The Gene as the Unit of Selection.* Oxford: Oxford University Press.
_____. 1986. *The Blind Watchmaker.* New York: Norton.

Durkheim, E. 1893 (1964). *The Division of Labor in Society*. Translated by G. Simpson. New York: The Free Press.

Fletcher, D.J.C., and C.D. Michener (eds.). 1987. *Kin Recognition in Animals*. New York: Wiley.

Goodall, J. 1986. *The Chimpanzees of Gombe: Patterns of Behavior*. Cambridge, MA: Harvard University Press.

Hamilton, W.D. 1964. "The Genetical Theory of Social Behavior: I and II." *Journal of Theoretical Biology* 7:1-52.

––––––. 1971. "Geometry for the Selfish Herd." *Journal of Theoretical Biology* 31:295-311.

Higashi, S., and K. Yamauchi. 1979. *Japanese Journal of Ecology* 29:257.

Lenski, G., and J. Lenski. 1987. *Human Societies: An Introduction to Macrosociology* (5th ed.). New York: McGraw-Hill.

Lincoln, R.J., G.A. Boxshall, and P.F. Clark. 1982. *A Dictionary of Ecology, Evolution and Systematics*. London: Cambridge University Press.

Lopreato, J. 1984. *Human Nature and Biocultural Evolution*. Boston: Allen and Unwin.

Marx, K. 1867. *Capital*. 3 vols. Translated by S. Moore and E. Aveling. New York: International Publishers.

Merton, R. K. 1968. *Social Theory and Social Structure*. New York: Free Press.

Oster, G.F., and E. O. Wilson. 1978. *Caste and Ecology in the Social Insects*. Princeton, NJ: Princeton University Press.

Parsons, T. 1951. *The Social System*. Glencoe, IL: Free Press.

Perrow, C. 1986. *Complex Organizations*. New York: Random House.

Porter, S. D. and C. D. Jorgensen. 1981. "Foragers of the Harvester Ant, *Pogonomyrmex owyeei*: A Disposable Caste?" *Behavioral Ecology and Sociobiology* 9:247-256.

Schutz, A. 1967. *The Phenomenology of the Social World*. Translated by G. Walsh and F. Lehnert. Evanston, IL: Northwestern University Press.

Simmel, G. 1900 (1978). *The Philosophy of Money*. Translated by T. Bottomore and D. Frisby. London: Routledge and Kegan Paul.

––––––. 1950. *The Sociology of Georg Simmel*. Translated and edited by K. Wolff. New York: Free Press.

––––––. 1971. *George Simmel: On Individuality and Social Forms*, edited by D. N. Levine. Chicago: University of Chicago Press.

Smith, A. 1776 (1976). *The Wealth of Nations*, edited by R. H. Campbell and A. S. Skinner. Oxford: Clarendon Press.

Spencer, H. 1898. *The Principles of Sociology* (3rd ed.). New York: D. Appleton and Company.

Tönnies, F. 1887 (1963). *Community and Society*. Translated and edited by C. P. Loomis. New York: Harper and Row.

Trivers, R. L. 1971. "The Evolution of Reciprocal Altruism." *Quarterly Review of Biology* 46:35-57.

––––––. 1985. *Social Evolution*. Menlo Park, CA: Benjamin/Cummings.

U.S. Department of Labor. 1977. *Dictionary of Occupational Titles*. Washington, DC: U.S. Government Printing Office.

Van de Waal, F. 1982. *Chimpanzee Politics: Power and Sex Among Apes*. New York: Harper and Row.

Veblen, T. B. 1914 (1964). *The Instinct of Workmanship and the State of the Industrial Arts*. New York: Norton.

––––––. 1915 (1966). *Imperial Germany and the Industrial Revolution*. Ann Arbor: University of Michigan Press.

Wallerstein, I. 1974. *The Modern World-System*. New York: Academic Press.

Weber, M. 1904-1905 (1958). *The Protestant Ethic and the Spirit of Capitalism*. Translated by T. Parsons. New York: Charles Scribner's Sons.

––––––. 1925 (1978). *Economy and Society*. Translated by E. Fischoff, H. Gerth, et al., edited by G. Roth and C. Wittich. Berkeley: University of California Press.

Wilson, E.O. 1962. "Chemical Communication among Workers of the Fire Ant *Solenopsis saevissima* (Fr. Smith). 1. The Organization of Mass-Foraging. 2. An Information Analysis of the Odour Trail. 3. The Experimental Induction of Social Responses." *Animal Behavior* 10(1-2):134-164.
_____. 1968. "The Ergonomics of Caste in the Social Insects." *American Naturalist* 102:41-66.
_____. 1971. *The Insect Societies*. Cambridge, MA: Harvard University Press.
_____. 1975. *Sociobiology*. Cambridge, MA: Harvard University Press.
_____. 1984. *Biophilia: The Human Bond with Other Species*. Cambridge, MA: Harvard University Press.
_____. 1985. "The Sociogenesis of Insect Colonies." *Science* 228:1489-1495.

SEPARATION VERSUS UNIFICATION IN SOCIOLOGICAL HUMAN ECOLOGY

William R. Catton, Jr.

ABSTRACT

Despite Darwin's emphasis on interrelationships in the web of life, which laid the foundation for ecological science, a drift away from biology occurred as human ecology developed. Separatism became conventional among sociological human ecologists, who adhered to Durkheim's exclusion of nonsocial facts from the panoply of explanatory variables. Separatist human ecology embraced and catered to the hubris of industrialism as it focused on spatial patterns in cities, while perceptions of urban dominance obscured urban dependence on life support systems. It is now recognized that the unification of human ecology with general ecology requires the comprehensive study of human involvement in ecosystems. Part of this involvement includes the interspecific community structure of occupational niches. Seen as an extension of speciation, occupational differentiation among humans becomes meaningfully linked to studies of ecosystem dynamics. Specialized populations are threatened when an environment's niche composition is changed, whether the change is due to social or nonsocial causes. A unified human ecology needs to consider the comparability of the fate of animal populations and human populations hit by range compression (or its equivalent), the fact that specialists occupying niches may

Advances in Human Ecology, Volume 1, pages 65-99.

or may not be human, and the fact that occupational specialization can be a source of vulnerability to niche closure.

INTRODUCTION

As East and West Berliners battered into souvenir chunks the wall that had kept their city divided for more than a quarter century, their chisels and hammers struck sparks of potential insight for human ecology. As we shall begin to see below, we have an opportunity, using such insights, to move toward resolving a long-standing division among human ecologists.

Among sociological human ecologists there have been separatists and there have been unifiers. The former have insisted, while the latter have denied, that human ecology requires fundamentally different concepts and must involve distinctively different principles from those developed in the ecology of plant and animal communities. Taking some consequences of the recent change in Europe as a springboard, this paper will address that issue. We shall consider, first, the development of the separatist approach and clarify its stultifying effect and, then, look at an example of a potentially unifying concept, and explore a promising but unconventional way of using concepts developed in the study of biotic communities to illuminate human division of labor. In conclusion, the knowledge enhancing potential of unified ecology will be highlighted by means of a series of research challenges for human ecologists posed by findings from bioecology studies.

HUMAN ECOLOGY:
SOCIOLOGICAL SPECIALTY OR BRANCH OF BIOLOGY

Before we come back to some ecological lessons implicit in the smashing of the Berlin wall, let us review a series of intellectual events that erected a barrier of separation between human ecologists. Writing fifty years ago in the *American Journal of Sociology*, James A. Quinn (1940, p. 192) contrasted the view of sociologists that human ecology is "a phase of social study" with a tendency of biologists "to regard human ecology either as a branch of biology or as a marginal field that combines biological and social aspects." That cleavage has persisted.

Ecology, as a biological field of inquiry, was defined very broadly for the first two or three generations of its existence: the study of relationships between organisms and their environments. One of the leading textbooks simplified this to "environmental biology" (E. P. Odum, 1971, pp. 3,5) and suggested that if we were to think of a biological spectrum comprising, in order, genes, cells, organs, organisms, populations, and communities, then the focus of ecology was upon the latter portion of this spectrum.

Foundations for a science of ecology were laid by Charles Darwin when he made abundantly evident the importance of interrelationships in the web of life. Botanists, whose taxonomic efforts were in Darwin's time farther advanced than those of zoologists, were readier to begin developing ecological principles. Animal ecology nevertheless soon followed the initial development of plant ecology. Less than a decade after publication of Darwin's *Origin of Species*, Ernst Haeckel applied the word ecology to the relationships between plants and their environments. Books on plant ecology were published in the 1890s and early in the twentieth century. Theoretical concepts began to develop. The important concept of succession, for example, emerged from work by the Danish botanist, J. E. B. Wärming (1896), and by the University of Chicago's H. C. Cowles (1899). Ecological relations of Lake Michigan sand dune vegetation were studied. Frederic Clements (1916) published a systematized treatise titled *Plant Succession*, reflecting the early theoretical maturation of plant ecology.

Within only a year or so, Robert E. Park, in sociology, had read the volume by Clements and had begun to see the importance of its principles for understanding human phenomena. Meanwhile two books on animal ecology appeared: C. C. Adams (1913) *Guide to the Study of Animal Ecology*, and V. E. Shelford (1913) *Animal Communities in Temperate America*. By 1921, Park had introduced the term human ecology in the massive textbook by himself and Ernest W. Burgess, *An Introduction to the Science of Sociology*.

Primarily because of the influence of Park and Burgess (1921, 1924) sociologists came to think of human ecology as a specialty *within* their own academic discipline. They became so accustomed to its inclusion within a social science context that the efforts of others to develop human ecology as a branch of biological science either went unnoticed by them or seemed far-fetched. Few sociologists took any note, for example, of Paul B. Sears' *The Ecology of Man* (1957) or Lee R. Dice's *Man's Nature and Nature's Man* (1955). Sociologists largely lost sight of the processes of biogeocoenosis—the combined functioning of organisms and the earth, the concept now embraced by the term ecosystem. Such phenomena continued to affect human life but they had been defined as not sociological, and hence they seemed alien to the version of human ecology known to most sociologists.

Despite Park's own acquaintance with the early literature of plant and animal ecology, the legacy of Park and Burgess drifted in this nonbiological direction at two subsequent forks in the academic road. First, in the pacesetting sociology department at the University of Chicago in Park's time, a subtle conceptual dualism was developing in the thoughts and works of department members. Students were encouraged by Ellsworth Faris and others to absorb all they could of George Herbert Mead's insights in social psychology. Mead's Philosophy Department course, entitled Advanced Social Psychology, emphasized linguistic communication as a shaper of human nature (see Faris 1967). At the same time, Chicago was establishing sociology as a *research* discipline and Park was greatly influential in this effort. His selection of researchable topics for his graduate students was influenced by his interest in ecology. Sociologists from Chicago thus sometimes followed Mead's focus on analyzing symbolic interaction and sometimes followed Park by investigating interaction on a nonsymbolic level. When efforts were later made to *define* human ecology as a specialty, it seemed necessary among sociologists to stress the contrast between Mead's ideas and Park's. So human ecology was distinguished from the rest of sociology in that way. Instead of learning to regard language and culture as human techniques of adaptation used by our species in responding to biological challenges, sociologists came to think of ecological interaction as distinct from cultural interaction.

There was another fork in the road as well. When one of Park's influential students, R. D McKenzie, defined human ecology as "a study of the spatial and temporal relations of human beings as affected by the selective, distributive, and accommodative forces of the environment" (Park, Burgess, and McKenzie 1925, pp. 63-64), there were two very different ways of construing this definition. Emphasis *could* have been given to the idea that selective, distributive, and accommodative forces of the environment were to be studied by sociologists and would be important determinants of the spatial and temporal relations of human beings. This would have enabled sociological human ecology to remain united with plant and animal ecology. Instead, sociologists tended to notice the phrase "a study of spatial and temporal relations" and to disregard the clause about environmental forces. So, for many sociologists, human ecology came to be regarded as a study of spatial patterns in human affairs—with occasional attention to their sequence.

Sociological human ecology thus became separatist; it was divorced from biology. The divorce was doubtless motivated partly by the embarrassing sociological heritage of so-called Social Darwinism, in which a previous generation of sociological writers had built doctrines upon a foundation of badly misconstrued biological analogies. Thinking of *Homo sapiens* biologically became anathema to sociologists.

Two textbooks on human ecology by sociologists appeared in 1950. The introductory chapter of the one by James A. Quinn listed seven different points of view as to the nature and scope of human ecology (Quinn 1950, pp. 4-11). While he presented them in no meaningful order, they can be easily arranged to represent a continuum, ranging from the one that most nearly regards human ecology as a branch of general bioecology down to the one that regards human ecology as essentially unrelated to bioecology:

Type 1: Human ecology as an application of biological principles to human life, especially principles from plant and animal ecology. Examples include Allee (1938) and Adams (1935).

Type 2: Human ecology as coterminous with studies of communities and regions. "Within a community or a region the population, the environment, and the culture are bound together in an intricate complex so that no part can be understood except in relation to the whole" (Quinn 1950, p. 10). Examples include Mukerjee (1928) and Odum and Moore (1938). Note, too, that the subsequently provocative P-O-E-T scheme of Duncan (1959 1961) is foreshadowed by Quinn's delineation of this type.

Type 3: Human ecology as a study of sub-social relations among humans; that is, "those aspects of human interrelations that do not involve direct mental interstimulation and response among the participants, and especially those that do not involve interaction through symbolic communication. Impersonal, subsocial interaction occurs typically through the medium of the natural environment on which participants depend . . . " (Quinn 1950, p. 7). Here Quinn has epitomized the un-Meadian view of Park's legacy. Examples include McKenzie (1934) and Park (1936).

Type 4: Human ecology as the study of spatial distributions. No example was cited by Quinn at this point, but much of the work of Calvin F. Schmid and his students would exemplify this type. (It should be noted that the early studies in plant ecology had drawn their principles from analyses of spatial distributions; sociologists may have simply mistaken the accident of the earliest promising procedures for the essence of the ecological perspective.)

Type 5: Human ecology as the study of sociocultural areas. Examples include the "natural areas" in Chicago, each described in one or more monographs by students of Park and Burgess.

Type 6: Human ecology viewed as identical with human geography. An example is Barrows (1923).

Type 7: Human ecology as an inclusive synthesis of all the human sciences. An example is Bews (1935).

Types 1 and 2 would unify human ecology with ecology, whereas type 3 was incipiently separatist, and types 4, 5, 6, and 7 more definitely so.

Quinn himself opted for a combination of areal patterns of group life, as he put it, and especially . . . the subsocial aspects of community and regional organization, or types 3 and 4 above. By so opting, he contributed to the subsequent conclusion of Gibbs and Martin (1959, p. 30) that "human ecology is viewed by sociologists as nothing more than a method or as a field concerned only with the spatial distribution of phenomena, whether cemeteries or crimes," a conclusion they documented by analyzing 68 articles indexed as "ecology" in the *American Journal of Sociology* and the *American Sociological Review*.

Amos Hawley, on the other hand, subtitled his *Human Ecology* (1950), "A Theory of Community Structure." In his preface, Hawley said the book marked completion of a work begun by McKenzie before his death in 1940, and described the volume as an attempt to develop "a full and coherent theory of human ecology" by working from the assumption that "there is continuity in the life patterns of all organic forms." In saying this, even at mid-century, Hawley was going against a strong antibiological current in sociology, and, as we shall see, subsequent publications of his reflect the influence of that current upon his views. However, he began the 1950 book with an account of the contributions of plant and animal ecologists, so that theoretically he was working close to type 1. Substantive chapters of the book cited empirical studies that ranged from type 2 to type 5.

The antibiological current in sociology was vividly reflected in the critical book by Milla A. Alihan (1938). Alihan deplored the effort of sociological human ecologists (referred to simply as "ecologists" in the book) to distinguish organic interactions from cultural interactions. Instead, however, of concluding that cultural phenomena are, for humans, fundamentally involved in their solution of organic challenges, Alihan merely insisted that serious contradictions arise in the theoretical statements of "the ecologists" from their efforts to sever into two distinct entities the two aspects actually so intertwined. Valid as some of Alihan's specific criticisms may have been, their cumulative severity probably contributed mainly to reinforcing further the predilection of sociologists to remain aloof from biology.

SEPARATISM ENTRENCHED

Failing to see that human ecology had passed those forks in the road, sociologists acquired the habit of using the word ecological almost as a synonym for spatial. To study any sociological topic "ecologically" was to study its spatial aspects, or the spatial distribution of the phenomenon. At the same time, sociologists took the word community as a synonym for town or city, missing deeper implications of its usage in ecological literature. Human settlements were seen as if they were aggregates of a single species, *Homo sapiens*, whereas to biologists a community was an association of diverse and interdependent species (Mukerjee 1932; Stephan 1970).

Most sociological human ecologists long ago virtually ceased to read bioecology literature, though they sometimes continued to read (or at least cite) the early works of Park, Burgess, and McKenzie, and may have recognized sometimes the fact that Park, at least, had cited some writings of plant and animal ecologists. At least from the time when Alfred McClung Lee (1946), a nonecologist, revised August Hollingshead's human ecology chapters in Park's (1939) *Outline of the Principles of Sociology* (after Park was dead and when Hollingshead was in military service), sociological human ecology became regretably ingrown and dysfunctionally unmindful of bioecology.

Sociological advocates of "regional" studies (e.g., Mukerjee 1928, 1932) were commonly misunderstood as proponents of mere localism in sociological inquiry. One of them, Howard W. Odum of the University of North Carolina, pointed out how this misconception prevented recognition of regionalism as an interdisciplinary investigation of the interdependence of culture, social behavior, social structure, and environmental factors (H. W. Odum 1951, pp. 353-358).

As a consequence of the disciplinary history sketched above, sociologists were not in the vanguard of efforts around the time of the 1970 Earth Day (and for a time thereafter) to comprehend the causes and consequences of ominously changing global and localized environmental conditions. Few sociologists responded to the earliest signs of global warming, of loss of biodiversity, and other monumental changes in the ecosystems supporting human societal life. Most sociologists continued adherence to Durkheimian precepts that excluded such nonsocial changes from consideration as important causes of social change, believing in the face of much contrary evidence that "a social fact can be explained only by another social fact" (Durkheim 1950, p. 145).

Other scholars were not bound by the same taboo. Two sons of regional sociologist Howard W. Odum became ecologists—outside the sociological discipline. In 1963, Eugene P. Odum dedicated a small book on *Ecology* (in the Holt, Rinehart and Winston "Modern Biology Series") to his father "whose life works on 'Southern Regions' and 'American Regionalism' early inspired me to seek more harmonious relationships between man and nature." A considerably enlarged edition of this book came out a dozen years later, with a subtitle added: "The Link Between the Natural and the Social Sciences." The subtitle was a clear repudiation of separatism. A photograph in the first chapter of this edition showed a modern city dominated by high-rise buildings, industrial facilities, and limited-access highways. It bore this caption: "The city, a high-energy fuel-powered ecosystem that requires large areas of solar-powered ecosystems for its life support maintenance" (E. P. Odum 1975, p. 3). The caption succinctly reflected the sort of idea that has come to seem essential in a biologist's conception of human ecology, but it is an idea neglected (if not rejected) until recently by sociological human ecologists.

Howard T. Odum, the other ecologist son of Howard W., seems also to have seen the links between biology and sociology that were implicit in his father's work. He has elaborated upon the energy aspects of human ecology epitomized in his brother's picture caption. In the opening pages of *Environment, Power, and Society* (1971, pp. 1-2, 6) he wrote of matters so generally ignored by traditional sociological human ecologists that a newer group were impelled by events of the 1970s to label themselves *environmental sociologists* (Dunlap and Catton 1979).

H. T. Odum said this book was about nature and man. Nature consisted, he said, of animals, plants, microorganisms, and human societies, and these living parts of it were connected by unseen channels "over which pass chemical materials that cycle round and round being used and reused . . . and over which flow potential energies that cannot be reused . . . " (1971, p. 1). Now familiar patterns of human culture, he went on to say, had developed when human societies evolved as a significant part of the systems of nature. Humans at first had to adapt to the food and fuel energy flows available in nature. Folkways, mores, religious and ethical teachings evolved to guide individuals in their participation in the group and to provide means for using energy sources effectively. Energy from sunlight was spread out so evenly that it was not directly available for human tasks except as it had been concentrated (with much loss) by plants and animals. Societies had to gather and distribute food and other energy sources to survive; to do this they developed organization. But now, said Odum, the energetic relation of *Homo sapiens* to the natural environment has changed. Our new industrialized societies now derive enormous portions of their energy from flows of concentrated fossil fuels (coal and oil). Much of this energy they feed back into the environmental system to obtain greatly enlarged yields of food and other critical materials.

Reliance on fossil energy sources and on the resulting enhanced exploitation of ecosystems came about so fast, said H. T. Odum, that human customs, mores, ethics, and religious patterns were ill-adapted. "Man's role in the environment is becoming so enormous that his energetic capacity to hurt himself by upsetting the environmental system is increasing" (1971, p. 6).

The ideas put forth by the Odums are clearly human ecology—if this is defined as the study of ecosystems involving human beings. (An ecosystem is, of course, a comprehensive web of interrelations between organisms, other organisms, and their environment.) Yet these ideas are clearly alien to the separatist version of human ecology that persists in sociological literature. They are either unfamiliar or peripheral to human ecologists of a more moderately separatist middle level of sophistication, for whom human ecology comprises the study of human communities (i.e., cities) in a manner that regards them as *analogous* to ecosystems. Such scholars pay *some* attention, perhaps, to literature of bioecology but tend to regard it as a source of "models" which may be taken to have "human counterparts." This approach has been deplored by Duncan (1961, p. 143) who, while acknowledging that an "ecosystem analogy" might be an improvement over the nineteenth-century organismic analogy that fed so-called Social Darwinism, insisted that the ecosystem concept was "much too valuable . . . to be sacrificed on the altar of metaphor."

THE URBAN EMPHASIS:
ITS DISTORTING EFFECT

One serious flaw in separatist human ecology has been its excessive preoccupation with urban life. Even when it has not just reduced "ecological" studies of urban phenomena to mere spatial analyses, this preoccupation has distorted perception of the interdependence of *Homo sapiens* with the rest of the biosphere. For example, the study of "urban-regional hierarchical systems" sees cities as the center of influential forces that radiate outward and diminish with distance (Berry and Kasarda 1977, p. 280). Not only do impulses of economic change appear to originate in large cities, from which they are transmitted "downward" through a hierarchy so that "economic backwardness" will persist longer in more "peripheral" areas, but even along axes between cities the growth potential supposedly depends on the intensity of interaction between the cities at the ends of the axes. According to "modern growth theory," it appears that "continued urban-industrial expansion in major metropolitan regions" should cause growth impulses and economic advancement to spread out to smaller places and "ultimately infuse dynamism into even the most tradition-bound peripheries" (Berry and Kasarda 1977, p. 281).

As separatist thinking sees the matter, hinterlands are dependent upon cities, rather than vice versa. By staying aloof from mainstream bioecology this separatist version of human ecology has deprived itself of understanding that would flow from concepts well known to biologists but unfamiliar to many social scientists. One such concept is *carrying capacity*. For any use of any environment by any population of organisms there is a volume and intensity of use that can be exceeded only by degrading that environment's future suitability for that use. Carrying capacity is the name for this maximum *sustainable* use level. It *can* be exceeded, but the excess load will exist only temporarily. Overshooting carrying capacity means subsequent load reduction—unless the carrying capacity available from elsewhere can be tapped. These fundamental ideas are missing from the separatist way of thinking. For separatist human ecologists, the *dependence* of cities (whose population loads clearly exceed the carrying capacity available within city boundaries) upon carrying capacity from areas elsewhere hardly seems "ecologically" significant. Even when hinterlands specifically are considered, it is said that "once the core-periphery pattern is set the core region becomes the lever for development of peripheral regions, reaching out to them for resources as its input requirements increase . . . ." Differently endowed hinterlands become specialized then, it is said, according to the needs of core cities. "Cities are the instruments whereby specialized subregions are articulated in a national space economy" (Berry and Kasarda 1977, p. 389).

These statements are not false; they are biased. Collectively they reflect hubristic notions about the relation between man and nature. That hubris and anthropocentrism (indeed, the *ethno*centrism of scholars born and educated in an urban industrial society) have kept separatist human ecologists (e.g., those trained in and affiliated with departments of sociology) unresponsive—even unreceptive— to the "limits to growth" literature (see, e.g., Hawley 1975, pp. 6-10).

NICHE LOSS AND HABITAT DESTRUCTION

Now let us return to Berlin and the insights obtainable from its reunification.

For nearly three decades, two portions of Berlin's human population had been artificially segregated. As one of the concepts often used in the early Chicago literature of sociological human ecology, segregation had denoted patterns of spatial distribution more or less spontaneously arising from processes of competition by city dwellers for advantageous sites (Park and Burgess 1924, pp. 252-254, 525-545; Burgess 1928). The long imposed division of Berlin between two antagonistic political entities had to have severely distorted its previous spatial patterns. Students of the conventional (separatist) style of sociological human ecology (see, e.g., Berry and Kasarda 1977; Theodorson 1982) would now certainly expect some remarkable processes of readjustment—of labor markets, commuting routes, land values, uses of buildings and building sites, and some shifts to a new and more spontaneous pattern of residential location.

But a deeper ecological insight was available to those who might consider one of the incidental sparks arising from Europe's new birth of freedom. Removal of that major barrier to human mobility across Germany, known to Westerners as the Iron Curtain, meant that scores of trained attack dogs, formerly used for patrolling the artificial border between the Federal Republic of Germany and the German Democratic Republic, were made redundant ("Periscope" 1989). The specialized *niche* for these canine border guards had ceased to exist.

Inclusion of the niche concept in the lexicon of their version of human ecology had received no more than lip-service from Berry and Kasarda; it was mentioned only once in their introductory chapter "The Ecological Approach" but it is neither defined nor subsequently used in the remainder of the book. Mainstream ecologists have gone to great lengths to make the concept clear and useful. Hutchinson (1965a) developed an abstract mathematical definition: Given a set of coordinates $(X_1, X_2, X_3 \ldots X_n)$, each of which represents a relevant variable in the life of a species, its "fundamental niche" is the hyperspace in which no competitors are present and all its needs are provided for. If competitors are present, some smaller hypervolume occupied by the given species constitutes its realized niche. Hutchinson's definition was an elaboration of an earlier version. For our purposes the earlier notion of niche (Elton 1927), a species' "habits, food, and mode of life"—in short, the role it plays in an ecosystem—is nearly sufficient. Even this seemingly simpler version entails three broad components (into which the multiple coordinates of Hutchinson's version could be clustered): the kinds of resources the species takes from its environment, the kinds of relationships it must have with other organisms to go on living, and the kinds of things it must do to (or put into) its environment in the process of living (cf. Orians 1972).

At the Berlin wall, elimination of their niche destined the guard dogs for elimination. Ineradicable killer habits had been instilled in them by human trainers. The niche for creatures with those habits had been a human contrivance, as well. On-going processes of human history had now done away with that niche.

Although historically special, what makes the plight of these German dogs ecologically instructive is that it is an instance of a common pattern (recognizable by nonseparatist human ecologists). Another representative example of that pattern has befallen a furry marsupial in Australia. It just happened to be mentioned in a news article contemporaneous with, but overshadowed by, celebration of the astonishing developments in Europe in the final months of 1989 ("Koala's in Wild Imperiled" 1989). An ecological phrase that is key to comparison of the two instances is habitat destruction. History's erosion of the Iron Curtain (which had been the institutional source of the niche for those trained attack dogs) sealed their fate. A Germany without the dividing wall was no suitable habitat for such creatures. Meanwhile, half a century of human "development" of lands along Australia's eastern coast had eliminated almost 80% of the natural habitat and food supply for koalas. Accordingly, these marsupial "teddy bears" had dwindled in number from an original several million to an estimated 400,000. And their decline continues.

Among ecologists, wildlife managers, and livestock people, it is common knowledge that protection of the range or habitat is essential to protecting an animal population's continued existence. Allowing habitat to be destroyed (i.e., seriously changed) endangers any population dependent on it (in its previous condition). Niches are lost when environments are changed. All too often, "humanitarian-minded" efforts to defend a game species have prompted elimination of its predators, with the result that "innocent" grazers and browsers have then multiplied until their numbers exceeded carrying capacity and their numbers destroyed their own habitat by overuse (Dasmann 1970, p. 239).

The two cases described above are similar and yet different. Both involved a population of animals endangered by loss of the kind of habitat their existence required. In the koala case the requirements were determined by the natural characteristics of the species. In the case of the German guard dogs the requirements were impressed upon the genetic potential of the canines by human culture. But in both instances, human action closed down the niche the animals happened one way or another to require.

The Human Employment of Animals

Now let us give attention to what all this means for *human* ecology. Undoubtedly many *human* border guards were destined by the wall's reopening to lose their jobs too. The similarity of the canine redundancy and this instance of human redundancy, taken together with the similarity of the guard dogs' niche elimination and the koala loss of habitat, should enable us to see anew that human ecology is integrally connected with general ecology. Ordinarily, loss of their niche by a population of dogs would hardly be seen as "unemployment," and loss of employment by an occupational category of people would not always be seen as an ecological phenomenon. The comparability is important, however, and we shall come back to it.

Range compression is one of the processes by which loss of habitat can occur. In Africa, for example, elephants have been forced by increasing human numbers to retreat permanently onto full-time sanctuaries—areas they used to move freely in and out of according to seasonal variations in availability of food and water. This human compression of the elephants' range results in pachyderm herds exceeding the carrying capacity of lands they cannot leave. If separatist human ecologists do not commonly see the overstocked elephant sanctuaries' resemblance to cities, perhaps recalling the problems of cities under a blockade will highlight the comparability. Consider the prodigious airlift required to supply West Berlin's needs when Soviet Forces shut off surface supply routes in 1948. The city's hinterland dependence was then blatantly evident. The Berliners would have suffered the consequences of human range compression had there been no airlift.

Throughout most other parts of the African continent there are other large mammal species suffering the same circumstance as they are crowded by human land use changes into shrinking residual areas. An animal population subjected to range compression remains too numerous to be supported by the available plant community. The herd's overutilization of the vegetation on its limited range destroys that resource—and, by niche closure, imperils the herd (Hanks 1979, pp. 15-16).

Wildlife populations have niches that are essentially functions of the species' inherent needs. Habitat destruction may be, for such populations, self-inflicted—because a population that has somehow come to exceed the carrying capacity of its available range simply cannot curtail its use of resources from that range, so it uses more than can be *sustainably* supplied there. We must not fail to understand the serious ecological nature of this predicament just because the range compression leading to it happens in certain instances to be human driven. Nor should we imagine it just happens to nonhuman populations.

For the canine border guards in Germany, the niche was special, not characteristic of all dogs. It was manmade (both through the specialized training of those particular dogs and through the cold war's creation of the political circumstances that gave them employment). In this instance the loss of habitat by these hapless animals was *not* self-inflicted, any more than was the loss of *access to hinterland* by West Berliners at the time of the blockade, or by the people of Leningrad during the 900-day siege in World War II.[1] Nor, however, was it the first instance of fatal unemployment for canine servants of human employers. Other dogs that once pulled Eskimo sleds lost out as snowmobiles powered by internal combustion engines displaced them. Likewise, tractors have deprived farm horses in many countries of the niche they once had.

Nonseparatist human ecology would not neglect these phenomena. The niches humanly assigned to nonhuman animals have been far more various than the mention of these few examples might suggest, and systematic consideration of the diversity could broaden the intellectual horizons of human ecologists. We should not forget such additional examples as the use of canaries in mines to test for poisonous gases, or the human use of the valuable homing instinct of pigeons domesticated as message carriers. Further, the fact that predator-prey relations have been a principal factor in the balance among species in biotic communities has figured in the development of multispecies communities dominated by *Homo sapiens* (misleadingly called, simply, "human communities" as if consisting of a single species). As Bowman (1977, p. 10) has pointed out, "Man has made use of [natural predator-prey relations] to control some of the animal species he finds undesirable. Thus in Southern Asia man has used the mongoose to hunt and control snakes. In many parts of the world he has used variously dogs, cats, and ferrets to kill rodents and rabbits."

Even for purposes of traction and transport, quite a number of different species have been thus employed by humans: for example, reindeer, onagers, camels, dromedaries, yaks, buffalo, and elephants (Bowman 1977, pp. 5-7). These nonhuman members of the labor force have pulled implements for cultivating and harvesting domesticated plants. They have pulled assorted vehicles in peace and war, carried loads, and turned machinery. Horses, of course, have also been widely employed at such tasks. It could serve human ecology well were some of us to cross disciplinary boundaries freely enough to achieve somewhat systematic knowledge of the development of equine niches in human communities (see, e.g., Lawrence 1985; Edwards 1987; Wissler 1914). In fact, the broad study of human domestication of plants as well as animals ought to be seen as a valuable contribution to our understanding of human community structure and processes (see, e.g., Ucko and Dimbleby 1969). Mutualistic interactions between assorted species as well as within species are a topic vital to human ecology (see Addicott, 1984).

The relevance of all these matters to human ecology stems from the biologist's meaning of the word community—a multispecies unit. Populations of the several species expand until they fill the niches available to them in the community's environment. These niches differ according to the constraints and opportunities for each type afforded by their interactions with each other, as well as by the resources available to each. In part, the various types *are* each others' resources. Clearly the structure of a community is a product of evolving balance among the mutual impacts of the interacting species populations upon each other and upon their common environment.

For human ecologists to appreciate fully the relevance of the biologist's conception of the community to their studies of human communities, it is important to see that the examples of human employment of animals cited above are not isolated instances. Living in a highly urbanized modern industrial society, it is too easy to imagine that we only "harvest" animals (for food, for clothing materials, etc.) and to forget how common it has been to assign various tasks to animal "employees." Division of labor—long a topic of sociological study—needs to be seen as a feature of the multispecies community. Tasks (or functions) are not just divided among the members of a human population; it has been too easy for sociologists to limit their analyses as if all relevant tasks were performed by human members of a one-species labor force. Even in human communities (where many different niches have human—but socially differentiated—occupants), some niches are assigned to nonhumans.

Human Range Compression

Presumably most of the human border guards within Germany who were affected by the reopening of the Cold War frontier would be shifted into new niches in a revised occupational structure. It is usually possible in principle, though not always easy, for a redundant human to be retrained and fitted into a different niche. Humans are, quite clearly, a multiniche species (Hutchinson 1965b; Hardesty 1972). Reassignment possibilities are, of course, an important difference between human occupations and natural species niches.[2] A seal cannot become a dog, but a scuba diver can be retrained to serve on dry land as a prison warden. The difference must not, however, prevent us from achieving the ecological recognition that loss of niche space, or loss of habitat, or range compression, can happen to human as well as to nonhuman populations.

Back again to Australia: Consider the plight of the aborigines. Or, in North America, the Indians. Or, black Africans, who, on their continent have likewise suffered range compression in the lands that became white settler societies as Europeans expanded into a "New World." Habitat remaining available to these various indigenous peoples was insufficient to support their remaining populations by precontact patterns of resource use after European take-over on these continents. No one should see or hear the American term Indian Reservation without recognizing a tragic human instance of range compression. Newcomer populations compressed the range allotted to prior inhabitants. The plight of the displaced indigenous peoples became aggravated, of course, by the fact that the lands "reserved" for their use generally tended to be of insufficient quality as well as quantity for supporting their populations even by the ostensibly more "productive" modern lifestyles (or patterns of resource use) imposed by the displacers. ("Productive" is enclosed in quotes because of the serious difference in the meaning of "production" in social science usage versus the meaning it has in bioecology literature.)

Racial or ethnic differences have commonly confounded these human tragedies, but the ecological process—loss of niche, or destruction of habitat—need not depend on such differences. Occupational specialization, so intrinsic a feature of modern human living, suffices even in a racially homogeneous population to put people into niches that may expand or contract. In a society with an extensive division of labor, scarcely anyone is self-sufficient. The interdependence that is entailed by division of labor was seen by Durkheim (1933) as a new form of social solidarity, but it is also a new source of vulnerability. Problems of redundancy can arise whenever a change of circumstances (of any sort—climatic, geological, political, economic, technological) reduces the availability of jobs of whatever kind people have been fitted to by training.

In the mid-1980s, for example, there came to be an "oil glut" whose repercussions bear this out. Such factors as a recent worldwide economic recession caused it, arising partly from the sharp escalation of oil prices following the oil embargo imposed earlier in the 1970s by oil-exporting Arab countries seeking to pressure allies of their enemy, Israel. One consequence of the so-called glut was a curtailment of previously expanded drilling activity by American oil companies as oil prices fell back. A 1986 survey conducted by the American Association of Petroleum Geologists found 35% unemployment among its Colorado and Oklahoma members, while 26% of its Louisiana members and 24% of its members in Texas were also without jobs (*Spokesman-Review* 1986).[3] Although the cases are different, from a truly ecological perspective we see what is common to the redundancy of the German guard dogs and the redundancy of the petroleum geologists: Niches can be lost differently, but loss of niche endangers a population regardless of the cause (see Ehrlich and Ehrlich 1981, pp. 155-212; Hughes 1975, pp. 68-86; Koopowitz and Kaye 1983).

HUMAN ECOLOGY AND THE COMMUNITY CONCEPT

In the preceding paragraphs I have sought to convey a sense of the clear applicability of certain ecological concepts and principles to human and nonhuman species alike. Large-brained, slow-maturing, group-living *Homo sapiens* indeed does differ, as sociologists have steadfastly insisted, from other species. Humankind possesses, shapes, and is shaped by, a nongenetic form of inheritance called culture. This fact is vital and undeniable, and has many ramifications. However, it does not make ecological processes irrelevant for understanding human experience. It does not make ecological principles inapplicable to human social patterns, processes, or destiny.

To suppose human individuals or collectivities are somehow exempted by their special culture-bearing nature from ecological influences is a serious error. It is hubris that endangers human ecology as a discipline as well as endangering the human ability to cope with future changes of circumstances.

Human social organization and culture *become involved* in an ecological web of influence. In that way the ecology of ecosystems in which humans participate must differ from the ecology of ecosystems devoid of human involvement. Even though we therefore need *additional* ideas (ideas that would be inapplicable to whales, weasels, or wolves) if we want to understand the human condition, biological sciences (including ecology) are highly relevant for illuminating human experience and behavior. The point to be emphasized, then, is that the uniqueness of the human species puts no impermeable (Berlin wall-like) barrier between human ecology and other branches of ecology. Ecology is ecology; it is inclusive. Human ecology must not be exclusive (cf. Darling 1963).[4]

By now it should be abundantly clear that a major aim of this paper has been to advocate, and exemplify the possibility of, extricating human ecological thinking about community structure from the rut into which sociologists had thrust their version of it by mid-century, forty years ago. In particular, human ecologists ought not, as sociologists have so largely done, regard the phrase "community structure" as meaning chiefly the spatial organization of cities.

At mid-century one of the important sociological human ecology textbooks (Hawley 1950) did partially transcend that myopic view. Proceeding from the premise that among all organic forms there is continuity, Hawley in those days believed the nature and development of community structure (a fundamental sociological problem) could be illuminated by pursuing the logical implications of general ecological theory based on contributions of plant and animal ecologists.

Hawley used the phrase community structure not only in the subtitle of his book but also as the title of a chapter. Significantly, there were also chapters on "Organism and Environment," on the "Interrelatedness of Life," and one in which the relation of human ecology to general ecology was explicitly addressed. The latter was a revision of an earlier paper (Hawley 1944), and in retrospect one can already see in the revision some foreshadowing of Hawley's later backsliding from his once-staunch insistence that "most of the difficulties which beset human ecology may be traced to the isolation of the subject from the mainstream of ecological thought" (Hawley 1944, p. 399).

Ecological interest in biotic communities, said Hawley (1950, p. 42), is concerned with the form of community organization and the way communities develop. In a footnote, the idea that there exist "close and vital interactions and interdependencies" between plant, animal, and human communities was stated as a basis for considering "biotic community" as a concept that includes "all that is germane to the description of the adaptation of life to a given habitat" (Hawley 1950, p. 41).

Unlike those who then equated human ecology with plotting social variables on census-tract maps of a city, Hawley recognized that a community could be usefully viewed as an organization of niches. Each species in the community fitted into a niche, and the various species, organized into a hierarchy of dominance, exerted different amounts of influence upon each other through their differing impacts upon their common habitat (cf. McNaughton and Wolf 1970). Niches were also linked into food chains. A consequence of these considerations was a grading of niches with regard to the number and size of the types of organisms occupying them. Processes regulating the number of niches and the numbers of organisms in each niche were an important topic for ecological study.

How resistive other sociological human ecologists have been to this view of their field of inquiry is stunningly indicated by the fact that in Theodorson's (1982) "Index of Persons Cited and Topics" there is no listing of niche at all, and in the "Subject Index" of Berry and Kasarda (1977) there are just two entries under "Niches." One is an error, citing a page on which there is no occurrence of the word or concept. The other single occurrence is embodied in a brief description of Robert E. Park's followers analyzing functional and residential segregation of city populations.

What little usage of the term niche there has been by human ecology separatists seems indicative of mere lip-service to the notion that, as Hawley said in the 1950 textbook, *Homo sapiens* is "inextricably involved in the web of life." Separatists have not really believed that, so they have not really *used* such ecological concepts as niche. Moreover, they have misunderstood and misused other ecological concepts in giving much more attention to the idea that humankind is differentiated from other life forms by the possession of culture and is, thus, able to exploit an unprecedentedly diverse assortment of resources. Culture is said to have fostered such human dominance in biotic communities that they were subject to "reconstruction" in which human influence largely determined "the kinds and abundance of life forms" of which a community would consist (Hawley 1950, pp. 44-61).

As we shall presently see, "kinds and abundance of life forms" serves as a fair definition of community structure, among biologists. And, as we shall also see, it reflects the fact that a topic traditionally claimed by sociology—division of labor—is not an exclusively human phenomenon.

Three and a half decades later, in another book with *Human Ecology* as its main title, but subtitled "A Theoretical Essay," Hawley (1986, pp. 3, 126) laid more emphasis on *divergence* of human ecology (at least its sociological version) from bioecology. And in the mean time various other writers (e.g., Form 1954) had sought to divorce human ecology from ecology. For Theodorson (1982) the study of urban spatial organization apparently remains the essence of human ecology, even though new techniques of analysis have replaced earlier ones, and data from a more varied (international) assortment of cities are now analyzed.

Hawley (1986, p. 3) reiterated (but no longer seemed serious about) the idea that we could learn from plant and animal ecologists a valuable lesson—that individuals or species do not separately and independently achieve workable adaptation to their environments but rather do so collectively "through an organization of their diverse capabilities." To learn this *from plant and animal ecologists* would mean recognizing that division of labor is characteristic of all biotic communities, not just those so dominated by their human members that we call them human communities and allow ourselves to fall thereby into neglecting their nonhuman components. Hawley was not now taking care to avoid the fall.

SENSITIZATION TO BIOECOLOGY'S CONCEPTS

Between the time of my first reading of the 1950 book by Hawley and my first reading of his 1986 book, I had acquired much additional familiarity with ecological literature by biologists. Having learned what biologists mean by "ecological diversity" (species richness, and species abundance) in biotic communities, I was struck upon reading again Hawley's 1950 chapter on "Community Structure" with a hauntingly ambivalent assessment of it—a sense of near breakthrough and yet also a sense of lost opportunity.

I noticed in the rereading that most of the sources Hawley cited in that chapter were by sociologists and anthropologists (despite his having dealt in an earlier chapter with the idea that human communities are humanly dominated biotic communities). Only two citations were to sources in biological literature, one of which was, in fact, written by a social anthropologist. And yet, Hawley set forth in that chapter some conceptual tools that were uncannily similar to concepts that have become standard in the bioecology literature.[5]

Meanwhile, Gibbs and Martin (1959) had advocated redefinition of human ecology as the study of "sustenance organization," so as to recapture its continuities with mainstream ecology. And a paper came out in a regional sociological journal (Stephan 1970) which recognized that when human communities are taken as special instances of (multispecies) biotic communities, this challenges sociologists to consider socioecological implications of the species concept.

Unfortunately, to respond to the challenge he was pointing out, Stephan (1970) argued that we should regard occupations as sociological species. Sociologists were not open to such a suggestion. A biologist (Hutchinson 1965b) had noted that the cultural differentiation of human populations enabled them to occupy many different niches. He had spoken of differently specialized (behaviorally isolated) humans as "quasi-species." Sociologists' terminological resistance notwithstanding, Stephan's paper astutely elaborated substantial justification for considering occupational differentiation as an extension of speciation and went on to demonstrate the kinds of insights that would follow from such an approach.

Speciation and Differentiation

As premises for his argument, Stephan (1970) cited Hawley's (1950, p. 67) contention that ecology's subject of inquiry is the community, and Duncan's (1959, p. 684) statement that a sociological conception of human ecology has to focus interest upon studying organization. He quoted the further explication by Duncan and Schnore (1959, p. 144) that what human ecologists seek to account for is the forms taken by social organization "in response to varying demographic, technological, and environmental pressures."

Duncan (1961) had repudiated the "myth" that human ecology is thus merely a different name for what sociologists could perfectly well do without resorting to ecological ideas. Following this repudiation, Stephan noted how sociologists, by using the term community to refer to the organization of a single population (*Homo sapiens*) instead of concurring with biologists that a community consists of a number of populations or species in interaction, deprived social science of the concept's "intrinsic utility." Leo Schnore (1958, p. 626), mindful of Durkheim's reliance on Darwin's explanation of speciation, had, as Stephan pointed out, actually called Durkheim's treatise on division of labor a study of the origin of social species. To take advantage of the ecosystem concept in our analyses of social organization, Stephan wrote, we need such a concept of social species to work with. "The human . . . aggregate must be somehow differentiated into 'species populations' . . . which interact with one another and form an ecological community" (1970, p. 221). The closest sociological equivalent to biology's use of the species concept would be occupations, said Stephan, because that concept identifies the way in which a class of human beings make their living. How they make their living, Stephan was implying, is what is *ecologically* important about members of a species, that is, how they interact with other species and what they take from and put into their surroundings.

But Stephan went farther, insisting it would be illogical to restrict the social species concept to occupations. Human ecology should also take into account "quasi-occupational categories" such as children, thieves, property owners, housewives, and so forth, whose typical patterns of activity constitute distinctive ways of making a living. In addition, other activities that may or may not be means of livelihood for their practitioners—such as vacationing, stamp collecting, patriotism—may represent "social types" whose interactions with other social types have ecological repercussions.

It was probably unwise for Stephan to substitute the phrase social species for the more palatable (to sociologists) phrase social types—or even for the word occupations. Not much was gained by mere renaming, and it was too easy to miss the insights toward which he was aiming; sociologists could simply object that one person changing from one role to another would thus be a member of two or more "species," and could insist that was absurd. Clearly there *are* differences between an occupation or a social type and a species. But it was important to call attention to the neglected similarities, especially the functional interdependence among social types that parallels species interdependence.

What Stephan was really driving at, following Kenneth Boulding (1958) and Lotka (1956), was the suggestion that an ecological community could be represented in mathematical notation by letting $X_1, X_2, \ldots X_n$, stand for the sizes of various occupational or other populations, and writing a set of equations expressing the mutual interdependence at hypothetical equilibrium:

$$X_1 = f_1(X_2, X_3, \ldots, X_n),$$
$$X_2 = f_2(X_1, X_3, \ldots, X_n),$$
$$\ldots,$$
$$X_n \; f_n(X_1, X_2, \ldots, X_m).$$

Although Stephan did not mention it, a moment's reflection would suggest that when the form of these functions (f_1, f_2, etc.) is made explicit by research, the coefficients that would doubtless be attached to the various population terms in the equations would sometimes be positive, sometimes negative. In Stephan's words, the set of equations conveys the idea of the balance of nature. It describes an ecological community in terms of the population effects of interactions in a given habitat among occupants of different niches—be they actual species or quasi-species.

The interactions between one population and another may be of various kinds. The ith and jth populations may, according to Stephan, compete with one another, or complement one another, or they may be independent, or one may be predatory or parasitic upon the other. Human ecology should expect to observe all of these kinds of relations among socially differentiated human populations (i.e., occupations and other social types). Systematic study of the causes and consequences of the various relations could become a major quest of human ecology. Calling the types "social species" was meant to stimulate recognition of the human relevance of ecosystem principles; instead Stephan's use of the phrase may have aroused sociologists' antibiology convictions. These continued to impede recognition of the importance for human ecology of an interspecific concept of community.

Finally, Stephan devoted several pages to enumerating advantages he believed human ecology would gain from using the community concept in this way (essentially as mainstream ecologists use it). Such use conformed, he said, with Hawley's (1944) admonition about preventing isolation of human ecology from general ecology. The proposed model was, moreover, more directly suggestive of research problems than most approaches then in vogue. In addition, some perennial problems associated with the study of social organization and social change would be easier to resolve with this model. Examples he mentioned were similar to the niche closure or habitat loss examples mentioned earlier in the present paper. He spoke of the way various other social types had declined or become extinct as the farming population declined—fewer makers and sellers of certain farming equipment could find employment, certain summer job opportunities dwindled, Grange memberships declined, and so forth. At the same time, various "suburban species" such as trade union members, Little Leaguers, wearers and sellers of grey flannel suits, and so forth, increased. As these examples should indicate, the community model from bioecology would help both scientists and policymakers pay attention to the unanticipated consequences of purposive social action (Merton 1936).

I had myself tried to persuade sociologists to use the term quasi-speciation to refer to "nongenetic differentiation of a human population into differently specialized subgroups by use of alternative tools, customs, or symbols" (Catton 1980, p. 279; 1978). The idea of occupational differentiation as a human version (or human extension) of species differentiation was not really new anyway. In a treatise on *Animal Ecology*, Elton (1927) had called an animal's niche its "profession." Odum, Cantlon, and Kornicker (1960) pursued the idea to derive a "hierarchy postulate" that would account for the commonly observed logarithmic relation between numbers of species and numbers of individuals in communities. And a team of zoologists (not sociologists—not even sociological human ecologists!) pursued the niche-profession analogy (occupations in human societies as analogues to species in plant and animal communities) and found the distribution of 1,083 residents among 116 occupations in Ann Arbor was well fitted by the same logarithmic series as are the species distribution data from plant and animal communities (Clark, Eckstrom, and Linden 1964). Here was the point: Could the similarity between an occupational distribution and a species distribution (1) show that a town really was a community in the bioecologist's sense of the term, and (2) reflect the operation of similar distributive forces in the two cases? Could human ecology once again be conceived as the study of distributive forces in the environment operating upon human populations?

Recalling Another Unifier

The above comparison of an occupational distribution and a species distribution calls for contemplating again the very unorthodox (for sociologists) version of human ecology put forth in 1949 by George K. Zipf in his *Human Behavior and the Principle of Least Effort*. As Zipf had shown, many different kinds of phenomena seemed to fit a common pattern (the generalized harmonic series), and one could be impressed by the kinds of inferences he drew about this from a metaphor he devised in which effort was minimized by matching an assortment of tools to an array of jobs. When Zipf's book was new, human ecology was still widely equated (by sociologists) with the study of urban spatial organization. This made Zipf's subtitle ("An Introduction to Human Ecology") seem quite bizarre to sociological readers. But it was scarcely more bizarre than was, for them, his application of the generalized harmonic series to data as diverse as the rank-frequency distribution of words and the rank-size relation among a nation's cities.

What both Zipf and Stephan were taking into account might best be called "cultural polymorphism." The implications of the biological concept of polymorphism (Ford 1955; Ruffie 1986, pp. 3-133) needed to be broadened for purposes of modeling ecosystem processes when humans are involved. The simplest biological definition of polymorphism is the "occurrence of more than one distinct form of individuals in a population" (Rickleffs 1979, p. 877). The possible differentiation of functions among the interacting organisms in a community is limited when it has to depend either on biological polymorphism within a single species or on genetically based differences between the various species (Catton 1987, p. 415). Human societies, however, have transcended such limits. Ecologically speaking, what is distinctive about the human species is that we have substituted sociocultural differentiation and technology for biological polymorphism and interspecific differences. Recognizing this leads to the further recognition that the polymorphism that makes possible a highly ramified division of functions among humans is in the tools rather than in the hands that wield them. Human polymorphism is more in the socially instilled contents of the brains that control those hands and those tools than in the biological structure of those brains.

Having worked through to ideas like these, Zipf's insights may now be seen in a different light. Similar patterns do indeed show up in seemingly unlike and supposedly noncomparable data sets. In the biological literature various diagrams depict species abundance patterns. In these diagrams, the rank-ordered species in a community are plotted arithmetically on the abscissa, and on the ordinate the abundance of each species is plotted logarithmically. The resulting patterns visibly resemble many of the figures that appeared in Zipf's book.

Among the biologists' cases one sees bird species data from various European woodlands, species abundance of ground vegetation in an oak forest and in a conifer plantation, and the comparative number of moths of various species in those same wooded environments (Magurran 1988, Figures 4.1, 4.3, 4.4). The slopes of the lines differ, and Magurran was able to suggest ecological implications of the differences. So it may well be appropriate to concur with Zipf by construing a common pattern that shows up in such different categories of organisms in very different settings as an indication that there may truly be a common mechanism pervading many instances of community structure. Variations on the common pattern thus become interpretable as indicators of situational (environmental) differences. Sociologists who would be human ecologists had better take Zipf seriously after all.

Expunging the Aversion to Analogy

Many sociologists are still likely to resist these ideas, decrying them as reasoning by analogy.[6] Some human ecologists with academic departmental identities other than sociology may share the same strong aversion to interspecific comparisons. Comparisons between humans and other species (especially including the experimental psychologist's maze-running or lever-pressing rats) have long seemed repugnant to orthodox sociological thought. But social scientists have overdone their rejection of *all* comparisons across species boundaries, responding too categorically to some misguided examples of interspecific comparison committed by so-called Social Darwinists three or four generations ago.

It is time to reconsider just what is involved in comparing occupational differentiation with speciation. Table 1 is meant to lay to rest conventional objections that decree human ecology should remain a strictly social science and must not borrow biological concepts.

Differentiation is simply not entirely a biological concept. It is more general than that. There are manifestations of the process in the various domains studied by the various sciences. Speciation is a biological special case of the general phenomenon. Sociocultural differentiation is no more and no less truly a special case. As the table indicates, we may reasonably regard biology and sociology as each studying its own special case of a more general process. When subject matters of two disciplines are related in this manner, it is to be expected that each discipline might advance by accurately understanding the other discipline's discoveries. It is also to be expected that in studying its own portion of the overarching common type of phenomenon, each discipline might occasionally forge ahead of the other in conceptualizing and investigating the shared phenomenon. How foolish it would be for either discipline to consider the other's advances permanently preemptive of any related inquiry by itself!

Table 1. Differentiation as a Subject in Two Sets of Disciplines

General Process	Differentiation	
Special case	genetic differentiation (speciation)	sociocultural differentiation (quasi-speciation)
Disciplines	Biological Sciences	Social Sciences

Consider, then, the fact that Durkheim drew upon both Darwin and Haeckel to assert that the multiplicity of species in a finite habitat was due to the ability of many more unlike than like individuals to coexist inasmuch as their differences reduced the acuteness of competition between them. Then he went on to assert that humans "submit to the same law" so that, for example, the "oculist does not struggle with the psychiatrist, nor the shoemaker with the hatter, nor the mason with the cabinet maker, nor the physicist with the chemist, etc." (Durkheim 1933, pp. 266-267). The division of labor, he said, results from the struggle for existence. In proportion to its development, the division of labor "furnishes the means of maintenance and survival to a greater number of individuals" than could be supported in more homogeneous societies (1933, p. 270).

Biologists have also learned by using sociological concepts. Is there really any sound reason they should not? Must sociologists be so parochial as to assume the word sociology can apply only to studies of interactions among members of one species (and must that one species be *Homo sapiens*)? Others have used the word to refer to patterns of association and interaction among other types of organisms—for example, Braun-Blanquet (1932) on *Plant Sociology*, and Reid (1962) on *The Sociology of Nature*, a book on animal ecology. Reid, in fact, asked a fundamental sociological question: Just what is it that constitutes social behavior? His answer was that "when animals behave differently in association than they do when isolated from their kind, then their life is to that extent social." Adding that the dividing line between social and nonsocial is not well-defined, he said division of labor is seen among both highly social and only slightly social species (Reid, 1962, p. 120).[7]

Ecological Diversity:
Species Richness and Species Abundance

Arguing that division of labor is measured by the amount of difference among individuals in their sustenance activities, Labovitz and Gibbs (1964) suggested that *two* dimensions must be considered—both the number of occupations and the distribution of workers among them. There would be less division of labor in a society with 99% of its labor force in one of ten occupations than in a society with only five occupations but with each accounting for 20% of the labor force. In effect, they were recognizing the importance of both dimensions of ecological diversity—species richness and species abundance. No biological literature was cited in their paper, and Labovitz and Gibbs may or may not have been aware that biologists distinguish between those two components of the ecological diversity concept.

If we follow Elton (1927), the ecological diversity alluded to in biological literature is much like the division of labor Durkheim saw as a major aspect of human community structure. By citing Darwin, Durkheim implied that occupational diversity results from evolution. Although the existence of millions of distinguishable species is indeed a result of evolution, the ecological diversity of a particular biotic community is achieved in a much shorter time than it took for all those species to evolve. The ecological diversity of a community thus has to be largely the result of a process that proceeds much faster than evolution. Succession is the bioecologists' name for that faster process. Although it is a process that, like evolution, is guided by environmental selection pressures, succession refers to a sequence of additions and substitutions of already existing species into a particular (changing) habitat, not a sequence of origins of new species—such as would be implied by evolution (Preston 1960).

Conceivably, in human communities ecological diversity (division of labor) might be attributed to *cultural* evolution, a faster process (potentially) than biological evolution. But if sociological human ecologists had not distorted the meaning of succession when they took over the term from plant ecology, it might have been recognized before now as a more likely explanation for the occupational structure existing at a particular time in a particular human community.

Sociologists' use of the word succession clearly reflects the perils of separatism. Due to what Hawley (1944, p. 309) termed the "failure to maintain a close working relationship between human ecology and general or bioecology" succession came to mean in sociological human ecology literature a very different kind of process than was denoted by the same word in the studies of biotic communities. An essential component of the succession process was called "reaction" by Clements (1916, p. 79), but this component was seriously misunderstood and the term was used much differently by Burgess (1928). The misinterpretation was mentioned in a footnote by Alihan (1938, p. 173): "The term 'reaction,' although used by both plant and human ecologists, has a different meaning in each case. In plant ecology, it means 'the effect which a plant or a community exerts upon its habitat' . . . while in human ecology it represents the resistance of the inhabitants to the invaders."

Despite that lucid footnote, Alihan (1938) went on to claim it was "evident that succession as interpreted by Burgess and invasion as understood by McKenzie are synonymous" even though "McKenzie does attempt to differentiate between invasion and succession by saying that invasions enact successions." In plant communities, according to Alihan's understanding of McKenzie, "successions are the products of invasion." To compound the confusion, Alihan then asserts that succession, as used in these statements, stood for "the final stage of invasion—the 'climax.'" (1938, p. 174).

The confusion arose from, and was representative of, the sociologists' assumption that invaders (the newcomers to an area) drive the process of community change. Burgess clearly supposed that. If McKenzie thought plant ecologists viewed succession as invader-driven, he was wrong. Clements (1916) had clearly described the process as one in which a plant community's reaction upon its environment reduces that environment's suitability for supporting that association of species, often making it more suitable for supporting a somewhat different association. *Then* newcomers can find a niche. Reaction facilitates invasion, as the terms are understood in bioecology. In separatist human ecology, reaction is thought to be an impediment to continued invasion. Succession as seen by plant ecologists was *not* an invader-driven process. Its essence was missed by sociological human ecologists; their separatism enabled them to misconceive succession as invader driven.

But even if we now were to suppose succession, correctly understood, had more to do with accounting for the occupational diversity of community structure, Durkheim's invoking of evolution was important. And had Darwin's study of the origin of species not been available to support Durkheim's interpretation of division of labor as a means of limiting the range of competition or mitigating the struggle for existence, subsequent ecological literature would have provided such support. Studies of "species packing" can sound very much like Durkheim, even though they were done by biologists. According to Robert May (1974, p. 322), "the total number of species packed into an interval on the resource spectrum is greater if they are specialists . . . than if they are generalists. . . ." In the biotic community "there is an effective limit to niche overlap. . . ." This means there is "resource partitioning." According to Jonathan Roughgarden (1974, 1976), so-called guilds of competing species thus limit their competition.

On the other hand, biologists have learned some things about factors shaping the division of labor in biotic communities that should call into question some of Durkheim's inferences. For example, because Durkheim seemed to attribute human specialization to the inventiveness of *Homo sapiens* he thus seemed oblivious to possible environmental constraints on the process. Biologists, however, see the closeness of packing dependent on an environment's resource diversity and stability (May and MacArthur 1972). Can we really suppose no such constraints affect human division of labor? A correlation of ecological diversity with latitude is an impressively well-established pattern in bioecology (Fischer 1960; Johnson and Raven 1970; Orians 1975). Species richness tends to be markedly greater in communities nearer the equator and markedly less in communities at higher latitudes, although exceptions do occur which can be instructive. This diversity gradient largely holds for amphibians, for birds, for reptiles, and for mammals. Why not then assume, in the manner of Zipf, some common mechanism operating alike among all types of organisms?

According to Fischer (1960, p. 68), diversity gradients are evidently "related to gradients of environmental factors—temperature, humidity, etc." Temperature and humidity are *physical* conditions, but obviously they affect *biological* processes. This ought to suggest to sociologists that biologists have learned not to adhere (as sociologists have tried to adhere) to a methodological rule prohibiting any resort to independent variables from a "lower" science when trying to account for dependent variables in their own science. Even though Durkheim put a curse on explaining social facts by relating them to anything but other *social* facts, it seems imperative now to learn the futility and unwisdom of continuing to respect that curse.

CONCLUSION: SOME INTERESTING QUESTIONS

Once freed from that taboo, human ecologists of even the sociological persuasion can put aside traditional separatism and rejoin the ecological mainstream. New vistas may open to our sociological imaginations. Some examples of ecological insights and ecological questions worthy of fresh and imaginative consideration by liberated human ecologists will serve as an appropriate conclusion to this paper.

In biotic communities undergoing succession, the future species composition of a community will depend not only on the soil and climate at the site and on the environmental impacts of prior occupants of the site. It will also depend on the availability, in the vicinity, of plants and animals capable of occupying the niches that come into existence. Even if such organisms have already evolved elsewhere, they cannot become part of this particular community if there is no proximate "seed source." We should recall the direct sociological parallel: The difference between endogenous invention and diffusion from another culture parallels the contrast between evolution (by mutation and selective retention) and succession.

As we have seen, the occupational structures of human societies have commonly involved assignment of various niches to nonhuman functionaries. In view of that fact, the biologist's conception of a community as a multispecies unit ought not to remain unacceptable to human ecologists. Once accepted, that view of community ought to make more nearly acceptable Stephan's extension of the species concept to occupational (and other socially defined) categories of persons. We need not *call* occupations social species. We need only recognize that occupational (and other social) differentiation results in mutualistic, parasitic, predatory, and other relations between types, just as do the biological differences among species. The effort by Hawley (1950) to contrast "symbiotic" and "commensalistic" relations in human communities was a worthy beginning in the study of such issues, but we have to be careful not to abort it by supposing those two categories were exhaustive and Hawley's interpretations definitive and final.

We should take the similarities between the distributions of occupational types in human communities and the distributions of species (and niches) in plant and animal communities as confirmation of the essential soundness of Stephan's suggested approach, even if we resist his vocabulary. Sociologists should at last outgrow the traditional disregard for the writings of nonsociologists. Separatism wrought its damage upon the thinking of some sociological human ecologists when citations of biological literature began to be systematically deleted from textbook treatments of human ecology for sociology students—for example, in the revision by Alfred McClung Lee (1946, 1951) of Robert E. Park's (1939) *An Outline of the Principles of Sociology*. In Hollingshead's (1934) chapters therein on human ecology, Lee inserted many new citations to sociological literature that bore little direct connection with the text; much text that would have sustained the linkage between human ecology and bioecology was deleted; virtually *all* biological source citations were eliminated.

Social scientists have much to learn from biologists' studies of community structure; these could provide valuable concepts and hypotheses for human ecology. To illustrate: Even Marxist sociologists might learn from reading a paper by two members of the Animal Behavior Research Group at Oxford (Barnard and Sibly 1981). The desperate need today in the Soviet Union for "perestroika" to rebuild that country's faltering economy, as explained by Mikhail Gorbachev (1987), may reflect a cumulative rise during postwar Soviet history in the ratio of "scroungers" to "producers." As Barnard and Sibly (1981, p. 543) put it, "Scroungers apparently reduce the cost of exploiting a resource by letting producers invest the necessary time and energy in foraging, building, incubating, defence, etc., and then usurping the results of their efforts." As Gorbachev sees it, expropriation of a surplus produced by others' labor is not an activity confined to capitalist countries. It has become an insidious feature of Soviet life. Perestroika seeks to reduce the scrounger/producer ratio. As biologists have found, if that ratio becomes too high the scrounger role ceases to be viable.

Can the USSR move toward what biologist Maynard Smith (1982) has called an Evolutionarily Stable Strategy (ESS)? Will human ecologists who cease to separate their work from general ecology increasingly find the study of evolutionarily stable strategies an important and fruitful way to proceed? This ESS concept has been touted as the most important recent development in evolutionary theory (Parker 1984). The strategy concept in such a context may remind us again of Zipf's tool-arrangement metaphor. Was Zipf (1949) on to something more fundamental than was immediately apparent?

In studying the distribution of labor force members among occupational categories in various human communities, can we find (did Zipf, in fact, find) patterns best described by the canonical lognormal curve that recurs so widely in biotic community studies (Preston 1962; May 1975; Sugihara 1980)? If so, will we find indications that it is a mere statistical artifact, as suggested by May (1975), or will it be found to be the result of a hierarchically structured set of niches influenced by many interacting variables (Sugihara 1980)? Can we find contrasts between "immature" and "mature" human communities corresponding to those enumerated by E. P. Odum (1969) for these two types of biotic communities? Will it turn out, as Richerson (1977) believed, that although culture can be treated as a system of inheritance (with Lamarckian qualities) enabling humans to specialize more readily than other creatures, humanly possible specializations may all too often conflict with ecological stability? Is that sort of conflict at the heart of the ecological predicament currently confronting mankind (in the views of increasing numbers of scientists in various fields)?

May we find it useful to classify occupations according to the varying degrees of "parasitism" they seem to involve? Would it be revealing to look for human counterparts (in the exploitation of others' efforts and skills) to kleptoparasitic species, to brood parasitism, and even to kleptogamist mating behavior (Barnard and Sibly 1981)? Have sociological human ecologists, for that matter, adequately explored human versions of the ecological concept of dominance? Have the exchange theorists in sociology said all there is to say about the relations between occupational categories that must derive satisfaction of their own needs by obtaining goods and services from others?

If questions like these strike social scientists as too far-fetched (because of their ingrained habit of staying safely within the bounds of sociological purity as defined by Durkheim's rules), would it not be prudent to consider the interesting use by biologists of concepts *they* borrowed from physics? "Viscosity" is a notable example. Biologists refer to a population as viscous when it is sufficiently sedentary so that it becomes highly endogamous. In such a population with little out-marriage, the principles of kin-selection can foster a high degree of mutual aid activities. But populations can vary in viscosity, and the kin-selection principles would operate differently (or with less promotion of mutual aid) in less viscous populations (Wynne-Edwards 1977, pp. 12-13).

Human ecologists from any of the social sciences may not immediately reach out that far to augment familiar vocabularies, but a vocabulary change can be a stimulus to new insight. Sociologists who have studied power relationships between human groups have perhaps sometimes imagined that the ecologists' studies of dominance relationships were addressing essentially the same issues under merely different nomenclature. To her credit, however, Ward (1978) recognized that power and dominance are *not* just interchangeable terms. Insofar as power and dominance are different, then sociological studies of power relationships are likely to miss the distinctively ecological insights obtained from studying relations of dominance between one species population and another. The disinclination of social scientists to grasp and appreciate such additional insights is not overcome just by calling power "dominance." It can only be overcome by paying attention to ecological studies of dominance as such.

The key element to distinguish dominance from power is the concept of environment. In sociological literature, power has meant something like the extent to which some person of group can more or less directly influence or control the actions of other persons or groups, with or without their consent. In bioecology, dominance refers to the extent to which a particular species or group of organisms affects the *environment* shared by that species or group with other organisms. Dominance tends to refer especially to the control of energy flow in the ecosystem. Plant ecologists commonly use the term dominant (as a noun) to refer to the tallest plants in a biotic community, for those plants determine the availability of sunlight to the understory.

Human ecology would benefit from giving serious consideration to biologists' analyses of the ways species diversity may originate (Ross 1972) and the way it may be affected by environmental changes (MacArthur 1975). Human communities, surely, will undergo in future years considerable structural change that may be more readily understood if we arm ourselves with these ecological insights, because some of the most serious changes are bound to result from alterations now being inflicted by industrial civilization upon our planet—our habitat. As Hawley (1944, p. 399) once told us, "Probably most of the difficulties which beset human ecology may be traced to the isolation of the subject from the mainstream of ecological thought." It is still true!

NOTES

1.   Dependence of the city of Leningrad on its hinterland became painfully evident when the siege reduced its supply lines to an intermittent trickle of imports across icy Lake Ladoga. More people lost their lives in Leningrad during those 900 days of deprivation than the total of all U.S. military fatalities in all wars.

2.   From an ecological perspective, new meaning can be seen in a classic sociological study. Thomas and Znaniecki (1918-1921) clearly showed how difficult and nonautomatic is the readaptation to new niches (as old ones close up) even among members of the relatively flexible human species. The Polish immigrants who were the subject of their massive study had come to America after absorbing Old World folkways; in the New World they were faced with the necessity of adapting to unfamiliar circumstances. Old ways of behaving and thinking were not easily abandoned or changed. When new ways contradicted the immigrants' old-country upbringing they were learned only with difficulty. Thomas generalized from the immigrants' situation, reaching the conclusion that *generally* an accustomed way of behaving tends to persist as long as circumstances allow. If circumstances change and make familiar and comfortable ways unworkable (or unacceptable), some degree of crisis is inevitable. Readaptation hurts and is resisted. A term that has since become familiar for denoting the enervating disorientation and bewilderment associated with moving into unfamiliar societal contexts is "culture shock." As a tourist one can feel it when one travels abroad. Half a century after Thomas and Znaniecki studied the phenomenon among Polish peasants resettled in America, Alvin Toffler extended the concept when he popularized another phrase: "future shock." This apt new term expressed the fact that forced adjustment to *new* ways can be as traumatic as forced adjustment to *foreign* ways.

3.   By comparison, the unemployment rate for the entire U.S. civilian labor force in 1986 was 7%.

4. An excellent (nonexclusive, nonseparatist) definition of human ecology has been provided by an historian (Hughes 1975, p. 3): "Human ecology . . . is a rational study of how mankind interrelates with the home of the human species, the earth; with its soil and mineral resources; with its water, both fresh and salt; with its air, climates and weather; with its many living things, animals and plants, from the simplest to the most complex; and with the energy received ultimately from the sun."

5. In a long chapter on human ecology in *The Handbook of Modern Sociology*, intended "primarily as an extension of [such] elements in Hawley's work," Duncan (1964, p. 40) declared: "Only a hopelessly anthropocentric view of the universe . . . can overlook the continuity of man's uses of materials, energy, and information with those of preceding and associated forms of life."

6. For some illuminating remarks about legitimate versus illegitimate reasoning by analogy, see the chapter on "Induction, Analogy, and Intuition" in Quine and Ullian (1978, pp. 83-95).

7. There has long existed among some biologists (with acceptance by a very few sociologists) the idea of a "general sociology"—the study of social living patterns among whatever animal species typically live in collectivities. This long antedates the more recent (and controversial) field of sociobiology. See, for example, Allee (1931). That work, together with Allee (1932) and Wheeler (1934), received citation with approval in George Lundberg's *Foundations of Sociology* (1939).

REFERENCES

Adams, C.C. 1913. *Guide to the Study of Animal Ecology.* New York: Macmillan.

────────. 1935. "The Relation of General Ecology to Human Ecology." *Ecology* 16(July):316-335.

Addicott, J.F. 1984. "Mutualistic Interactions in Population and Community Processes." Pp. 437-456 in *A New Ecology*, edited by P.W. Price, C.N. Slobodchikoff, and W.S. Gaud. New York: Wiley.

Alihan, M.A. 1938. *Social Ecology: A Critical Analysis.* New York: Columbia University Press.

Allee, W.C. 1931. *Animal Aggregations: A Study in General Sociology.* Chicago: University of Chicago Press.

────────. 1932. *Animal Life and Social Growth.* Baltimore, MD: Williams and Wilkins.

────────. 1938. *The Social Life of Animals.* New York: W. W. Norton and Co.

Barnard, C.J., and R.M. Sibly. 1981. "Producers and Scroungers: A General Model and Its Application to Captive Flocks of House Sparrows." *Animal Behavior* 29(May):543-550.

Barrows, H.H. 1923. "Geography as Human Ecology." *Annals of the Association of American Geographers* 13(March):1-14.

Berry, B.J.L., and J.D. Kasarda. 1977. *Contemporary Urban Ecology.* New York: Macmillan.

Bews, J.W. 1935. *Human Ecology.* London: Oxford University Press.

Boulding, K.E. 1958. *Principles of Economic Policy.* Englewood Cliffs, NJ: Prentice-Hall.

Bowman, J.C. 1977. *Animals for Man.* The Institute of Biology's Studies in Biology No. 78. London: Edward Arnold.

Braun-Blanquet, J. 1932. *Plant Sociology.* Trans. by G. D. Fuller and H. S. Conard. New York: McGraw-Hill.

Burgess, E.W. 1928. "Residential Segregation in American Cities." *Annals of the American Academy of Political and Social Science* 140(November):105-115.

Catton, W.R., Jr. 1978. "Understanding Social Differentiation." *Contemporary Sociology* 7(November):695-698.

────────. 1980. *Overshoot: The Ecological Basis of Revolutionary Change.* Urbana: University of Illinois Press.

────────. 1987 "The World's Most Polymorphic Species." *BioScience* 37(June):413-419.

Clark, P.J., P.T. Eckstrom, and L.C. Linden. 1964. "On the Number of Individuals per Occupation in a Human Society." *Ecology* 45(Spring):367-372.

Clements, F.E. 1916. *Plant Succession: An Analysis of the Development of Vegetation.* Washington, DC: Carnegie Institution.

Cowles, H.C. 1899. "The Ecological Relations of the Vegetation of the Sand Dunes of Lake Michigan." *Botanical Gazette* 27:95-117, 167-202, 281-308, 361-391.

Darling, F.F. 1963. "The Unity of Ecology." *Advancement of Science* 20(November):297-306.

Dasmann, R.F. 1970. *A Different Kind of Country.* New York: Macmillan (Collier Books).

Dice, L.R. 1955. *Man's Nature and Nature's Man: The Ecology of Human Communities.* Ann Arbor: University of Michigan Press.

Duncan, O.D. 1959. "Human Ecology and Population Studies." Pp. 678-716 in *The Study of Population: An Inventory and Appraisal,* edited by P.M. Hauser and O.D. Duncan. Chicago: University of Chicago Press.

_____. 1961. "From Social System to Ecosystem." *Sociological Inquiry* 31(Spring): 140-149.

_____. 1964. "Social Organization and the Ecosystem." Pp. 36-82 in *Handbook of Modern Sociology,* edited by R.E.L. Faris. Chicago: Rand McNally.

Duncan, O.D., and L.F. Schnore. 1959. "Cultural, Behavioral, and Ecological Perspectives in the Study of Social Organization." *American Journal of Sociology* 65(September):132-146.

Dunlap, R.E., and W.R. Catton, Jr. 1979. "Environmental Sociology." *Annual Review of Sociology* 5:243-273.

Durkheim, E. 1933. *The Division of Labor in Society.* Trans. by George Simpson. New York: Macmillan.

_____. 1950. *The Rules of the Sociological Method.* Glencoe, IL: The Free Press.

Edwards, E.H. 1987. *Horses: Their Role in the History of Man.* London: Willow Books.

Ehrlich, P.R., and A. Ehrlich. 1981. *Extinction: The Causes and Consequences of the Disappearance of Species.* New York: Ballantine Books.

Elton, C. 1927. *Animal Ecology.* New York: Macmillan.

Faris, R.E.L. 1967. *Chicago Sociology 1920-1932.* San Francisco: Chandler.

Fischer, A.G. 1960. "Latitudinal Variations in Organic Diversity." *Evolution* 14(March):64-81.

Ford, E.B. 1955. "Polymorphism and Taxonomy." *Heredity* 9(August):255-264.

Form, W.H. 1954. "The Place of Social Structure in the Determination of Land Use: Some Implications for a Theory of Urban Ecology." *Social Forces* 32(May):317-323.

Gibbs, J.P., and W.T. Martin. 1959. "Toward a Theoretical System of Human Ecology." *Pacific Sociological Review* 2(Spring):29-36.

Gorbachev, M. 1987. *Perestroika: New Thinking for Our Country and the World.* New York: Harper & Row.

Hanks, J. 1979. *The Struggle for Survival: The Elephant Problem.* New York: Mayflower.

Hardesty, D.L. 1972. "Human Ecological Niche." *American Anthropologist* 74 (June):458-466.

Hawley, A.H. 1944. "Ecology and Human Ecology." *Social Forces* 22(May):398-405.

_____. 1950. *Human Ecology: A Theory of Community Structure.* New York: Ronald.

_____. 1975. *Man and Environment.* New York: New Viewpoints, a Division of Franklin Watts, Inc.

_____. 1986. *Human Ecology: A Theoretical Essay.* Chicago: University of Chicago Press.

Hollingshead, A.B. 1939. "Human Ecology." Pp. 63-168 in *An Outline of the Principles of Sociology,* edited by R.E. Park. New York: Barnes & Noble.

Hughes, J.D. 1975. *Ecology in Ancient Civilizations.* Albuquerque: University of New Mexico Press.

Hutchinson, G.E. 1965a. "The Niche: An Abstractly Inhabited Hypervolume." Pp. 26-78 in *The Ecological Theater and the Evolutionary Play.* New Haven, CT: Yale University Press.

_____. 1965b. "Prolegomenon to the Study of the Descent of Man." Pp. 78-94 in *The Ecological Theater and the Evolutionary Play.* New Haven, CT: Yale University Press.

Johnson, M.P., and P.H. Raven. 1970. "Natural Regulation of Plant Species Diversity." *Evolutionary Biology* 4:127-162.

"Loalas in Wild Imperiled." 1989. *New York Times* (December 3), p. C-16.

Koopowitz, H., and H. Kaye. 1983. *Plant Extinction: A Global Crisis.* Washington, DC: Stone Wall Press.

Labovitz, S., and J.P. Gibbs. 1964. "Urbanization, Technology, and the Division of Labor: Further Evidence." *Pacific Sociological Review* 7(Spring):3-9.

Lawrence, E.A. 1985. *Hoofbeats and Society: Studies of Human-Horse Interactions.* Bloomington: Indiana University Press.

Lee, A.M. 1946. *New Outline of the Principles of Sociology* 2nd ed. New York: Barnes & Noble.

Lotka, A.J. 1956. *Elements of Mathematical Biology.* New York: Dover.

Lundberg, G.A. 1939. *Foundations of Sociology.* New York: Macmillan.

MacArthur, J.W. 1975. "Environmental Fluctuations and Species Diversity." Pp. 74-80 in *Ecology and Evolution of Communities,* edited by M.L. Cody and J.M. Diamond. Cambridge, MA: The Belknap Press of Harvard University Press.

Magurran, A.E. 1988. *Ecological Diversity and Its Measurement.* Princeton, NJ: Princeton University Press.

May, R.M. 1974. "On the Theory of Niche Overlap." *Theoretical Population Biology* 5(June):297-332.

————. 1975. "Patterns of Species Abundance and Diversity." Pp. 81-120 in *Ecology and Evolution of Communities,* edited by M.L. Cody and J.M. Diamond. Cambridge, MA: The Belknap Press of Harvard University Press.

May, R. M., and R. H. MacArthur. 1972. "Niche Overlap as a Function of Environmental Variability." *Proceedings of the National Academy of Sciences* (USA)69(May):1109-1113.

Maynard Smith, J. 1982. *Evolution and the Theory of Games.* Cambridge: Cambridge University Press.

McKenzie, R.D. 1934. "Demography, Human Geography, and Human Ecology." Pp. 58-64 in *The Fields and Methods of Sociology,* edited by L.L. Bernard. New York: Ray Long and Richard R. Smith, Inc.

McNaughton, S.J., and L.L. Wolf. 1970. "Dominance and the Niche in Ecological Systems." *Science* 167(January 9):131-139.

Merton, R.K. 1936. "The Unanticipated Consequences of Purposive Social Action." *American Sociological Review* 1(December):894-904.

Mukerjee, R. 1928. "Social Ecology of a River Valley." *Sociology and Social Research* 12(March):341-347.

————. 1932. "The Ecological Outlook in Sociology." *American Journal of Sociology* 38(November):349-355.

Odum, E.P. 1963. *Ecology.* New York: Holt, Rinehart and Winston.

————. 1969. "The Strategy of Ecosystem Development." *Science* 164(18 April): 262-270.

————. 1971. *Fundamentals of Ecology* (3rd ed.). Philadelphia: W. B. Saunders Co.

————. 1975. *Ecology: The Link Between the Natural and the Social Sciences* (2nd ed.). New York: Holt, Rinehart and Winston.

Odum, H.T. 1971. *Environment, Power, and Society.* New York: Wiley-Interscience.

Odum, H.T., J.E. Cantlon, and L.S. Kornicker. 1960. "An Organizational Hierarchy Postulate for the Interpretation of Species Individual Distributions, Species Entropy, Ecosystem Evolution and the Meaning of a Species Variety Index." *Ecology* 41(April):395-399.

Odum, H.W. 1951. *American Sociology: The Story of Sociology in the United States through 1950.* New York: Longmans, Green and Co.

Odum, H.W., and H.E. Moore. 1938. *American Regionalism.* New York: Henry Holt & Co.

Orians, G.H. 1972. "The Strategy of the Niche." Pp. 169-188 in *The Marvels of Animal Behavior,* edited by T.B. Allen. Washington, DC: National Geographic Society.

_____. 1975. "Diversity, Stability and Maturity in Natural Ecosystems." Pp. 139-150 in *Unifying Concepts in Ecology: Report of the Plenary Sessions of the First International Congress of Ecology, The Hague, The Netherlands, September 8-14 1974*, edited by W.H. van Dobben and R.H. Lowe-McConnell. The Hague: Dr. W. Junk B. V. Publishers.

Park, R.E. 1936. "Human Ecology." *American Journal of Sociology* 42(July):1-15.

_____. 1939. *An Outline of the Principles of Sociology*. New York: Barnes & Noble.

Park, R.E., and E.W. Burgess. 1924. *Introduction to the Science of Sociology*. Chicago: University of Chicago Press.

Park, R.E., E.W. Burgess, and R.D. McKenzie, eds. 1925. *The City*. Chicago: University of Chicago Press.

Parker, G. A. 1984. "Evolutionarily Stable Strategies." Pp. 30-61 in *Behavioral Ecology: An Evolutionary Approach* (2nd ed.), edited by J.R. Krebs and N.B. Davies. Sunderland, MA: Sinauer.

"Periscope" 1989. *Newsweek* (December 4), p. 6.

Preston, F.W. 1962. "The Canonical Distribution of Commonness and Rarity: Part I." *Ecology* 43(Spring):185-215.

Quine, W.V., and J.S. Ullian. 1978. *The Web of Belief* (2nd ed.) New York: Random House.

Quinn, J. A. 1940. "Topical Summary of Current Literature on Human Ecology." *American Journal of Sociology* 46(September):191-226.

_____. 1950. *Human Ecology*. New York: Prentice-Hall.

Reid, L. 1962. *The Sociology of Nature*. Harmondsworth, Middlesex, UK: Penguin Books.

Richerson, P.J. 1977. "Ecology and Human Ecology: A Comparison of Theories in the Biological and Social Sciences." *American Ethologist* 4(May):1-26.

Rickleffs, R.E. 1979. *Ecology* (2nd ed.). New York: Chiron Press.

Ross, H.H. 1972. "The Origin of Species Diversity in Ecological Communities." *Taxon* 21(May):253-259.

Roughgarden, J. 1974. "Species Packing and the Competition Function with Illustrations from Coral Reef Fish." *Theoretical Population Biology* 5(April):163-186.

_____. 1976. "Resource Partitioning Among Competing Species—A Coevolutionary Approach." *Theoretical Population Biology* 9(June):388-424.

Ruffie, J. 1986. *The Population Alternative: A New Look at Competition and the Species*. Trans. by Laurence Garey. New York: Pantheon Books.

Schnore, L.F. 1958. "Social Morphology and Human Ecology." *American Journal of Sociology* 63(May):620-634.

Sears, P.B. 1957. *The Ecology of Man*. Eugene: University of Oregon Press.

Shelford, V.E. 1913. *Animal Communities in Temperate America*. Chicago: University of Chicago Press.

Stephan, E.G. 1970. "The Concept of Community in Human Ecology." *Pacific Sociological Review* 13(Fall):218-228.

Spokesman-Review. 1986. "1 in 4 Petroleum Geologists Out of Work." Spokane, WA: SpokesmanReview, October 9: p. A-13.

Sugihara, G. 1980. "Minimal Community Structure: An Explanation of Species Abundance Patterns." *American Naturalist* 116(December):770-787.

Theodorson, G. W., ed. 1982. *Urban Patterns: Studies in Human Ecology* (rev. ed.). University Park: The Pennsylvania State University Press.

Thomas, W.I., and F. Znaniecki. 1918. *The Polish Peasant in Europe and America*. Boston: R. G. Badger.

Ucko, P.J., and G.W. Dimbleby, eds. 1969. *The Domestication and Exploitation of Plants and Animals*. Chicago: Aldine.

Ward, S.K. 1978. "Human Ecology, Community Studies, and Comparative Sociology: Common Ground for Future Work." Paper presented in a session on "New Directions in Human Ecology" at the annual meetings of the Population Association of America.

Wärming, J.E.B. 1896. *Lehrbuch der okologischen Pflanzengeographie*. Berlin. [English trans. 1909, *Oecology of Plants*. New York: Oxford University Press.]

Wheeler, W. M. 1934. "Animal Societies." *Scientific Monthly* 39(October):289-301.

Wissler, C. 1914. "The Influence of the Horse in the Development of Plains Culture." *American Anthropologist* 16(January-March):1-25.

Wynne-Edwards, V.C. 1977. "Society versus the Individual in Animal Evolution." Pp. 5-17 in *Evolutionary Ecology*, edited by B. Stonehouse and C. Perrins. London: Macmillan.

Zipf, G. K. 1949. *Human Behavior and the Principle of Least Effort: An Introduction to Human Ecology*. Cambridge, MA: Addison-Wesley.

THE NATURAL ECOLOGY
OF HUMAN ECOLOGY

Jeffrey S. Wicken

ABSTRACT

All forms of life take their identities within self-enabling systems of relationships in which parts and wholes mutually constitute each other. I explore how this theme of ecological relationality became rooted in historical time and process through the works of Kant, Darwin, Marx, and Freud. The theme and its development has significant implications for an ecologically based evolutionary ethics in which humans are neither endowed with hubris nor reduced to reciprocal exploitation. The ecological relationality in which human experience is embedded provides a cooperative fit with nature in which humans are both products and formers of, and jointly ends and means for, our own history.

INTRODUCTION

Ours is an age of both differentiation and integration. As individual disciplines cut deeper into their own fields, they discover more and more commonalities of principle with other fields as well. This is hardly surprising. From the time

Advances in Human Ecology, Volume 1, pages 101-118.
Copyright © 1992 by JAI Press Inc.
All rights of reproduction in any form reserved.
ISBN: 1-55938-091-8

101

of Galileo on, it has been understood that general answers were best obtained by asking limited questions. The answers cross disciplinary boundaries; hence, the recent proliferation of interdisciplinary journals that attempt to organize what, for want of better terminology, might be called the "whole" of epistemology.

My interest in this paper will be to explore the theme of ecological relationality, which began solidly in the nineteenth century. We are constituted, as humans, by systems of relationships which include families, cultures, and histories, and reach downward to include the biophysical matrix of life itself.

Nucleic acids, for example, owe their identities as repositories and transmitters of genetic information to their coevolution with proteins in the context of microspheres (Fox 1980; Wicken 1987) that self-assemble in hydrophobic tension with aqueous environments. Their informational capacities emerge in the context of autocatalytic systems in which each part is given identity by participation in a "whole" that, as a whole, is able to process materials and energy for the propagation of the system itself. At the other end of nature's spectrum, no human life can be understood in isolation from other lives. Life, from its simplest to its most complex, is relationally constituted. It is for this reason that I have engaged what might seem an eclectic cast of characters to carry the arguments.

Darwin, naturally, will be a central character. So too will Marx, Freud, and Kant. The thematic focus will be on the ecological relationality that comes from historical process. Understanding our lives as productions of evolutionary history, and as active participants in the future that history makes possible for us, is an extremely important theme for human ecology. Bringing life fully into an evolutionary nature through the biophysical and social sciences is preconditional to understanding ourselves in relationship to the larger ecological household that birthed us, that sustains us, and toward whose maintenance we are both accountable and responsible.

I use these words with care. Accountability and responsibility are normative concepts outside the usual framework of science. They traditionally belong to the domain of ethical philosophy. However, that domain, in the absence of connection to the biophysical world, has not accomplished very much over the millennia. Ethical philosophy has made little progress since Plato—in no small measure because it has divorced its concerns from the biophysical sciences. I am no great advocate of sociobiology, because of its predilection to elevate DNA from its informational role in biology to a determinative God for biology and the social structures that issue therefrom. But at least sociobiology aims for a "whole" nature, in which values have organic connection with our biological identities.

The particular aims of this paper will be to discuss the temporalization of ecological relationality that began in the nineteenth century and continues through our own. While delineating the thematic identity of any century is perilous business, that century's special genius was to show how time and history, no less than physics and chemistry, are the stuff of our constitution. Hegel, Marx, and Darwin all participated in the process of temporalizing ecology for our present age. So too has thermodynamics.

THE DISCOVERY OF TIME

Ludwig Boltzmann referred to his century as the Age of Darwin (Prigogine and Stengers 1984). This is an interesting and revealing remark from a man who had contributed so much to understanding time from a perspective—thermodynamics—that many felt to run antiparallel to the Darwinian revolution. Thermodynamics was widely considered the spoil-sport of biology: Nature ran downhill, and life struggled gamely upstream against an entropic tide.

This has been a big problem for the philosophy of biology ever since Lord Kelvin instructed Darwin about the limitations of his Lyell-inherited uniformitarianism that wanted, in effect, unlimited time for variation and natural selection to deliver the fruits of diversity of life on earth. Since this early adversarial start, evolutionary theory and thermodynamics have been steadily moving together as seekers of that common thread of conceptual coherence that science, by its nature, requires. From his own efforts to understand thermodynamics in statistical terms, Boltzmann knew the value of Darwin's populational approach to evolution, and was sufficiently impressed by its power to give him the credits.

Scientific credits are meted out parsimoniously, and often mean-spiritedly. Boltzmann knew, however, that this thermodynamic understanding of time had much in common with Darwin's. Each, of course, wanted to explain large phenomena in terms of simple laws. Those laws had to be accountable to the Newtonian paradigm for correct science, and they had to deliver the empirical goods. For Darwin, these goods were the diversity of life. For Boltzmann, they were the classical equations of thermodynamics—including entropic irreversibility—by reduction to statistics and mechanics. Evolution and thermodynamics were natural allies, and the past two decades have resolved most of their early differences to mutual benefit. Thermodynamics is no longer the "dismal science" of heat-death, but of creation in Darwin's own ecological arena. It is through ecological energy flows that organisms emerge, compete, and diversify. In the sections that follow, I will introduce, and develop as I can, this connective tissue.

THE REVISION OF ECOLOGY

The study of ecology began, as did so many fields, with Aristotle. For Aristotle, function was so tightly knit with form that there was no room for evolutionary change. Relationality became "essentialistic" (Mayr 1982), and remained so until Darwin. Organization had to be its own cause, because mechanics could not explain its origins. Aristotle, therefore, founded ecology on the premise of the timeless organizational fit of life to its environment.

Kant, two millennia later, used the mechanistic sciences of his day to argue that whatever we could possibly understand about the workings of organisms would not be sufficient to understand how they emerged. Time may have been an a priori category of perception for Kant, but it was certainly not the currency of creation. For both Aristotle and Kant, evolution was epistemologically forbidden. We will examine these arguments, and let them set the stage for resolution in the century of time.

In the early nineteenth century, the temporalization of ecology was moving on several fronts. Mainly, they were directional, and often had questionable social agendas. Time was a vehicle in which *progress* was made. Hegel's "geist" "strove" for articulation in the dialectic of knowing ourselves relationally, and the Kantian categories correspondingly became developmental ones. That they led, in Hegel, to the fixity of the German state is unfortunate, but Hegel had plenty of company in that regard. Herbert Spencer, too, saw the evolutionary process as delivering a final "good"—namely a Utopian state delivered from the hardships of natural selection by a Lamarckian struggle up a scale of being. Deliverance issued from *work*. Such "moralistic" competitive fitness could only achieve the utopian ends if the indigent (construed sometimes as the lazy) were not aided by state relief from their poverty.

Darwin pioneered the new ecology by replacing "progress" with *simple adaptation*. That the *corpus* of his work emphasized competition more than cooperation is unfortunate, because relationality is the bigger part. Each life is a nexus of relationality, and cannot be understood apart from that formative field. The field of ecology was born from the simple human recognition that all lives are constituted by relationships to others.

This recognition that parts are relationally defined by their participation in wholes guided much of Artistotle's work, and allowed him to effectively use social structures as metaphors for understanding biology. Aristotle's greatness as a thinker was very much connected with his feel for wholeness. For Aristotle, the ordering of parts under natural laws was an expression of wholeness. Science's predilection for cutting life's relationality to disciplinary pieces runs against this noble enterprise—which, simply stated, is to bring conceptual coherence to life within a broad framework of value. The conceit that science is a value-neutral enterprise is foolish, and should be abandoned. Science is value-loaded, the former of our contemporary mythos. Our aim should be to synthesize science and philosophy with the values of human ecology. It is in this spirit that Kant, Darwin, Marx, and Freud are discussed here, with an effort to see how the power of their visions illuminate the paths of human ecology for our own age.

The importance of reconciling these men is as follows. Kant chopped nature into epistemological bits, because the science of his day provided no way around it. We could know with authority only that which presented itself to our deductive reason, namely, phenomena that could be mapped into the a priori categories of space and time. Biology did not fit his scheme, nor did ethics. But Darwin pulled the world together naturalistically with such incontrovertible documentation of life's evolutionary connection that biology was finally unified as a science—permanently. There remain immense controversies in the evolutionary reconstructions of our pasts. The questions of how much respective weight should be given to natural selection, the sources of variation, and the constraints on those sources continue to bedevil rapprochement among evolutionary theorists. All this controversy notwithstanding, descent with modification remains intact as the basic idea of modern biology.

Still, Darwin failed to theoretically resolve Kant's epistemological objections to the possibility of a "full" science of biology. Partly this owed to the fact that his principles of variation and natural selection were ad hoc in ways that science just could not ignore. Darwin did not understand the basis of heredity. Nor did he understand the physical principles by which organisms utilize energy for their own maintenance and reproduction. The resolution of the former problem has come from the sturdy work in genetics, and then in molecular genetics, that began with the rediscovery of Mendel's wheel in 1900. The resolution of the latter problem has come from ecological thermodynamics (Wicken 1987). Kant, meanwhile, saw life as so indivisible to the ordinary world of process and change that an evolutionary ecology was virtually unthinkable.

KANT

Kant separated life from what we could conclusively know about nature on what seemed, in the early nineteenth century, to be sound epistemological ground. We could hope to describe eventually how organisms worked in an extended Cartesian physics, but not how they emerged. The origin of biological organization was outside the province of science for Kant. So, too, were the origins of the moral sense, which struck him as no less remarkable than the physical cosmos that excites and invites our imaginations. Each were outside the scope of the a priori deductive conditions for certain knowledge set out in the *Critique of Pure Reason*. In the *Critique of Judgment*, Kant wrote about living systems and tried to reconcile their purposiveness with what could, in fact, be known with certainty.

Kant described organisms as "natural purposes"—their own causes and effects, their own ends and means. This remains (teleology included) a most useful definition for life. After all, everything an organism is *for* functionally involves the survival and reproduction of its organizational form.

A few words, then, on teleology. Since science had, from the time of Galileo, been systematically engaged in the business of banishing teleology from its course, Kant took life's manifest purposiveness as an admission that there would never be a complete science of biology: We might understand how organisms operated, but we could never understand how they came to be. Kant understood that, in discussing life in teleological terms, he was excluding biology from the realm of the phenomenally knowable as spelled out in the "Pure Knowledge" critique, and it framed the basis of his philosophical rejection of evolution. As natural purposes, organisms were outside the power of science to understand. Biology would never have its Newton, able to explain the existence of "a single blade of grass." However great his accomplishments, Darwin was not biology's Newton, for he could not account for the origins of biological organization.

Kant had a more difficult problem—understanding the "moral sense" *without* physics or biology as its underpinnings. Once biology is cut from a knowable nature, the "moral sense" must be taken as a given, a bequest from God. In this way, Kant takes Descartes' ontological separation of nature into knowing mind and knowable matter to its necessary conclusions. The "categorical imperative" was the fruit of that bifurcation. Kant took the empirical fact that humans possess moral feeling from the bosom of David Hume, but he could not reconcile it with either biology or physics. The empirical reality of the moral sense could not be justified by pure reason, which for Kant was that which could be mapped into Cartesian coordinates. It could only be felt, and known in the immediacy of that feeling. The moral imperative is simple, wonderful, and true: Act, so as to use humanity, whether in your own person, or the person of another, always as an end, never as a means merely, said Kant. That this edict is sufficiently close to the golden rule to lack declarative novelty does not detract from its value. Unless we can learn that message, and assimilate it within the broad scope of Darwinian competition, we will perish as a species.

What is special, and also very troublesome, about the way in which Kant systematically separates morality from biology, and biology from physics, is that his moves are made on what seem, at first sight, to be solid epistemological grounds. We cannot know ourselves in the kind of way that we can know the trajectories of physical objects in gravitational fields. We cannot prove the moral cosmos within. Hence the "imperative" part of the categorical imperative. Morality runs against the nature that we can know with Cartesian clarity; but, since we feel it so absolutely, we must recognize its truth: The moral law within supersedes, finally, the stars above. Kant understood that our lives are drawn outward—not just for limited proximate goals, but for our condition of knowing beyond reason that we are relationally constituted by history and by an ecology of interaction with the extended "others" of our lives whose full embrace insists that we know ourselves as morally purposive beings.

This "drawing out" of life for purposes beyond survival and reproduction is of enduring importance philosophically no less than is Kant's "giveness" of the moral sense. The pinioning of that moral sense in biology is essential to the broad Darwinian vision.

RELATIONAL ECOLOGY

Fitting life's teleology into the framework of science has been a major problem for the philosophy of biology ever since Darwin. On one hand, Darwin realized that the only way to move the evolutionary vision from speculative philosophy to science was, in effect, to take life as a given, and then use the principles of variation and selection to generate its diversity.

Darwin was not happy with this solution, because it cut life from the nature that birthed it. However, with the New Synthesis in evolutionary theory (loosely, neo-Darwinism) the problem became really acute. A philosophy of biology, independent from the philosophy of physics and chemistry, was judged necessary to legitimize teleology for the life sciences (Mayr 1982). While this "autonomy of biology" posture may have had its historical usefulness a while ago, it has badly obstructed dialogue between the physical and biological sciences (Wicken 1985) and has led to a communication impasse that is not only antiecological, but supportive of the old Kantian distinctions that an evolutionary cosmos is required to bridge. If life is a product of nature, then everything that leads to life and supports it is part of its relational ecology. Biological purpose must have antecedents in physical nature; and moral purpose must have its sources in biological nature.

The latter synthesis has been an important achievement of sociobiology. The failures of sociobiology to do that theme sufficient justice owe to its "genes first" ontology that regards living systems as derivative from informational programs. The paradox inherent to this line of reasoning is that life emerged ecologically. Replacing the first cause of divine design by the first cause of informational programs maintains the "autonomy of biology" progam that separates life from the rest of nature.

Aristotle remains seminally helpful here. That his arguments have been terribly misunderstood over the centuries does not subtract from their enduring importance. For Aristotle, teleology *was* nature. Final causes provided 'whys,' and efficient causes provided the 'hows' to get there. These were not separate causal principles for Aristotle, and his abuse in the post-Galilean literature leading to the contemporary philosophy of science is a direct result of failing to understand teleology within its own Cartesian terms. Aristotle's causal framework was seamless: Final causes were nothing other than nature's manifestly functional order, and efficient causes were the precipitating events to get there. Organisms for Aristotle, no less than for Kant, were "natural purposes" or "natural organizations" in contemporary parlance. That is, they were their own causes and effects, their own ends and means. For Aristotle, this made an evolutionary ecology ontologically impossible. For Kant, it made it epistemologically impossible.

Kant had a point. If science was incapable of knowing purpose, it could not know life in "Pure Reason" terms. Kant was right to this degree, and only to this degree: The knower can never fully know itself in analytic terms. Godel's incompleteness theorem put this problem formally to rest, by showing that axiomatic systems could not be verified within the framework of their own propositional structures.

Epistemological barriers notwithstanding, it is surprising that Kant did not appreciate the affinity of his definition of life with his definition of morality. Both are teleological, and both are ecological. In this sense, Kant's collective work constitutes a kind of philosophic creationism imposed by his era. Life could not be understood in terms of physics, and morality could not be understood in terms of life. Ergo, separation of life from nature.

The Darwinian revolution changed all this empirically, but its theoretical structure requires the engagement of ecological thermodynamics which link life with physical sources. The Darwinian revolution requires bridging life with the rest of nature. But whereas it is no longer empirically possible to separate human nature from physical nature, the theoretical infrastructure for making these connections has only recently begun to solidify with ecological thermodynamics (Prigogine 1980; Wicken 1987).

Considering his rather monastic personal ways, it is interesting that Kant reveals himself as an Epicurean where normative issues are concerned. That is, Kant did not see the "ought" of human nature as conformable to the "is" of physical nature. From this separation, Kant felt that the moral act must be done in "pain" against our instincts. He said, and took it to be a matter of a priori knowledge, that moral law determines the will by thwarting all our inclinations, and must produce in us a feeling we call pain.

These words should give us pause. If morality is pain, we are in deep trouble. Echoes of original sin will not help us resolve the problems of living together as a species in harmony with the nature that birthed us and to which we are finally accountable. People, utilitarian beasts that we are, prefer to minimize pain and, if morality is pain, we will minimize morality in our lives. This is wrong-headed, antiecological thinking. Fortunately, there are avenues out.

The following sections will discuss the broad message of Darwinism for human ecology through sciences of process that originated with the nineteenth century discovery of time. These are ecological thermodynamics, Marxian social evolution, and Freudian psychological development.

DARWINISM AND THE ECOLOGY OF HUMAN VALUE

Ludwig Boltzmann and Charles Darwin contributed powerfully to the major leitmotif of the nineteenth century: the discovery of time as that which is irreversible and fundamentally constitutive of the world. Yet Boltzmann conceived his own work in statistical thermodynamics to be secondary to Darwin's work in evolution. Partly this was because he used Darwin's populational thinking as an access to his own work in treating molecules as populations. But mainly, I suspect, it was because Boltzmann knew that Darwin dealt most singularly with the nineteenth-century understanding of time as irreversible process. Boltzmann was largely correct in this intuition. This remains the age of Darwin, and the humanities and social sciences are still assimilating his biological lessons.

The social sciences and humanities are becoming increasingly wed to the biophysical sciences. The conditions of that wedding are, however, still under tense negotiation. The biophysical sciences have behaved overmuch as the blustering suitor in this relationship, claiming territory that they have not earned in the human sphere. As humans, we are motivated in our enterprises by two opposing forces: the desire for clarity and the need for meaning. The former points downward toward theory reduction; the latter points upward toward synthesis and transcendence.

For the past half century, the neo-Darwinian program has looked for clarity by attempting to reduce the social-psychic world to "selfish genes" (e.g., Dawkins 1976, 1982). Under this program, even the most preciously human feelings of kindness for others are expressed as epiphenomenally derivative from the all-embracive mandate of reciprocal exploitation. The humanities are properly wary about handing over the human torch to this molecular message. They cannot do that effectively, outside of scared, uninformed criticism of sociobiology, without engaging this male conquistador on his own terms. Resistance against reduction to that which is not human requires that the humanities take science more seriously.

Ernst Mayr (1982) writes with pride bordering on hubris about his own importance as a synthesizer. Along with a few other Darwinian naturalists, Mayr was able to absorb the nonnegotiable understandings of the emerging science of genetics, and the synthetic theory of evolution emerged from this negotiation. However, having once done this hard act of listening, Mayr and other framers of the synthetic theory have largely closed the door on future discourse by developing an "autonomy of biology" posture which has proved unprofitable for dialogue with the physical sciences at one end of the spectrum and with the social sciences and humanities at the other. Such historical inertia impacts greatly on what evolutionary theory can contribute to understanding the human condition.

The disciplinary chauvinism of the physical and biological sciences in matters human is not to be underestimated as an impediment to getting a correct synthesis of nature's polarities. Whereas social thinking ought never to be divorced from physical-biological realities, it is equally and conversely true that any biophysical commentary on the human constitution is spurious if it does not address what it "feels like" to be human. This is where I take greatest objection to sociobiology, as presently conceived. For example, E.O. Wilson (1978) urges us to look at the human species through an "inverted telescope," so that we can see its objective status in the large picture of nature. Whereas that kind of objectivity is taxonomically and perspectively valuable, it short-changes the human condition of persons knowing their own relationalities through experiencing the world existentially. The telescope must be removed to get a proper picture of ourselves as humans.

It is in this sense—connected with the selfish-gene motif—that current sociobiology is a crude, first-order approach to interweaving the biological and the social. Its problem is not just that it attempts to do this unilaterally and reductionistically. The fundamental problem is that it appeals to a flawed neo-Darwinian ontology of what it means to be an organism. In its tilt toward genetic reductionism, sociobiology taps overmuch into the myth, born from the central dogma of information flow from DNA to RNA to protein, that behaving phenotypes are "produced by" genetic programs, which ultimately own their existences to replicating strands of nucleic acid. This antiecological view of life leads finally to an antiecological view of morality.

A real concept of organism is lacking in neo-Darwinism, and many (e.g., Gould 1980) have pointed out this omission very forcefully. Conceiving organisms as intermediaries between genes and selective environments is poor science, poor philosophy, and delivers poor messages about life's relational constitution. Extrapolating the "genes first" premise into the human-social arena has been ethically disastrous. Scientifically, it suffers the paradox of building lives from concatenations of points or of generating motion from rest. There is a lifelessness about neo-Darwinism that its advocates urge us to ignore by appealing to the autonomy of biology as a discipline. The sense of this appeal is that, evolutionary visions of nature's continuity notwithstanding, we should bracket the problem of life's emergence from the body of evolutionary theory and begin with the genotype-phenotype dichotomy expressing itself in selective environments. The ineluctable conclusion of this reasoning is that the entire sentient dimension of life has its primal antecedents in nonliving matter.

The primitive assumptions of neo-Darwinism lead to conclusions about social structures, and about ethics, that just do not fit with experience. If ethical systems are conceived as extended phenotypes, to use Dawkins' (1982) expression, then they are in no essential ways different from somatic phenotypes. Each serves the general project of survival and reproduction. The upshot of this reasoning is that selfish interests become the basic bits of neo-Darwinian transaction, and we are then obliged to explain altruistic behavior and ethico-religious systems as derivative from this fundamental selfishness. However important kin-selection and game-theoretical models are for this task, we are much closer to the project of understanding life if we regard it as an ecological phenomenon than as the production of selfish genes.

Much work has been done in recent years to connect evolution with thermodynamics. Contemporary developments in evolutionary theory proceeding from irreversible thermodynamics cement the Kantian picture by making life continuous with the rest of nature. Living systems are informed autocatalytic organizations (Wicken 1987) that maintain themselves through energetic exchanges with their environments. This was the center of Schroedinger's theme that organisms maintain their organizations by feeding on negentropy. The environment-organism interface is a porous one; and organisms are relationally constituted by internal processes interacting with selective environments. They are not gene machines. Rather, genes play information roles within autocatalytic wholes that pull resources into themselves for growth, homeostasis, and reproduction. Those wholes both depend on, and provide a selective context for, the existence and operation of their parts. Species coevolve with environments, and genetic programs coevolve with systems of internal relationships in interaction with environments. There is no ontological priority in this relational network. Priority belongs to the system itself, and parts differentiate within its framework.

The same general reasoning applies to the relationship between the biological and social sciences. The context of meaning provided by the higher hierarchical levels coevolves with the operational principles at the lower levels. The relational identity of organisms fuses self-interest with ecological interest. Of course there are mavericks, parasites, and outlaws. But the strategy of life is the coevolution of autocatalytic selves with the environments that sustain them. Selected informational programs bear the impresses of their environments, and "selfish genes" are contextualized within organisms whose strategic best interests are served by replenishing their environments. Selfishness coevolves with cooperative participation in the ecological whole.

Darwin's immense accomplishment was to show, conclusively, that the diversity of life on earth was the product of history, variation, and natural selection within an ecological household. The significance of this achievement cannot be overestimated. With Darwin, essentialism and special creation were gone for good. Our natures issue from millennia of hard, historical work. They contain the baboon's nature and the crocodile's nature, all tested for function in the ecological arena. We humans are big neocortical elaborations of a nature that evolves. We are accountable to that nature for our survival, and we are responsible for its survival.

Because of this replacement of Aristotelian essences by history and selection, responsibility is not moralistically imposed on the human condition in Darwinian metaphysics. Rather, it is selected for function. And here sociobiology makes some extremely important contributions to an evolutionary ethics. Since we are products of history in an ecological arena whose very contours we form as decision makers, responsibility comes with the turf. With the emergence of our reflective noosphere (Teilhard de Chardin 1975) comes the realization that the future is a decision landscape—not blindly deterministic, but open and self-determining.

Our Judeo-Christian myths ring clearly on this. Milton's *Paradise Lost* is partly a polemic against the hubristic self-determination that comes with separation from God. In trying to justify God's ways to Man, it implicitly asserts the importance of the spiritual ecological household in which we find our individual meanings. The Darwinian scheme does this more explicitly, for it locates human nature meta-ethically in ecological nature. Unfortunately, the early ethical interpretations of Darwinism opposed the theme of fitting cooperatively with nature.

If we follow nineteenth-century prescripts on ethical and political matters that claim their base in Darwin, and regard ourselves as blind participants in a struggle for existence, we get ethics only through an epiphenonemal back door. If struggle is all, then we revert to a "justice is the interest of the stronger" mentality criticized by Plato. Understanding evolution more broadly, as Herbert Spencer in his better moments did, as the adjusting of internal relations to external conditions, the Darwinian-ecological approach vindicates in real-world terms Plato's understanding that justice is that which benefits all and allows the maximum space for improving all. It vindicates, too, Kant's understanding that one can never regard humans simply as means for some abstract end. In all moral matters, the ends *are* the means. Humans are jointly ends and means for their own engagement of history, both as its products and as its formers.

This philosophically reconciles Kant's understanding of organism with evolutionary process. If organisms, ecosystems, and societies are each jointly ends and means of their own activities, then the teleology that had always been central to defining normatively the place for man in the world fits right into the Darwinian scheme and gains therein real-world justification. Teleology is brought into the domain of science through thermodynamics, since organisms are systems of kinetic relationships that maintain their organization by degrading energy. The purposiveness of life is a part, and a consequence, of ecological energy flows (Wicken 1987).

MARX AND FREUD

Now, let us turn to the specifically human dimensions of this relational ecology. Here, the works of Marx and Freud are truly seminal.

Crassly stated, Marx regarded humankind as an abstraction that emerged under historical forces with the aid of apposable thumbs. On one hand, he was enthusiastic about Darwin as providing a natural-world analog for his own struggle schema on the societal level. On the other hand, Marx's materialism is eschatological in the sense of involving a "fall from initial grace" with the institutionalization of exploitative relationships that, in an important way, marks the beginning of civilization as understood in textbooks, followed by the dialectical resolution of conflicts pointing toward an ideal society which maximized freedom for all. This is not far from the Hegelian Geist struggling for articulation, since the freedom enjoyed by the liberated society is a self-conscious one, having assimilated its history for its own use. Marx's evolutionary progession toward freedom is a nice utopian theme, in contradistinction to the oppressive ones of Plato, Hobbs, and Moore. The want of progressive eschatology in Darwin's nature denies a simple mapping of Marx into Darwin. This does not mean that there is no possibility for a concept of progress in the Darwinian scheme. Evolution opens doors for experimentation and, in this, leads to increasing dimensions of freedom that are relationally constituted from ecological interactions.

An interactionally emerging ecology of freedom contrasts sharply with Kant's categorical imperative. For Kant, freedom could only exist in the moral realm, because it had no basis in the biophysical world. Hence, the "pain" of moral choice. Hegel and Marx on the other hand, were beginning to understand freedom as an emergent quality of life, of its coming naturally to consciousness.

While freedom and cooperation have not been emphasized parts of the Darwinian research program, one needs only to look at the general structure of the phylogenetic tree to see their reality. Life starts minimally and consciouslessly. It elaborates where there is room for organisms to circumscribe their environments through informed behavior. Humans have moved along the most productive branch of this tree by behaving cooperatively and ethically with the gift of choice.

With human reflectivity comes a truly new evolutionary phase, in which moral agency counts tremendously. We live in, and create, a noosphere in the broadest of senses. Regardless of the determinism one assigns to the evolutionary process or the ontology of consciousness to which one subscribes, evolution led from the insentient to the spiritual and the choosing. Through progressive evolution, the world has become a conscious, self-guiding place where freedom shares a codefinitional domain with responsibility. Teilhard de Chardin (1975) may have been off-base scientifically, but he was right about the freedom of our activities in the emerging noosphere. That much is in our hands.

The spaciousness of the Darwinian program lies in its value-neutrality. It is nonideological and, therefore, nonprescriptive. In this, it gives room for the articulation of values, including those enunciated in the Marxist and Freudian visions. It provides a meta-naturalism for dealing optimally with determinism, freedom, and responsibility. None of us knows the room freedom plays in her or his life. None of us knows how much the ostensible freedom we experience each day is determined through genetic predisposition, chemicals, hopes, fears, and cultural learning. We do know the importance of feeling free. We want to be free, and demand furthermore that the societal context of our lives grants us that freedom for self-actualization.

Plato would have approved of this contemporary updating of his own most serious reflections, since a major theme of *The Republic* is self-actualization. Plato was stuck, however, in atemporal categories that were unable to deal properly with freedoms at a personal level. Even the philosopher-king had to act "freely" with the world of forms telling him what to do. The world of forms is gone.

In physics, quantum mechanics said a resounding "no" to a Platonic world that might be known behind the mask of nature. What we know is interactional, and what we can claim in behalf of objectivity is finally accountable to the interaction of knower and known. Knowing, in effect, is ecological. Perceived phenomena are the joint construction of observer and observed. Kant was correct in denying the possibility of a Knowable without a Knower. Reality is interactional, and we are explorers of this interaction.

The theory is easy compared to the praxis. So much conflicting talk has emerged from both the sciences and the humanities that we should take care to know what the major themes truly are. Evolutionary theory has told us convincingly that there are no essences beyond the productions of history in ecological contexts. Similarly in literature, deconstructionism tells us there are no meanings beyond those of the experienced interaction of self with script. The context is ecological for all cases, and meaning comes from that interaction.

The social-humanistic thought relevant to the Darwinian revolution can only be interactive, historical, and process-oriented. Wholes, in this ecology, are not sums of parts. Neither, on the converse side, are there parts that exist in independence from the wholes to which they contribute. Parts are relationally constituted by wholes and are functionally invested with meanings by them. The components of the nitrogen cycle coevolve with the ecological system that must get nitrogen from heterotrophs back to autotrophs. The selective pressure on species flows from this relationality. We live now in a very perilous part-whole world, where the survival of each part is increasingly nested in the survival of the whole. Conversely, the survival of the whole is predicated on parts performing their relational functions. Coevolutionary, developmental processes lead ecologically to the human scene and its ethical dilemmas.

This is reflected in the individual human psyche. The forming psyche encounters an ecology of relationships early on. Parents and children interact in mutually formative ways, with the historical substrate of biology breathing through the whole process. Our psyches are built on individual experiences playing themselves out in a larger history of long-term evolutionary experience in long-term ecological arenas.

Freud's special importance as a scientist was in taking account of these forces for the development of the responsive dimension of humankind. We respond in certain ways because we develop within an ecology of experience, an experience that is relationally structured. Although Freud was only superficially influenced by Darwin, understanding Freud's work properly requires that we locate his message within the broad Darwinian framework. Libinal forces, power forces, and survival forces all play themselves out for Freud in an arena of developing human nature adjusting itself and forming itself in response to subterranean forces.

Whereas Freud's special contributions are not subsumed by a Darwinian view of nature, they do fit into its spacious fabric of mutually adjusting relationships. The ecology of mind, of social progress, and of nature all require an understanding of how parts and wholes are mutually defined. Everything in Darwin's nature must be relationally understood. Just as nitrogen fixing bacteria achieve their identities by ecosystem participation, so do humans achieve their identities by participation in larger communities. The guiding hand of consciousness and morality is finally an ecological hand.

Selfish genes have nothing much to do with this. Since a community united by a common will is all that can keep this most important evolutionary experiment in consciousness on track, what is essential in planning for the future is to understand that self-actualization is inseparable from global actualization. Accordingly, any worthy definition of "self" must be embedded in a developing system of relationships that is formative of the human psyche. Only with those understandings can an appropriate sociopolitical stage for freedom and responsibility be built.

Any social planning enterprise must deal with Plato's question about the nature of justice and the just fit between individual and society. Plato was at his most pregnant when he searched for that optimality and eschewed easy answers in favor of meta-ethical observations. Justice could not involve making a person worse. Whereas Plato understood the practical ways in which people could be made better or worse, he had to rely on an "essential" educational agenda about timeless forms. If our nature was fundamentally ahistorical, that nature could be helped or hurt only by the study of subjects such as mathematics, music, and astronomy.

This Weltanschauung played through the eighteenth century. For Locke, humans were slates for the impression of ideas, both normative and scientific. For Hobbes, they were mechanical determinations. For Hume, they were bundles of sensation seeing causation as constant conjunction. All these classical modifications of the timeless Platonic order were both ahistorical and stipulative: Section off a place in the sun, as it were, and build a society that impresses the needs of the macrocosm into the behaviors of the normative actors. The actors always came out bleakly in that arena, having plenty of responsibilities but few freedoms. The Darwinian revolution irreversibly reset that stage by showing that any ecology, human or otherwise, was rooted in historical struggle for survival and reproduction. Interpreting that struggle for human societies has been a subject of hot debate ever since.

Herbert Spencer's Social Darwinism sanctioned the crushing oppress of a laissez-faire capitalism that looked at the economically poor as the necessarily unfortunate detritus of the evolutionary process. Poverty was a wonderfully moral thing in that regard, for it provided a steely mechanism by which to sort out the genetically deficient and the lazy from the sturdy achievers. Hence Spencer's opposition to any kind of relief for the poor: If they cannot propagate, then eventually the achievers will inherit the earth and a steady-state Utopia will come to pass, with 2.0 perfect children for each perfect couple.

This "redness of tooth and claw" understanding of the Darwinian scheme bothers me very much, and Darwin himself did not press that programmatic language. Like Marx, his ideas have been used to advance and underwrite (in the hallowed name of science) the very worst of human inclinations. Our age requires more. It requires an ecology of spirit, that is neither resentful toward the double-edged sword of science, nor absurdly capitulative to its disclosures. As Kant pointed out very clearly, science can know what it can know. It has its limits, and this magnificent wonder of humanity is worth preserving not just for our children or our "selfish genes" but for itself. We, as carriers of that progressive torch of evolution to a "noosphere," have an obligation to see that the ideas that have moved and influenced us to accomplish so much do not fail us now, when our footsteps grow so heavy on our planet that the biosphere yells back that *it* has had enough of our hard technology. Our age requires the enlistment of ideas to fuel the practical marketplace of keeping this planet alive. The selfish-gene, exploitative interpretation of the Darwinian bible will not do anymore.

AN ECOLOGY OF SPIRIT

Darwin had no specific moral agenda. Therein lies his central place in the formulation of post-essentialistic metaethics. He was a naturalist, an explainer of nature's historical processes. In that role he influenced much social and normative thought. If Darwin had had an agenda, its theme would have been that all value is necessarily relational, since populations are units of selection and individuals gain their identities through the historical and ecological conditions of evolution. In this way, Darwin provided many thinly-populated categories for others to fill in: individual, population, society, history, environment. What do these concepts mean, and how are they to be weighted in thinking about the future? Marx and Freud paved some important avenues.

Marx emphasized the formative power of history on human nature. For Marx, the natural history of man *was* history. Darwin would not have disagreed. We are formed not by environmental impresses on essentialistic canvas, but by the interactions of our own histories with those many forces of social evolution that point toward freedom. Marx did not address what those forces were at the psychological level. Humans were blank-slated for historical impress. The individual for Marx thus became an abstraction and historical process the concrete reality.

Freud's insights were complementary to Marx's, for he regarded society as an abstraction against which the concreteness of the individual could be developed. The framework, however, remained ecological. Freud asked what those forces within the individual were that placed boundary conditions on her or his capacity to be a sane, functioning member of the world, and he understood the ways in which we can get truly damaged by the "important others" that enter this ecology. Marx gave society a historical deep structure in which humans participated as pale beings driven by economic forces. But Freud inverted this relationship, by presenting an ecology of mind whose forces might devour us. Society for Freud became the abstraction—that which oppressed, that which required sublimative activity.

Personal ecology was concretely developmental within a Darwinian world. The important dialectic interplay here is that individuals are accorded opportunities for well-being only in the context of societies that seek appropriate human bases for well-being. Marx saw those forces in historical terms. Freud saw them a bit more biologically. Each, however, can only be understood properly in relationship to Darwin, for Darwin set the stage of relationality. Parts and wholes, humans and their environments, must be seen as mutually constitutive if we are to take Darwin's teachings into the future.

In this regard, a caveat is in order: The authority of science is powerful and can, if not vigilantly attended, be a source of myths that close reality to the most fundamental of human experiences. The "selfishness motif" plays dangerously into what we do as humans and the manner in which we conceive our futures. If the deliverances of science tell us that all our outreachings to others are epiphenomenal to selfishness, then we may tend to behave that way (Wicken 1989). The Darwinian theme must be interpreted with unbowing fastidiousness to what the human condition means in relational terms. The reading of the Darwinian Bible has been drastically polarized toward the "red in tooth and claw" motif; and it is time for a Gestalt change.

Darwin changed the subject of ecology forever. Whatever order there is in biological nature must be earned by success in the ecological arena. Still, the ironies are immense. Darwin turned away from the "Great Chain of Being" in no small measure because he saw nature's opportunistic cruelty very clearly. Wasps lay eggs in virgin meat. Humans exploit each other, with the terrible and strange notion that they are islands with destinies of their own apart from the common weal. However, the idea that survivors and reproducers get the spoils is not the central Darwinian message for our age. The bigger dimension of Darwinism asks that we understand the conditions of our contingency within a world whose principles of operation are honed within an ecological framework in which parts are invested with meaning by wholes. So construed, evolutionary theory asks our participation in delivering a world where self-interest meshes with global interest.

We are, by virtue of the felicitous burst of neocortical growth that accompanied our descent from the trees, carriers of a moral torch reaching for the future. That Promethean torch is part of the human spiritual ecology. Using it to light a sane and caring path to the future is our responsibility.

REFERENCES

Dawkins, R. 1976. *The Selfish Gene*. Oxford: Oxford University Press.

————. 1982. *The Extended Phenotype*. Oxford: Oxford University Press.

Fox, S. 1980. "Metabolic Microspheres." *Naturwissenchaften* 67:378-383.

Gould, S. 1980. "Is a New and General Theory of Evolution Emerging?" *Paleobiology* 6:119-130.

Lotka, A. 1922. "Contribution to the Energetics of Evolution." *Proceedings of the National Academy of Science* 8:147-155.

Mayr, E. 1982. *The Growth of Biological Thought*. Cambridge, MA: Harvard University Press.

Prigogine, I. 1980. *From Being to Becoming*. San Francisco: Freeman & Co.

Prigogine, I., and I. Stengers. 1984. *Order Out of Chaos*. New York: Bantam Books.

Teilhard de Chardin, P. 1975. *The Phenomenon of Man*. New York: Harper and Row.

Wicken, J. 1985. "Thermodynamics and the Conceptual Structure of Evolutionary Theory." *Journal of Theoretical Biology* 117:363-382.

————. 1987. *Evolution, Thermodynamics, and Information: Extending the Darwinian Program*. New York: Oxford University Press.

————. 1989. "Toward an Evolutionary Ecology of Meaning." *Zygon* 24:153-184.

Wilson, E.O. 1978. *On Human Nature*. Cambridge, MA: Harvard University Press.

BETWEEN THE ATOM AND THE VOID:
HIERARCHY IN HUMAN ECOLOGY

Gerald L. Young

ABSTRACT

This paper examines the concept of hierarchy as it is used in various disciplines and explores its potential in human ecology. Commonalities and shared problems are scrutinized, with stress placed on the utility of hierarchy theory to address ecological questions, especially those of connectivity and holism. Emphasized is the utility of hierarchical organization to organize, understand, and connect to the various environments—natural, social, and built—with which humans interact. In addition a catalogue of problems and a survey of issues are presented, along with some ideas bearing upon them that have appeared in the literature, all with the idea in mind of providing the reader an outline of some theoretical issues that keep arising in hierarchy theory and that ought to be studied more closely to correctly assess this concept, its connection with other ideas, and its utility in ecology and human ecology.

Advances in Human Ecology, Volume 1, pages 119-147.
Copyright © 1992 by JAI Press Inc.
All rights of reproduction in any form reserved.
ISBN: 1-55938-091-8

In truth, nothing exists but the atom and the void.

Democritus

Democritus of course was wrong: We humans exist between the atom and the void! We hold ourselves to be of some significance, and everything we hold near and dear stands there with us: family, friends, the earth itself, even the relative familiarities of the solar system stand between the atom and the void. Our stance at that midpoint shapes, and limits, our understanding—of ourselves, of the world, of the universe.

We modern, knowing humans stand in awe and disbelief at the complexity of it all—at the millions of atoms that make up each of our bodies—and at the millions of celestial bodies that make up the universe. We stand rooted in the middle, but disconnected, in perception if not in fact, from the millions at either end.

To simplify complexity, and to comprehend it, humans early on invented a connective God, a micro-macro God: awe-inspiring Creator of the universe but still comfortable companion to the individual kneeling in prayer before going to bed. Disconnect the easy junction of an all-knowing God and you disconnect many human individuals from the micro- and the macro-cosmos. With the step from ignorance to knowledge, from magic to science, many humans faced that disconnection. Increased awareness meant, for many, decreased belief in the safety of deities. Knowing of the atom, knowing of the void—knowing how much we humans do not know—created the chasm between the two extremes and displaced humans as significant beings. The immense complexity now revealed still overwhelms many people and alienates them from a world and universe that no longer submits to simple, easy, deistic explanations.

Part of the burden of science and scholarship in the late twentieth century is to help people reestablish connections, to help them find again the linkages that do connect them to each other and to the world and even the universe. Of all the disciplines, ecology is among the most promising in the quest to reestablish lost connections and human ecology even more so, because it is more interdisciplinary and makes better use of realms beyond science.

Ecology has emerged slowly from its parent disciplines in the biological sciences. Most ecologists would claim it is now established as a discipline in its own right, though few ecologists identify themselves apart from a parent field. In a similar way, but less successfully, a human ecology has struggled to find its own voice somewhere between biology and the social sciences. The struggle is often less than successful and many students of human ecology retreat, pulling it with them back into their specific disciplines. Because of this, human ecology is often relegated to a peripheral status in established disciplines, left to wither as a marginal subfield.

The struggle goes on, however, because some scholars see that connective need not met by the orthodox disciplines. This struggle is truer of human ecology in its amorphous status than for ecology as an accepted field in biology. Of the numerous rationales for ecology—and human ecology—as distinct from more narrow and specialized disciplines, two are of particular relevance here. One is the argument for a trans- or interdisciplinary perspective, a response to a need for connective inquiry, for scholarship that builds on connections and commonalities. The other is for holism, for a holistic approach complementary to the entrenched reductionism so successful in contemporary science and scholarship. Both of these are broached as responses to that need for explication of connections, for the study of relationships between organisms, including humans, and their fellow organisms and the surroundings or environment.

Can human ecology help achieve such connections? How successfully has human ecology achieved an interdisciplinary perspective? Is a holistic approach to human-environmental relationships a realizable goal or an unrealizable ideal? Can common ground be identified for scholars in human ecology to work, ground fertile to scholars from all the disciplines from which human ecology is emerging? Are shared tools available to work such ground?

Hierarchy theory is one such tool, a conceptual tool that has been widely employed to make connections between humans and the world around them, to help them to organize that world, and to help them deal with its enormous complexity. As might be expected from its integrative, connective utility, the concept is common to numerous disciplines. The purpose in this paper is to examine this concept as it is used in these various fields and to explore its potential in human ecology.

Hierarchy theory has not been much developed as a directly identifiable human-ecological concept. Instead, human ecology must draw—as it usually has—from the use of a concept in many different disciplines. Hierarchy theory has developed in the literature of the physical sciences, in all of the life sciences, including those concerned with humans, in several applied fields, and even in the arts and humanities. This paper will explore the commonalities and shared problems, and stress the utility of hierarchy theory to address ecological questions, especially those of connectivity and holism.

CONTROVERSY: WORD AND CONCEPT

Hierarchy engenders controversy. The word elicits a long list of rather repugnant associations: patriarchy; the pecking order; master races and inferior peoples enslaved or slated for elimination; caste systems and untouchables; wicked Popes and Presidents above the law; the Mafia; the military; even the bureaucracies in which so many of us serve.

Much of the recent upsurge in controversy centers on that distaste for hierarchy as a label rather than actually on the concept, though many authors seem not to understand the difference. Most, after harsh denouncements of the concept, merely change the name, declaring that the "problem" is now solved. Heterarchies (Lincoln and Guba 1985) or LIMA's (Dyke 1988), for example, do not change the reality, though these writers try to persuade their readers that such name changes are a new approach to that reality.

Lincoln and Guba (1985) attempt to "move" from "older" hierarchic to heterarchic concepts of order, on the premise that if order does exist, then many orders exist side by side, their degree of predominance depending on any number of interacting factors. This is not a "paradigm revolution," as they claim, but simply an admission that hierarchy applies to many different sets of orders.

Dyke's "LIMA's, or "level-interactive modular arrays" are also just another word change, from hierarchy to levels. LIMA is a nonce word, created because Dyke (1988, p. 70) fears that "the word hierarchy is dangerous," leading to losses in human freedom. (Loss of degrees of freedom is discussed later in the paper.) LIMA does not work as a word either, because you have to remember the specialized and particular meanings intended by Dyke. It has no base in the vernacular; four words in the place of one or, alternatively, an awkward acronym that will never be picked up in popular, or probably even scholarly, usage.

Other controversies swirl as well around semantic misunderstandings. One of the bitterest denouncements of hierarchy comes from feminist authors. The problem they decry is a real one, and needs to be solved; the problem they create is an unnecessary one, and comes from synonymizing hierarchy with "patriarchy." Societal hierarchies of various kinds—especially those of family, religion, and politics—can take patriarchical forms, but the two are not synonymous. This criticism also assumes hierarchies are normative arrangements, which is true of some but not of most. The elimination of patriarchy, a realizable goal, does not require the elimination of hierarchies.

Some of the negative views of hierarchy come from surprising sources: Leshan and Margenau (1982, p. 98, 122), for example, claim that "in the physical sciences, the term 'hierarchy' is rarely used, it is in fact useless" and generally meaningless. This view is directly contradicted by wide use of the term to describe structure and relationships in the physical sciences: in physics (Purcell 1963; Bronowski 1970; Bohm and Peat 1987); in geology and minerology (Smith 1964, 1969, 1981); and in astronomy and cosmology (Oldershaw 1978, 1983).

Differences in viewpoint are also expressed by qualifiers attached to the word hierarchy, used to distinguish different kinds of hierarchies. Pattee (1970) based his case for the existence of hierarchical organization on explication of a typology consisting of *structural hierarchies* (lifeless); *functional hierarchies* (hierarchical organization in biological systems characterized by the presence of time-dependent functions); and *descriptive hierarchies* ("being hierarchical" requires control of system dynamics internally, with some aspects of 'self-observation'). Riedl (1978, p. 124) identifies three "forms" of hierarchy: a mass or collective hierarchy; a dichotomous hierarchy or "hierarchy of alternatives;" and the box-in-box or sequential hierarchy. Another example of differentiation of hierarchies by "type" is Eisler's (1987) critical distinction between *domination hierarchies*, human rankings in which the determining factor is force, and what she calls *actualization hierarchies*, the kinds of "systems within systems" of primary interest in the present paper, systems that evolve toward ever more complex levels. Her work is an attempt to clarify a common misconception, that of confusing "power" hierarchies, especially bureaucracies, with the more general usage, that is, treating power hierarchies as exhaustive of the concept— which they are not. Space permitting, other examples could be presented here, but the idea should be clear.

Additional critiques of the notion of hierarchy come from some educational reformers, from anarchists, deconstructionists, and the new "networkers." But, none of these have demonstrated how systems can remain functional without levels of order, how structures can be created without the combining of components into larger wholes, how constantly emerging levels of complexity can be understood without a concept of hierarchy.

The most commonly used alternatives to the term hierarchy are "levels-of-integration" or "levels-of-organization." I have not been able to identify any consistent differences between these three terms, so I continue to prefer hierarchy because it is less awkward and more incorporative. Sometimes, the others are useful, however—especially levels-of-organization in general biology and levels-of-integration in ecology—and where used, I intend the three interchangeably. Besides, the word "level" does not escape all the implications of hierarchy, that of higher and lower, for example, and itself has other implications that might not be immediately apparent.

Mario Bunge (1960), a philosopher/physicist, has explored the semantic implictions of the word level and was able to distinguish nine different meanings in contemporary science and ontology: level (a) as a synonym for degree; (b) as an indicator of complexity; (c) as a manifestation of analytical depth; (d) to designate an emergent whole; (e) as a poistem (meaning a "system or bundle of qualities, a group of interrelated properties," pp. 400-401); (f) as an expression of rank; (g) to designate layering or stratification, a stratum; (h) to suggest a telescopic system or what Bunge called "rooted layers"; and (i) as evolutionary series. All of these have utility of meaning for hierarchies defined as "levels" of integration or organization in human ecology.

A note here on analogy. Describing hierarchies in more than one kind of system or organization is often dismissed as "merely" analogy. Bunge (1981, p. 223), author of many works on a theory of levels, defined analogy as "an objective property of pairs of systems." The dictionary definition we are all familiar with is even more useful here: An analogy is resemblance in some particulars between things otherwise unlike; analogous is defined as susceptible of comparison either in general or in some specific detail. Describing hierarchies in a variety of systems as analogous avoids the need to match each one exactly, yet makes the point that the processes described herein, and the structures in which they result, are comparative, that they do resemble each other in general ways and in some particulars.

HIERARCHY THEORY IN ECOLOGY

The history of the concept of hierarchy stretches far back in the history of Occidental thought. Patrides (1973) traces an ancient and persistent human inclination to seek or "assert order," a search he relates to various conceptions of hierarchy. The word hierarchy is an old philosophical term but may or may not have, as Whyte (1969, p. 9) claimed, a new twentieth century meaning. Leibniz exclaimed, for example, in the eighteenth century, that "the whole of matter is connected . . . all created things with each, and each with all the rest." That does not sound too much different, except for the "created" part, from Barry Commoner's (1972, p. 33) widely repeated twentieth-century statement on ecology: "everything is connected to everything else." But, how is "everything" connected to everything else? That is the question addressed in ecology and human ecology. That is the reason hierarchical concepts are useful in ecology, because they have been used for centuries, and are still used, to characterize such connections, to outline sequence and progression, to illustrate relationships.

Whyte (1969, p. 9) asked "do the most comprehensive laws of nature generate hierarchies, when circumstances permit?" He answered his own question with a life-long, emphatic insistence that the most widely accepted *fact* about the universe is that very large parts of it are strongly ordered as a "system of subsystems," a hierarchy in which each unit and subunit and superunit is in turn an ordered system. Many biologists agree with him, though there is some controversy over levels-of-organization even in the life sciences (see e.g., Guttman 1976).

Ecology, like all sciences, seeks an understanding of natural order. Frank Egler (1942) early identified organism, community, vegetation and ecosystem as a useful ecological hierarchy and later (1970) expanded this to nine levels of integration as of interest in ecology: subatomic units; atoms; molecules; cells; multicellular organisms; populations; community; ecosystem; and the human ecosystem, taking humans and their total environment as one single whole. This kind of hierarchy has most often been used to create a reason-for-being for ecology, used as a device to justify it as a "separate" field specializing in the higher levels (population, community, ecosystem) of biological organization. Despite the long-established "use" of hierarchies such as Egler's—their use as a rationale—hierarchy theory remains in an embryonic stage in general ecology and even more so in human ecology.

A limited conception of hierarchy, usually in a form similar to Egler's, has most often shown up in ecology as the organizing device for general textbooks, dating back at least to Eugene Odum's earliest editions. Reference was common to "organization at the species population level" or at the "community level" but beyond that, no explication was offered. Odum provided the first brief details on the concept in the third edition of his *Fundamentals of Ecology* text (1971) and in the second edition of *Ecology* (1975). This was elaborated further in a separate chapter on "Levels of Organization" in his recent *Ecology and Our Endangered Life-Support Systems* (1989), including a brief examination of "the emergent property principle" (p. 30). Odum recognized the organizational utility of the concept but never developed it to any real degree.

More recent attempts have shown considerable sophistication, focusing especially on analysis of the ecosystem. Most of the recent work is available only in scattered articles (cf., Hirata and Ulanowicz 1985) but two book-length exceptions have been published: Allen and Starr's *Hierarchy: Perspectives for Ecological Complexity* (1982) and the work by R.V. O'Neill, D.L. DeAngelis, J.B. Waide, and T.F.H. Allen on *A Hierarchical Concept of Ecosystems* (1986). These are the first extensive treatments in English of hierarchy theory in ecology, both using the concept of hierarchy to deal with complexity. Both books focus on medium number systems, indicating that both less and more complex systems are adequately addressed in other ways, a point with which I disagree. O'Neill and his colleagues do point out (p. 99) that hierarchies in ecosystem research are not "arbitrarily imposed on the system [but] empirically derived from observations of the system." They describe hierarchical structure as "the consequence of evolution in open, dissipative systems" (p. 101). The central point is that hierarchy theory "helps elucidate the complex interactions among species populations in the community" (p. 123).

Coverage in human ecology is even thinner, and the challenge more formidable. Only Steward (1951) and Young (1978, 1989) have provided any real focus on the use of hierarchy theory in human ecology. Steward, though one of the founders of cultural ecology in anthropology, examined hierarchy as levels of sociocultural organization and did not much develop the ecological utility of the concept. Young used hierarchy explicitly as a key device in the development of an interdisciplinary conceptual framework for human ecology.

THE CONCEPT OF HIERARCHY IN UNDERSTANDING HUMAN-ENVIRONMENT RELATIONSHIPS

Conceived most simply, but also most comprehensively, human ecology is the study of the interactions or interrelationships between humans and environments of various kinds. At least some of the problems that humans are now having with the environments in which they live derives from the fact that so many people operate at a limited number of interactional levels or fail to grasp the consequences of their actions (at one level) on other levels further removed.

The conception of environment—and of what is "ecology," especially human ecology—begins with but is not limited to the natural environment (Young 1986). The environmental sciences deal primarily, if not exclusively, with human impacts—air quality, ground water contamination, depletion of natural resources, to name but a few—but human ecology must deal with the full range of human-environment interactions, including those made up of other humans (the social environment) and those that humans have created for themselves (the built environment). Problems resulting from human interactions with each of these environments share similar characteristics: increasing complexity; separation or alienation, a lack of connection; difficulty—of individuals and nations—in grasping the extent of the impacts of their actions; and others.

These are all the domain of human ecology. Limiting a conception of environment too narrowly in human ecology—for example, to the operational environment, that which physically impinges on the organism—is too restrictive and is one of the reasons that we face so many environmental problems today. The concept of environment has to be expanded in human ecology, not reduced or restricted, so that we can trace our impacts and take responsibility for them. Expanding the concept of environment—to that large complex entity which we do perceive, in which we do live, with which we interact, and which we so obviously impact in so many ways—also necessarily enlarges what "ecology" is. Ecology is the study of how we interact with that complexity, an enormous, almost incomprehensible complexity that ranges from atoms to outer space. That entire range is now the domain of the human spirit, the human mind, the human being—and thus of human ecology.

For each set of this complex range of human-environmental interactions, two points should be emphasized: (1) humans either discover, or impose, hierarchical organization on the environment in question; and (2) understanding the hierarchical nature of such organization can help to reconnect human beings to those environments and aid them in understanding—and ultimately correcting—misunderstandings, displacements, harmful impacts, or discontinuities in such relationships.

Connecting To and Organizing Complexity

The Natural Environment

The "natural environment" is nature in all its complexity. Atoms and molecules qualify as part of the nature with which humans interact and which they increasingly manipulate at every level. And, so is the universe, in all its infinite complexity, part of that same environment, though we are presently impacting only the edges nearest the earth.

Ludwig von Bertalanffy (1950, p. 164), the founder of general systems theory, described what he called *reality* in terms of a "tremendous hierarchical order of organized entities," the higher the level-of-integration, the more complex the organizational structure. In a widely cited paper, Kenneth Boulding (1956) described general systems theory as the "skeleton" of science, but that designation might be more appropriate to hierarchy theory, which has a more ancient tradition and which provides many of the bones used to construct a systems skeleton. Recent literature repeats these claims, with Riedl (1978, p. 176), for example, claiming that "hierarchy is a necessity . . . a general law of Nature."

Why hierarchies? I still like, and repeat for my students, Whyte's (1969, p. 9) simple statement that "they are interesting" . . . and further that they make the universe "more meaningful." Science since Bacon has been so long committed to a reductionist view of the world and the universe that many of the more capable minds feel confined. General systems and hierarchy theory free ecologists from the shackles of the analytical mode without requiring them to reject it and provide glimpses of a wider, more diverse world, a more "interesting" world.

A few simple examples from studies of the natural environment will illustrate the significance of the concept of hierarchy to human well-being and to human understanding of ecological relationships: (1) taxonomic relationships that set humans in the context of other life-forms; (2) the atomic and molecular combinations so essential as the base of all life, including human, and (3) the interface between hierarchy theory and the theory of evolution.

Taxonomies, so basic to science, are a common form of hierarchy. Taxonomic hierarchies have never generated much controversy (at least as to form rather than content), whereas other uses of hierarchy as a concept continue to be debated. Appropriately, taxonomy is derived from the Greek word for "arrangement" or "order." Most relevent here is the fact that we humans can locate ourselves in the taxonomic arrangements we have created to describe natural living order. Taxonomies provide us a family of relationships and, in so doing, allow us to connect ourselves as organisms to every other living being in the world. Most readers will be able, for example, to visualize the placement of the human species in relationship to other primates, biologically our closest relatives. Trying to visualize such relationships, most people would employ a taxonomic hierarchy to allow them to "see" the connections.

In contemporary biology, this connected grouping is the preferred order, what has been called the Linnaean Hierarchy. George Gaylord Simpson (1967) provided a classical description of (animal) taxonomy as a hierarchy, a systematic framework for zoological classification that embraces a sequence of classes, or sets, at different levels, with each class (except for the lowest) including one or more subordinate classes. We use it to identify every living thing, plant or animal, and to relate each to all the rest.

As noted, the use of taxonomic hierarchies in systematics is admitted without much controversy. The more general utility of hierarchy theory, however, or in many cases of the idea of levels-of-organization or integration, is under debate in many disciplines. To some scholars, it is the "old order," a tired, outmoded way of viewing the world. To an increasing number of others, however, it provides a key to understanding connections, especially the relationships produced by interactions, processes that result in more complex entities with more complex relationships.

Examples drawn from the atomic or molecular level may not seem "ecological" to some readers, dismissed as merely an elementary chemistry lesson. But, I agree with Egler (1970) that this level is of ecological interest and with Weiss (1971) who proposed a "molecular ecology" as a way of understanding the world hierarchically. Atoms and molecules provide the essential base for the human environment, the base from which life emerges, the base for creation of those elements of the environment, such as water, on which we depend for our very livelihood. Readers should also be reminded that many of the destructive feedbacks from the environment—in the form, for example, of carcinogens, mutagens, and teratogens—impact the molecular-cellular level of life. Understanding that this level is impacted by changes in the environment and that the very base of matter and life is also organized hierarchically means that we can reconnect to that base as well in a step-by-step fashion and that, in turn, will help us reconnect to the environment—to the world.

If we go one way on the hierarchy, into the atom, we discover its hierarchical substructure. Whyte's "meaningfulness" is exemplified by the hierarchical order of the "material" substructure of the natural environment, constituted, according to an as yet incomplete "standard model," of three fundamental families or types of matter composed of 12 fundamental particles: five are grouped as quarks (up, down, charmed, strange, and bottom) with a sixth quark predicted theoretically (called top); the electron, muon, and tau particles are grouped together; and three are categorized as neutrinos, different and elusive and associated with the electron, muon, and tau. These provide a basic hierarchical taxonomy of matter, but they also are "real" in that they impart real properties to the atom, properties that humans will increasingly take advantage of to arrange and rearrange their environment.

Going in the other direction, examining how atoms combine into more complex hierarchical arrangements, allows a look at the physical base of all matter and life, a look that can begin with just three atoms: hydrogen, oxygen, and carbon. Elements, of course, are composed of atoms, the smallest particles that have all the properties of the element. The array of ordered properties that allow interactions between the atoms of elements are demonstrated in the hierarchy of the periodic table. Interactions between atoms depend on the number of electrons the atoms have and involve the sharing of electrons or an electron moving from one atom to another. All matter and all life, including that of humans, builds on this atomic base.

A molecule is the next level of complexity beyond the atom. The standard example is water: "if there is magic on this planet, it is contained in water" (Eiseley 1957, p. 15). In a molecule of water, the oxygen atom has formed an electron-sharing bond with each hydrogen atom, an example of moving one step in a hierarchy from simple to more complex.

But, hierarchies can always be looked at in two directions. Decomposition of hierarchies in nature is a key to understanding structure and organization— and functional relationships, including those of humans with the complexities of the environments around them. Obviously, a molecule of water can be so decomposed, broken down again into its component parts, hydrogen and oxygen, though the strength of the bonding resists this change. Breaking it down in a slightly different way, however, *ionizing* it, produces a completely different result. Only an incredibly small percentage of water molecules ionize (perhaps 1 in 10 million) but all life processes depend on that small percentage. A water molecule ionizes into hydrogen and hydroxide ions, the former a single proton, the latter an oxygen atom, a hydrogen atom, and the extra electron. But, these two ions are involved in most of the reactions that occur in organisms, that maintain life as we know it. If more hydrogen ions than hydroxide ions remain after such reactions, the solution is acidic, if more hydroxide, then it is alkaline. These relative levels affect virtually every chemical reaction in an organism, including humans, and are described by the pH scale so important in chemical and environmental reactions in general.

By adding carbon to our consideration of the interactions of atoms up and down the hierarchies of nature, we can begin to describe the basic molecules of life: carbohydrates, lipids, proteins, and nucleic acids. Simple carbohydrates contain only the elements carbon, hydrogen, and oxygen, one element beyond water in complexity. Simple sugars, or monosaccharides, such as glucose, contain seven or fewer carbon atoms in each molecule. The more complex sucrose is a disaccharide because it is built with two simple-sugar units. Polysaccharides are larger compounds with many sugar subunits linked together. Polysaccharide starch, for example, is an important storage compound in plants, the basic unit in the hierarchical trophic structure that we all depend upon. Similarly, fats are synthesized from two smaller molecules, glycerole (a carbohydrate) and fatty acids. The latter are chains of carbon and hydrogen.

The subunit of a protein molecule is an amino acid. Amino acids contain the same three atoms—carbon, hydrogen, oxygen—plus nitrogen. To synthesize a protein, amino acids must be linked together. Two amino acids linked together form a dipeptide; add a third to form a tripeptide molecule, and a long chain is a polypeptide. The 20 different kinds of amino acids form one of the basic alphabets of life and can be combined in many ways to form thousands of kinds of proteins, including the special kind of protein called an enzyme so critical to catalyze life-maintaining reactions within the cells of organisms.

Ribonucleic acid (or RNA) is required for the synthesis of proteins, including enzymes; information stored in deoxyribonucleic acid (or DNA) controls all cell activities and also determines the genetic characteristics of the cell and the organism. These two nucleic acids, which control the activities of the cell, are synthesized in a similar way: Both DNA and RNA are made up of individual subunits called nucleotides. Each nucleotide is made up of three small molecules linked together: a combination of the elements noted earlier in the form of (1) a five-carbon sugar and (2) a nitrogen base, with the addition of (3) a phosphate group. Note that the same kinds of hierarchical linkages are exploited for creating units and for taking them apart, and that systems can be described similarly at every level.

Combine all of the above elements, and a complex of others—in ways not now fully known—and the cell, the basic unit of life, comes into being. As Linus Pauling noted, life is a relationship among molecules and not a property of any one molecule. One could add that it is a hierarchical relationship.

Beyond the cell are found groupings of cells called tissues; when several tissues are grouped together in a special arrangement to do a particular task, an organ is formed, and several organs are related in a general function to form an organ system, for example, the digestive system. Similar kinds of linkages are established for the creation of all of the above units, though it is obviously not as simple as described here. And, all of the reactions depend on atoms as the basic units of matter—and life—and on the hierarchical linkages between them.

In evolutionary biology, as in ecology, the concept of hierarchy has recently begun to provide an explanatory framework for the study of the evolutionary process (Gould 1982). Laszlo (1987, p. 27) even labels hierarchical concepts "the most fundamental concepts of a grand synthesis of the findings of the new sciences of evolution and complexity." Recognizing this, biologists have begun to examine the connections between biological hierarchies and modern evolutionary thought (Eldredge 1985), that is, to analyze evolving hierarchical systems (Salthe 1985). Salthe began his book on the premise that it is psychologically necessary for humans that the world exhibit a comprehensive but simply conceived pattern. This basic world structure must allow causal and control relationships, must engender complexity, must be stable (spontaneously) and must provide boundaries to make our interactions with it meaningful. In Salthe's view, that basic structure is hierarchical: The world is ordered hierarchically, an order emerging from the evolutionary process. He further claims that biology and, more particularly, evolutionary theory in biology, *require* hierarchical organization to make sense of the phenomena under study and especially to apply that study to human betterment.

Eldredge (1985) builds on Theodosius Dobzhansky's definite and admitted hierarchical view of the evolutionary process. Eldredge critiques the "modern synthesis" of evolutionary theory—even though hierarchical—as unfinished and incomplete, because it restricts the evolutionary process wholly within the purview of geneticists. The modern synthesis falls short, he thinks, because it is limited in attention to only a few of the lower-level biological entities existent in the world and involved in the evolutionary process. His revision of the synthesis divulges a "variable ontology" which is context-dependent and which he feels automatically forces a more incorporative hierarchical approach to the structure of evolutionary theory. He identifies two "process" hierarchies, one of genes, organisms, demes, species, and monophyletic taxa that contribute to the development, retention, and modification of *information* nestled in the genome and a parallel hierarchy of nested *ecological* individuals—proteins, organisms, populations, communities and regional biotal systems—that reflects the economic organization (in an ecological sense) and integration of living systems. To Eldredge, it is the processes within these two hierarchies, and the interactions between the two, that provoke the events and patterns of evolution.

Matter also evolves! So claimed Bronowski (1973). He tried to show how all matter evolves, as in living systems, as a slow increase in complexity, step by step from simple to complex. And, the evolution of matter occurs not only on earth but across the universe, in the stars: "If the stars had to build a heavy element like iron, or a super-heavy element like uranium, by the instant assembly of all the parts, it would be virtually impossible. No. A star builds hydrogen to helium; then at another stage in a different star helium is assembled to carbon, to oxygen, to heavy elements; and so step by step . . . to make the ninety-two elements in nature" (Bronowski 1973, p. 349). Oldershaw (1978, 1979, 1981, 1985) concurs: The most fundamental design in nature is a hierarchy. He adds that "the Hierarchical Principle" incorporates entities from the atomic, stellar and galactic scales that share many analogous morphological and dynamic properties. He assigns empirical, hierarchical order to the universe, labeling it a "self-similar hierarchical cosmology."

The Social Environment

The social environment is comprised of other human beings—individuals and aggregates. The social environment has also evolved from relatively simple to very complex, requiring increased organization and various means of dealing with that complexity.

To the increasing number of critics of society as organized hierarchically, and to those who do not know or understand the pervasiveness of this concept in nature and human thought, Stevens'(1983, p. 23) statement that "no human culture is known which lacked . . . status differentiation on the basis of a hierarchical social structure," must be surprising and disturbing. But, he also claims the existence of fundamental archetypal determinants which *demand* that social structures be hierarchical. He goes further, claiming that societies cannot exist without a hierarchical structure, that ingrained in human nature is an archetypal need to organize collectively into a social "pyramid."

Patricia Barchas (1984) and her colleagues go even further, tracing similarities of hierarchical forms of social organization across primate species, using hierarchical relational systems as "prototypes," interconnected structures through which small groups achieve social order. These writers make the assumption that hierarchies provide general rules for the generation of animal (including human) behavior. Their ideas are even tested on chickens, leading to the statement that "some of the most fundamental behavioral mechanisms for development of hierarchical relations may be independent of animal type" (Barchas 1984, p. xii).

Social scientists have not been slow to recognize these kinds of relationships, which is one of the reasons the debate is heating up. Examples span the globe, the only difficulty being which ones to choose. Dumont's (1980) classic study of Indian caste is a must, but it is necessary to note that his work does not just synonymize hierarchy with social stratification and levels of inequality but, in fact, sharply distinguishes between them. Dumont focuses on the "conception of hierarchical opposition . . . extending throughout the totality of the ideology of every society" (Barnes, de Coppet, and Parkin 1985, p. 1). Britan and Cohen (1980, p. 3) urge anthropologists to bring their analyses into the modern world by attempting to "understand the hierarchical relationships of social, economic, and political life within complex states." Howell (1984) studied hierarchical relationships among the Chewong and Duff-Cooper (1984) among the Balinese. Nader (in Britan and Cohen 1980, p. 5) takes it down to the family level, arguing that the family today is understandable only in context, "in relation to the broader hierarchical systems of which it is now a part."

The Built Environment

The built environment is that environment which we humans create for ourselves and in which most of us spend most of our time: It is not much discussed as an "environment" but it too has grown increasingly complex as humans have become more and more innovative and in command of a sophisticated technology to enable us to manipulate our environment(s) in a wide range of ways. Any one of us can conjure up the remarkable array of artifacts with which we humans have surrounded ourselves: cities and settlement patterns, time and space, music and language, to note only a few examples. It seems essential that we understand the way they are ordered, the way they clarify *and* complicate our lives.

The widely studied spatial pattern of towns and cities well illustrates how human activities even inadvertently result in hierarchical relationships. It is best described as an idealized, theoretical pattern that marks perhaps a tendency rather than a reality. This tendency has led to the construction of a rather elaborate hypothesis, developed by the German scholar Walter Christaller (see Young 1978) and labeled Central Place Theory, to help explain the size, number and distribution of human settlements—towns or *central places*—in the belief that some ordering principles govern that distribution.

In brief, Christaller's theory holds that the basic function of a town or city is to be a central place providing goods and services for a surrounding tributary area. The term "central place" is used because to perform such a function efficiently, a city locates at the center of minimum aggregate travel of its tributary area, that is, central to the maximum profit area it can command. The centrality of a city is a sum measure of the degree to which it is such a service center. The higher the order of goods provided, the fewer are the establishments providing them, the greater the trade areas, and the fewer and more widely spaced are the towns or cities in which the establishments are located. The greater the centrality of a place, the higher is its "order" in a *hierarchy* of such places. In some areas, especially the flat American midwest, the settlement pattern, including transportation lines, is further ordered by another hierarchical system, the nested survey squares of township and range, which connect any particular point to a central base-line and meridian and then into the global network of latitude and longitude.

Corresponding to this organization of space, humans have also invented a system of hierarchical units to measure time, a system dovetailed into the apparent natural systems character of sun-earth relationships and seasons: seconds, minutes, hours, days, weeks, months, years. Like other hierarchical systems, "time scales" provide context or dimension to human affairs, thereby adding meaning. The system could be furnished with further texture, for example, to link the relatively brief scope of human events with the enormous expanse of evolution, by adopting Julian Huxley's (1964) term *cron*, a million years, as the basic unit of evolutionary time. The result is a hierarchy of kilocron for a billion years, millicron for a millenium, perhaps centicron for a century, and microcron for a year.

Hierarchy implies a series or a set of levels, a scale, that is, a group of related entities tied together into a progression of some sort: Hierarchy has traditionally meant the formation of integrated systems. *Legato* is a musical term meaning a passing or gliding from one pitch or tone to another in a smooth and connected manner. This provides a metaphorical device to describe the connectivities, the integrity implicit in hierarchy theory, the assumption of a smooth progression from one level to another, thus emphasizing the continuity of the structure rather than its (always possible) separation into parts. Legato comes from the Latin word meaning to bind or tie, a derivation that reinforces the idea of context in hierarchical systems, the idea of a part or individual integrated into, or connected to, a larger whole. The English word *liege*, literally "bound man," has the same derivation, the same implications, though a less positive connotation.

Few artifacts of human creation are more integrated than a musical score, an artifact that has been consciously, and conscientiously, constructed to form a highly cohesive unit. But, musical notes are identifiably separate entities and must be so if the composer is to be able to arrange and rearrange them to create the proper sequences and relationships; to make *music*, however, they must be so arranged, ordered that is, into a composition. Notes are used as an alphabet, integrated one by one into phrases, phrases to musical lines, lines to themes, and themes into movements; a classical composition is made up of four movements.

Numerous terms in the language of music underline the hierarchical nature of such relationships: chord, for example, is a Greek word meaning "string" and may be combined with a numerical indicator to form tetrachord, for example, a string of four in sequence. The word scale, so essential in music, comes from the Italian word *scala* meaning ladder and signifying the structural basis of music in a hierarchical system. Octave, motif, bridge, and others, reinforce this interpretation: music as archetype of the integrated, hierarchical systems of human fabrication (see Arias 1982).

Musicians probably never achieve perfect integration; there are always discontinuities. And, they do not always want to. They retain the word *capriccio*, for example, to describe a loose, irregular composition, one usually lively and whimsical. But, it is still described as a *composition*, that is, composed of individual notes, ordered at least to a degree. Harmonic can be defined quite simply as "of an integrated nature" or it can be expanded to "a component frequency that is an integral multiple of the fundamental frequency." Harmonic derives from the Greek *harmozein*, which means to "arrange or to set in order." The same root leads to *harmost*, which in ancient Greece meant a Spartan governor, regulator, or prefect, one who controlled or ordered society. These interconnected meanings suggest ordered hierarchies, reflections of the ancient human quest and its realization in human artifact and in human society.

Examples from music are particularly vivid, since music is an environmental experience that we all share, from childhood on, in some form or another. But, even the imaginary artifacts of human design are created in hierarchical form, depending on the level of complexity that is wished or that can be tolerated. We seem better able to deal with a complex positive than a complex negative. Hell, for example, has been deconstructed. Once a complex hierarchy of devils and their legions, Hell became so complex that lay people could no longer comprehend it, so the Church simplified it. Now Lucifer apparently does his devil's work in solitary splendor, without need of rank or file (Paine 1972). Jehovah, on the other hand, is served by so many angels they must be organized into tiers. Considering the numbers of people one might expect to arrive at each place, that seems something of a contradiction. We remain enchanted with a heaven rich and diverse but evidently grew bored with a hell too complex, peopled by too many devils or devil's helpers. Even the hierarchies of heaven or hell—or the lack of them—illustrate this significant pattern that humans construct to order the world around them, to create comprehensible structure in their lives, and to organize complexity.

HIERARCHY THEORY: SOME PROBLEMS AND QUESTIONS

Hierarchy theory addresses some of the fundamental connective questions of the relationships between humans and their various environments. Hierarchy theory helps to resolve recurrent questions about the understanding of complex systems. This section provides a catalogue of problems, a survey of issues, and some ideas bearing upon them that have appeared in the literature, the purpose of which is not to solve any of them but to help organize future discourse on hierarchy theory. The catalogue is not intended to be complete nor is the survey of relevant ideas exhaustive. In effect, this section provides the readers of this paper an outline of some theoretical issues that keep arising and that ought to be studied more closely to correctly assess this notion of hierarchy and its connection with other ideas.

Among the questions that persist, that need additional explication, and that will be examined briefly here are: the question of joining micro- and macro-levels; the question of ontology; the problem of emergent properties; the problem of discontinuities at certain levels; and the nature of the bonding process.

The Micro-Macro Problem:
On Relationships Between Parts and Wholes

Since reading it ten years ago, I have worked from Orian's (1980, p. 79) declaration that "one of the great challenges over the next decade will be to build conceptual bridges between micro- and macroecology." That decade has now passed and I remain puzzled why so few ecologists have recognized the potential of the concept of hierarchy to bridge that gap, to attain and sustain the connection. Social scientists pose the same question: In a recent volume in sociology (Alexander, Giesen, Munch, and Smelser 1987), the central theme is represented as "struggling with problems and dilemmas that arise in attempting to move from the micro to the macro level, and vice versa" (p. 376). Similarly, Knorr-Cetina and Cicourel (1981) frame advances in social theory and methodology in terms of integration of micro- and macro-levels. I have tried to weave the micro-macro *theme* throughout this essay as well, so a separate section on that question should not be needed. But, then I confront statements like those by Orians and Alexander and feel forced to face the question more directly and separately than is allowed thematically.

At least three reasons can be identified as to why the question is worded as it was by Orians and Alexander: (1) they both pose micro and macro as oppositions to be resolved by connecting the two extremes directly, rather than by intermediate steps; (2) neither Orians nor Alexander and colleagues, or other authors exploring similar questions, recognize the role of the concept of hierarchy in providing a resolution, a step-by-step linkage of micro and macro; and (3) writers exploring this question frequently involve "interaction" on the periphery (or even as a level itself) but never seem to recognize its centrality as a process that generates levels and at the same time as a force that maintains the integrity of levels and the linkages between them.

Any one of us would admit without question that our foot is connected to the rest of our body; we can see how they are connected and how they functionally relate. This is the notion expressed by *Expede Herculem*, that from the foot one may judge Hercules, that is, that the part provides some functional index to the whole. But, how readily do we see the same kind of connections in less obvious systems? Every discipline shares the Herculean mandate involved in connecting Gregory Bateson's (1970) hierarchies of units or Gestalten and in reaching Pattee's (1973) goal of discovering a deeper relation between the parts and wholes, the micro-macro extremes, of hierarchies. Acceptance of the idea behind this objective—that parts are integers of larger wholes—introduces the idea that science can "no longer concede true 'independence' to things . . . but on the contrary, it must go on to establish the range and degree of dependence which interrelates things and events with their context" (Weiss 1971, p.7). The concept of hierarchy is a useful tool in this quest for understanding of interdependence, interrelatedness, and context.

Koestler (1967) presented a useable idea with his invention of the *holon*, a word created to provide a constant reminder that every entity, including the human being, constitutes both a micro- *and* a macro-level: Each is a whole in and of itself—a whole generally made up of parts, however—and each is also, and always, part of something else. The holon is a device that emphasizes the desire among theorists that the distinction between micro and macro be an analytic rather than a concrete one. Entering a hierarchy, any hierarchy, at any level, according to the level of analysis desired, allows relationships of any entities at any level to be analyzed from both perspectives—that of content or part (micro) and that of place or context (macro). Individual and aggregate are each identifiable but fused conceptually by Koestler's dialectic term.

Scientists remain atomistic in their approach to scholarship, with every field of study aspiring to the reductionist method. The micro is still too often analyzed without adequate reference to the macro; even the macro is taken to be an entity unto itself. A focus on hierarchical relationships reestablishes connections between the micro and the macro, reestablishes relationships and meaning in human ecology, places the human again in a part-whole context. This is more humanistic than is concern only with people as objects or statistics, as items reduced to their meanest dimensions. Micro-macro relationships viewed in a hierarchical perspective allow analysis (of content or parts) *and* synthesis (of context, the whole). Fear of not being able to know, especially with great precision, as well as the comfort of safe knowledge, has retarded synthesis. There is increasing room for a field of study—human ecology—that marries the meanest with the most meaningful.

The Question of Ontology in Hierarchical Systems

Human beings exist in the world, their being is defined by their presence there and the relationships defined or allowed by that presence and its particular conditions. We exist on more than one level; not recognizing that creates problems, problems of relationships between us and other levels to which we do not admit being connected. The content, and context, of human *being* is conditioned by the range of entities with which people share the world and how they relate or fail to relate to those entities, to that content and context. The concept of hierarchy helps humans to identify, understand, and relate to the rest of the world.

Hierarchies *are* real, revealed in those necessary relationships of every entity between substance, form and context. As Kisly (1984, p. 3) notes: "hierarchy is inseparable from order . . . is inherent in order on every level, on all scales— is an organic principle without which the world could not exist." The atom exists and so does the void—and so does the range of relationships that connect them.

L.L. Whyte (1965, 1969, 1974) repeatedly claimed the first fact about the physical universe is its organization as a system of systems, as a hierarchy. Marjorie Grene (1967, p. 444), attempting to sort out some of the philosophical problems in the life sciences, addressed particularly the problem of levels of existence and concluded bluntly that a "one-level ontology contradicts itself . . . is untenable." Whitehead (1929) incorporated *all* reality, nonorganic *and* organic, into a hierarchical scheme, as did Bronowski (1973), in evolutionary terms and, more recently, Soodak and Iberall (1978). The latter are physicists who reiterate the idea that the complex systems in nature are hierarchically linked by thermodynamic propositions based essentially on interaction processes and the relations between atomism and a 'continuum.'

Humans use the concept of hierarchies to organize nature, or at least to organize their perceptions of nature (and, noting again, heaven and hell, even the supernatural). This organization ranges from Weiskopf's (1979) "quantum ladder" at the subatomic level to Bronowski's (1973) hydrogen jump from star to star in the evolution of matter. It includes many of the taxonomic and organizing systems of science. When taking these materials of nature and transforming them into the stuff of the built environment, the structures again reflect human preoccupation with levels of organization.

And even if the structures examined and reexamined so often did not really exist, which I do not believe, they are still an increasingly important extension of the human mind and so must be apprehended to gain knowledge of the way humans perceive the various environments of earth and the universe. Note too that it is widely believed that the brain itself is hierarchically organized. The ontological question may never be answered to everyone's satisfaction, but reality, and human existence, derives as well from the intellectual prominence of the device and on that basis alone, it cannot be discounted.

Emergent Properties

Emergent properties are normally defined as those properties of a whole system not possessed by its parts. Egler (1970) called levels of integration (or, interchangeably, hierarchies) "sister" to the idea of emergent evolution, which results in new emergent qualities when parts combine in nature to form wholes. George Salt (1979, p. 145) has gone further and defined an emergent property (of an ecological unit) as "one which is wholly unpredictable from observation of the components of that unit." He adds the corollary that such an emergent property is discernible only by observation of the unit as a whole. The thrust of Salt's letter is that ecologists tend to confuse emergent properties with what he called *collective properties* which, unlike true emergents, can be determined through study of component characteristics. Both are properties of wholes not possessed by parts, but marked by radical differences in terms of explication. This is a useful differentiation, one widely confused in the literature. Salt contends that this confusion can deprive the concept of emergent properties of great prospective value. The real property of emergence thus becomes one of the rationales for studying entities, especially such whole entities as ecosystems, from an ecological perspective.

The question of emergent properties raises again the differences between reductionism and holism. If the orthodox scientific view that all wholes are at least in principle completely explainable in terms of their parts proves to be true at all levels, then emergent properties and collective properties will become one and the same. But, until then, as Cottrell (1977) noted, there are two qualifications: First, some explanations of wholes and their properties remain in the realm of principle and not yet possible in practice and, second, too little is understood at this time to be sure that the subject matter of the behavioral, psychological, and social sciences, that is, of human ecology, can yet—or ever—be completely reduced to chemistry and physics. That subject matter concerns the emergent properties of human life!

Emergence—or what D.C. Phillips (1976) called the theme of emergence—is difficult to deal with because of lack of information and because it may not thereby be accessible to either the analytic method or a holistic-integrative approach. It is difficult to predict properties that will truly "emerge" at the level of the whole, armed only with knowledge of the component parts—and it is almost impossible to have *complete* or total knowledge of the whole, knowledge necessary to satisfactory prediction of emergent properties. Without the contemporary knowledge of water, used as an example of hierarchical bonding earlier, who could have predicted that it was a combination of the two gases hydrogen and oxygen?

Still, emergent properties are what Odum (1989) called an important consequence of viewing the world in terms of levels-of-integration. Inability to predict or to achieve complete understanding is insufficient reason to neglect attempts at comprehension or to delay efforts to deal with important consequences if we are ever to solve larger, more complex societal and environmental problems. Laszlo (1987, p. 190) claims that progress has been made, noting that such concepts as entropy, feedback, the exclusion principle, and others, are "not laws of the behavior of particular components but of the [emergent] behavior of patterned assemblies."

Some scientists do admit that emergent properties at the human level of complexity are especially difficult to explain in reductionist terms. They argue, however, that successes up to now support the optimistic view that someday even these will be subsumed. Cottrell submits that the scientific method will soon take us right to the gap between the material and the mental world. The debate seems empty to me until the edge of that gap is reached. At that point, scientists and scholars will be better able to grasp whether the gap is illusory or profound. Until then, two assumptions seem reasonable: (1) the knowledge to explain, in a reductionist way, certain properties emergent at very complex levels is at present not available; (2) lacking the empirical tools to study whole systems, including their emergent properties, does not deny their existence or their importance but in fact gives credence to a total systems or holistic approach. This last point does not deny, either, the importance of continuing the search for a reductionist explanation in the physical sciences.

Cottrell presents two particularly intriguing examples of emergent properties relevant to the mental world of the human, properties not now explainable by reduction to physical components—subjective aspects apparently not so reducible. The first is time's arrow, which seems to be an emergent property of humans themselves. Cottrell notes that recent work supports the view, contrary to intuition, that the physical world holds no role for the flow of time or the concept *now* but that in the mental world of humans, these hold the status, the irrevocable conviction, of direct experience. The second example, the property par excellence of this kind, is consciousness, the human awareness of self.

We cannot ignore high-level properties of such significance—and we cannot wait for the physical sciences to explain them to us. However inadequate our methods, humans must begin to recognize the existence of such complexities, must think about them and try to comprehend. That attempt at comprehension becomes one of the central tasks of human ecology, a task addressed to considerable degree by approaching such complexities as hierarchies.

The Question of Discontinuities

Recognition of the existence of multiple hierarchies in every domain of human existence is not a quest for perfection. A perfect "great chain of being" is not being reinvented here. This is what Dyke (1988) seems to think necessary when he sets absolute "totalization" as a condition for a hierarchy. No one can study hierarchies, those of nature especially, without seeing great discontinuities. The most obvious one, of course, is in the sequence building from raw atomic elements through molecules to the emergence of life. There is nothing at the level of the atom or the element to explain or even to describe the powers of a living being: Life "is something quite new and additional, and the more deeply we contemplate it, the clearer it becomes that we are faced here with what might be called an *ontological discontinuity* or, more simply, a jump in the Level of Being" (Schumacher 1977, p. 16). Life is the ultimate emergent property, unexplainable in terms of those levels of structural components from which it emerges.

Few if any hierarchies exist without noticeable discontinuities. The world is a mixture of discreteness and continuity; that mix would have to be perfect to allow no discontinuities. Admitting that involves only recognition of irregularities in the world, not a total lack of relationship or pattern or order. If carpenters put together only walls and tried to make a house, they would surely fail; walls are not the same as a floor or a roof. So, at a certain point in the construction of a house, carpenters combine elements, elements of the same or different kinds, into a floor or a roof instead of a wall. That creates a discontinuity in the smooth flow or progression of events, but it does not deny that the house is created a component at a time, by bonding individual pieces together in ordered ways to create a whole. The alternative is to bring the diverse materials together on a site and throw them into a jumbled pile, but that does not result in the ordered structure we need as a house. We do not work that way. Nature does not work that way.

Bochner (1973, p. 499) traces ideas of continuity and discontinuity in the physical and life sciences, in mathematics and philosophy back through history, quoting even Aristotle as aware of the duality: "Nature passes little by little from things lifeless to animal life, so that, by continuity, it is impossible to present the exact lines of demarcation." Mayntz (1989) reinforces the notion that discontinuities exist across the levels of organization in both nature and society, noting that sudden changes of state have always occurred at all levels of society. He determines that the difference, what distinguishes social hierarchies from natural ones, is that human behavior is constantly changing, and thus affects the range of phenomena to which it relates and which in turn affect it. Jaques (1978), on the other hand, proposes a discontinuity theory of human functioning, as expressed in a hierarchical system of five discrete levels of extension in logic, relates these to an equivalent system of five discrete levels in the human capacity to work, and to five equally discrete levels in hierarchical social organization. He argues that these are as ordinary a feature of human phenomena as they are of natural phenomena. Working with discontinuity, these writers take for granted the existence of hierarchies and of associated emergent properties.

Questions of Control

Human ecology, like all ecologies, is the study of life, a branch of the life sciences. As Pattee (1970, pp. 119-120) notes, if there is to be any theory of the life sciences, "it must explain the origin and operation (including the reliability and persistence) of the hierarchical constraints which harness matter to perform coherent functions," functions we all depend on for our very survival. He goes on to claim that

> the problem is universal and characteristic of all living matter . . . it is the central problem
> of the origin of life . . . the central problem of development . . . of biological evolution
> . . . of the brain . . . this problem [is] fundamental, since hierarchical control is the essential
> and distinguishing characteristic of life.

Pattee's conception of hierarchical control focuses on the level of discontinuity where life emerges from matter (where matter is "harnessed" to perform life's functions), but it well illustrates the importance of control in hierarchy theory. Less mysterious, but also interesting in human ecology, is the question of control that emerges, for example, when a regional air quality authority is created on a new level to mediate the conflict between lower-level units about pollution that crosses boundaries and thus evades the authority of local officials.

Organization, or system, by definition includes a conception of control. Every writer on hierarchy theory known to me admits control factors in the formation and functioning of hierarchies. No controls, no organization: Anarchy, disorder, chaos, are the alternatives. Without controls, complexity could not have evolved: All would be mud or soup. Entropy would have no counters. Humans totally unfettered could not have created civilization in any form. As noted earlier, Dyke's (1988) fear of the word hierarchy apparently stems from his belief that using the term and accepting the fact of hierarchies, will lead to the subordination of individual humans to society with the result a diminishment of human freedoms.

This is almost startlingly naive. Viewing relationships in hierarchical fashion does lead to the admission that an individual in context—a part of or integrated into an aggregate or groups—loses some degrees of freedom. But, that has always been true of any organism: Ecologically, independence is impossible. Every organism is tied into its community and into its environment in a myriad list of ways. We are all liege, subject to a harmost of some form, bound by limits to our freedoms by the very nature of belonging. No human individual has ever been autonomous, totally free of dependence on the biological community (for food and energy) or on the human community, the social level, for identity, companionship, for work and play. The functioning of any stable human organization is a constant balancing act between integrative and self-assertive tendencies in human individuals. Stability is maintained by allowing neither tendency to get out of control.

Dyke's (1988) muddying of the conditions for what constitutes a hierarchy also contributes to his fear of the word, much of the confusion stemming from his notion of control in hierarchies. For example, he seems to believe that, although the authority vested in higher and higher levels in an organized church (which he mistakenly uses as a paradigm for hierarchy theory) does result in a hierarchy, the "constraints" placed on an atom in a more complex molecule do not make a hierarchy. Constraint is a form of control, as is authority, *both* issuing from placement in a hierarchy. Similarly, he makes "supersession"— of one level by the next highest—a condition of calling any organization a hierarchy; to be superseded is an ultimate form of control—by elimination. Setting such a condition results from and would foster fears of control by integration into a series of levels. We might say, as T.S. Eliot did of free verse, that there is no free order. There is only good order, bad order, and anarchy or chaos. Freedom *and* order come only with controls.

Also relevant here is the question of the limits of complexity. The upper levels of the periodic table illustrate the instabilities that can result when complexity reaches a certain point. Social scientists have asked similar questions about cities and nations: Did over-reaching complexity, extending beyond the boundaries of effective control, lead to the downfall of the Roman Empire? Are cities like New York too large and complex to be effectively governed as one unit? Will (or can) present nation-states and federations be amalgamated into a stable world community?

Interaction and the Bonding Process

I find it curious that so many writers on hierarchy theory spend so much space on the question of what generates new levels in a hierarchy. Such questions begin at least as early as Redfield's (1942, pp. 3, 8) "how are parts constituted into wholes throughout the range of life-forms?" Often the phrasing is "how does a [whole] come about out of its component parts?" And, the questions are still around in the latest inquiries into hierarchy theory. It is odd because that same literature is replete with statements such as Weiss's (1971, p. 11) comment that hierarchies "must be conceived as interconnected . . . by the all-pervading mesh of forces and *interactions*" and Pattee's concurrence that "the most common and most concrete concept we associate with hierarchical organization (is some conception) of *interacting* levels" (1973, p. 132, emphasis added).

Zee (1986) even refers to the components of physical nature as a hierarchy of interactions. Smith (1969) stated general principles for structural hierarchy in inorganic systems in terms of interaction: Assemblies of units will not form coherent aggregates unless the parts *interact*, and in such a way as to transform internal structures and energy. Further, structures at each scale must have types of *interaction* appropriate to that scale and the energy available. Finally, he claimed that complex aggregates may involve the superimposition of several different structural hierarchies, each responding to a different type of interaction between units. Interactions among the living—those systems of most interest in ecology—seem even more conspicuous—and obvious. At every level, in every system, interaction can be and has been used to describe and explain the bonding process—even at the atomic and molecular levels and at the level of solar systems and galaxies.

One of the keys may be the questions raised by strong and weak interactions akin to those that bond the subatomic particles and atomic elements mentioned earlier. Levels in a hierarchy do become differentiated by strong internal interactions and weak external interactions. Certainly the nature of the interactions between or across levels, the differences between interactions horizontally and vertically, also exert influence. For example, Haferkaup (in Alexander et al. 1987) uses "face-to-face [strong] interactions to distinguish the micro level" (p. 177), whereas the macro-level "has many actors who are not in direct (i.e., are in weak) interaction with each other" (p. 178).

In those systems of interest in human ecology, interaction is an unmistakable choice as the basis for the formation of new levels. Two individuals interact to form a couple and then a family; families interact to form a neighborhood, a community, people bonded together by the interaction process in space or by mutual interests. Patterns of interaction and exchange also connect people to supply sources of materials and energy. A nation is held together by the same process, and acceleration of interactions among humans has led to bonding at higher levels in the form of federations such as NATO, the European community, and the United Nations (Young in press).

As Simon (1973, p. 23) noted: "The world is a large matrix of interactions . . . in which, by ordering . . . a distinct hierarchic structure can be discerned."

CONSPECTUS

This paper has examined some of the similarities that exist—between the living and nonliving and between natural and human-created—in the hierarchical organization and human understanding of complex systems. It is not yet possible to do a detailed inquiry into the fundamental difference between the organization of the living and the nonliving world, except to mention the change as a discontinuity. Knowing how molecules are arranged to create living cells is still beyond human understanding, but the difference must be recognized. Do not short-change the concept of hierarchy or the power of the human mind, however; as Thoreau (1854, p. 197) noted, "the imagination, give it the least license, dives deeper and soars higher than Nature does." The concept of hierarchy lets it soar at least as high as nature and, either way, the similarities have a lot to teach humans about how they relate and connect to the world around. Ultimately, the patterns traced in this paper teach that humans are inescapably an integral part of nature.

Herbert Simon (1969, p. 108) has suggested that if there are " . . . important systems in the world that are complex without being hierarchic, they may to a considerable extent escape our observation and understanding." Recognizing that does not imply that the systems we study are evenly scaled and always predictable. Science and scholarship cannot retreat to the nineteenth-century search for a perfectly ordered, mechanistic world or universe. Interactions between entities or units or parts can be completely random and yet still result in bonding, in more complex combinations or aggregates. No one "plans" the atomic collisions in the sun, yet they happen and we live because of it. Contemporary problems of human-human and human-environmental relationships constantly become more and more complex. How complex? What degree of complexity? What degree of dependence, of integration, of freedom or fixation, of determination, of similarity and difference? Present knowledge indicates that concepts of hierarchy help illuminate and answer such questions.

The increasing complexities of human-environment relationships create a mandate, a more and more imperative one, for science and scholarship to increasingly shift their emphasis so as to utilize available tools, especially the concept of hierarchy, *to engage, and then integrate, micro and macro-level observations*. Human ecology should be at the forefront of this shift. To do this, students of human ecology can use the concept of hierarchy to focus on the coherence of substance, form, and context; on the specification of context and significance; on the dialectic connectiveness of part and whole; and on the mutual effects of agency and structure in human-environment relationships.

REFERENCES

Alexander, J.C., B. Giesen, R. Munch, and N.J. Smelser, eds. 1987. *The Micro-Macro Link*. Berkeley: University of California Press.

Allen, T.F.H., and T.B. Starr. 1982. *Hierarchy: Perspectives for Ecological Complexity*. Chicago: The University of Chicago Press.

Arias, E.A. 1982. "The Application of General System Theory to Musical Analysis." *The Music Review* 43(3/4):236-248.

Barchas, P.R., ed. 1984. *Social Hierarchies: Essays Toward a Sociophysiological Perspective*. Westport, CT: Greenwood Press.

Barnes, R.H., D. De Coppet, and R.J. Parkin, eds. 1985. *Contexts and Levels: Anthropological Essays on Hierarchy*. Oxford: JASO.

Bateson, G. 1970. "Form, Substance and Difference." *General Semantics Bulletin* 37:5-13.

Bertalanffy, L. von. 1950. "An Outline of General System Theory." *The British Journal for the Philosophy of Science* 1(2):134-165.

Bochner, S. 1973. "Continuity and Discontinuity." Pp. 492-504 in *Dictionary of the History of Ideas*, Vol. 1, edited by P. Wiener. New York: Scribner's.

Bohm, D., and F.D. Peat. 1987. *Science, Order, and Creativity*. New York: Bantam Books.

Boulding, K. 1956. "General Systems Theory—The Skeleton of Science." *Management Science* 2:197-208.

Britan, G.M., and R. Cohen, R. eds. 1980. *Hierarchy and Society: Anthropological Perspectives on Bureaucracy*. Philadelphia: Institute for the Study of Human Issues.

Bronowski, J. 1970. "New Concepts in the Evolution of Complexity." *Synthese* 21:228-246.

Bronowski, J. 1973. *The Ascent of Man*. Boston: Little, Brown.

Bunge, M. 1960. "Levels: A Semantic Preliminary." *Review of Metaphysics* 8:496-406.

———. 1981. "Analogy Between Systems." *International Journal of General Systems* 7(4):221-223.

Commoner, B. 1972. *The Closing Circle*. New York: Knopf.

Cottrell, A. 1977. "Emergent Properties of Complex Systems." Pp. 129-135 in *The Encyclopedia of Ignorance*, edited by R. Duncan and M. Weston-Smith. Oxford: Pergamon.

Davis, F.H., and V.H. Heywood. 1963. *Principles of Angiosperm Taxonomy*. Princeton, NJ: Van Nostrand.

Duff-Cooper, A. 1984. "Hierarchy, Purity, and Equality Among A Community of Balinese on Lombok." *Journal of the Anthropological Society of Oxford* 15(1):15-29.

Dumont, L. 1980. *Homo Hierarchicus: The Caste System and Its Implications* (rev. ed.). Chicago: The University of Chicago Press.

Dyke, C. 1988. *The Evolutionary Dynamics of Complex Systems: A Study in Biosocial Complexity*. New York: Oxford University Press.

Egler, F.E. 1942. "Vegetation a an Object of Study." *Philosophy of Science* 9:245-260.

Egler, F.E. 1970. *The Way of Science: A Philosophy of Ecology for the Layman*. New York: Hafner.

Eiseley, L. 1957. *The Immense Journey*. New York: Random House.

Eisler, R. 1987. *The Chalice and the Blade: Our History, Our Culture*. San Francisco: Harper & Row.

Eldredge, N. 1985. *Unfinished Synthesis: Biological Hierarchies and Modern Evolutionary Thought*. New York: Oxford University Press.

Gould, S.J. 1982. "The Meaning of Punctuated Equilibrium and its Role in Validating a Hierarchical Approach to Macroevolution." Pp. 83-104 in *Perspectives on Evolution*, edited by R. Milkman. Sunderland, MA: Sinauer.

Grene, M. 1967. "Biology and the Problem of Levels of Reality." *New Scholasticism* 41:427-449.

Guttman, B.S. 1976. "Commentary: Is 'Levels of Organization' a Useful Biological Concept?" *BioScience* 26(2):112-113.

Hirata, H., and R.E. Ulanowicz. 1985. "Information Theoretical Analysis of the Aggregation and Hierarchical Structure of Ecological Networks." *Journal of Theoretical Biology* 116(3):321-341.

Howell, S. 1984. "Equality and Hierarchy in Chewong Classification." *Journal of the Oxford Anthropological Society* 15(1):30-44.

Huxley, J. 1964. *Essays of a Humanist*. New York: Harper & Row.

Jaques, E., ed. 1978. *Levels of Abstraction in Logic and Human Action*. London: Heinemann.

Kisly, L. 1984. "Focus." *Parabola* 9(1):2-3.

Knorr-Cetina, K., and A.V. Cicourel, eds. 1981. *Advances in Social Theory and Methodology: Toward an Integration of Micro- and Nacro-Sociologies*. Boston: Routledge & Kegan Paul.

Koestler, A. 1967. *The Ghost in the Machine*. New York: Macmillan.

Laszlo, E. 1987. *Evolution: The Grand Synthesis*. Boston: Shambhala.

Leshan, L., and H. Margenau. 1982. *Einstein's Space and Van Gogh's Sky*. New York: Collier.

Lincoln, Y.S., and E.G. Guba. 1985. *Naturalistic Inquiry*. Beverly Hills, CA: Sage.

Mayntz, R. 1989. "Social Discontinuity." *Interdisciplinary Science Reviews* 14(1):4-15.

Odum, E.P. 1971. *Fundamentals of Ecology* (3rd ed.). Philadelphia: Saunders.

_____. 1975. *Ecology: The Link Between the Natural and the Social Sciences*. New York: Holt, Rinehart and Winston.

_____. 1989. *Ecology and Our Endangered Life-Support Systems*. Sunderland, MA: Sinauer.

Oldershaw, R.L. 1978. "On the Morphology and Dynamics of Galaxies." *Speculations in Science and Technology* 1(5):477-482.

_____. 1979. "The Atomic Scale in the Self-similar Hierarchical Cosmology." *Speculations in Science and Technology* 2(2):161-171.

_____. 1981. "On the Number of Levels in the Self-similar Hierarchical Cosmology." *International Journal of General Systems* 7(2):159-163.

_____. 1983. "The Continuing Case for a Hierarchical Cosmology." *Astrophysics and Space Science* 92(2):347-358.

_____. 1985. "Set Theory Applied to the Self-similar Hierarchical Cosmology." *International Journal of General Systems* 10:235-255.

O'Neill, R.V., D.L. DeAngelis, J.B. Waide, and T.F.H. Allen. 1986. *A Hierarchical Concept of Ecosystems*. Princeton, NJ: Princeton University Press.

Orians, G.H. 1980. "Micro and Macro in Ecological Theory." *BioScience* 30(2):79.

Paine, L. 1972. *The Hierarchy of Hell*. New York: Hippocrene Books.

Patrides, C.A. 1973. "Hierarchy and Order." Pp. 434-449 in *Dictionary of the History of Ideas*, Vol. II, edited by P.P. Wiener. New York: Scribner's.

Pattee, H.H., ed. 1973. *Hierarchy Theory: The Challenge of Complex Systems*. New York: Braziller.

_____. 1970. "The Problem of Biological Hierarchy." Pp. 117-136 in *Towards a Theoretical Biology*, Vol. 3., edited by C.H. Waddington. Chicago: Aldine.

Phillips, D.C. 1976. *Holistic Thought in Social Science*. Stanford, CA: Stanford University Press.

Purcell, E. 1963. "Parts and Wholes in Physics." Pp. 11-39 in *Parts and Wholes*, edited by D.S. Lerner. New York: Free Press.

Redfield, R., ed. 1942. *Levels of Integration in Biological and Social Systems*. Lancaster, PA: The Jaques Cattell Press.

Rowe, J.S. 1961. "The Level-of-Integration Concept and Ecology." *Ecology* 42(2):420-427.

Riedl, R. 1978. *Order in Living Organisms: A Systems Analysis of Evolution*. New York: Wiley.

Salt, G.W. 1979. "A Comment on the Use of the Term Emergent Properties." *The American Naturalist* 113(1):145-148.

Salthe, S.N. 1985. *Evolving Hierarchical Systems: Their Structure and Representation*. New York: Columbia University Press.

Schumacher, E.F. 1977. *A Guide for the Perplexed*. New York: Harper & Row.

Simon, H. 1969. *The Sciences of the Artificial*. Cambridge, MA: The M.I.T. Press.

Simon, H. 1973. "The Organization of Complex Systems." Pp. 1-27 in *Hierarchy Theory: The Challenge of Complex Systems*, edited by H.H. Pattee. New York: Braziller.

Simpson, G.G. 1967. *The Meaning of Evolution*. New Haven, CT: Yale University Press.

Smith, C.S. 1981. *A Search for Structure: Selected Essays on Science, Art, and History*. Cambridge, MA: The MIT Press.

Smith, C.S. 1969. "Structural Hierarchy in Inorganic Systems." Pp. 61-85 in *Hierarchical Structures*, edited by L.L. Whyte, A.G. Wilson, and D. Wilson. New York: Elsevier.

————. 1964. "Structure, Substructure, Superstructure." *Reviews of Modern Physics* 36:524-532.

Soodak, H., and A. Iberall. 1978. "Homokinetics: A Physical Science for Complex Systems." *Science* 201(4356):579-582.

Stevens, A. 1983. *Archetypes: A Natural History of the Self*. London: Routledge & Kegan Paul.

Steward, J.H. 1951. "Levels of Sociocultural Integration: An Operational Concept." *S. W. Journal of Anthropology* 7:374-390.

Thoreau, H.D. 1957. *Walden*. Ed. by Sherman Paul. Cambridge, MA: The Riverside Press.

Weisskopf, V. F. 1979. "Contemporary Frontiers in Physics." *Science* 203(4377):240-244.

Weiss, P.A. 1971. "The Basic Concept of Hierarchic Systems." Pp. 1-43 in *Hierarchically Organized Systems in Theory and Practice*, edited by P.A. Weiss. New York: Hafner.

Whitehead, A.N. 1929. *Process and Reality: An Essay in Cosmology*. New York: Macmillan.

Whyte, L.L. 1965. "Atomism, Structure and Form: A Report on The Natural Philosophy of Form." Pp. 20-28 in *Structure in Art and in Science*, edited by G. Kepes. New York: Braziller.

————. 1969. "On the Frontiers of Science: This Hierarchical Universe." *General Semantics Bulletin* 36:6-14.

————. 1974. *The Universe of Experience: A World View Beyond Science and Religion*. New York: Harper & Row.

Wiley, N. 1988. "The Micro-Macro Problem in Social Theory." *Sociological Theory* 6(2):254-261.

Young, G.L. 1978. "Hierarchy and Central Place: Some Questions of More General Theory." *Geografisker Annaler* Series B, 60(2):71-78.

————. 1986. "Environment: Term and Concept in the Social Sciences." *Social Science Information* 25(1):83-124.

————. 1989. *A Conceptual Framework for an Interdisciplinary Human Ecology*. Lund, Sweden: University of Lund. [Acta Oecologiae Hominis, No. 1].

————. In press. "The Idea of Environment in a Historical Perspective of Human Population." *International Journal of Anthropology*.

Zee, A. 1986. *Fearful Symmetry–The Search for Beauty in Modern Physics*. New York: Collier Books/Macmillan.

FROM ENTROPY TO ECONOMY:
A THORNY PATH

C. Dyke

ABSTRACT

At least since the pioneering work of Georgescu-Roegen and Kenneth Boulding, attempts have been made to splice the concept of entropy into economic theory. There are good reasons to make the attempt. There are many more difficulties in succeeding than are usually recognized. I set out a series of ground rules that have to be observed for the concept of entropy to be used coherently, and discuss the conditions under which the extension of entropy to economic systems could be both sound and useful.

In the orthodox tradition economic systems are normally thought of, following Robbins, as systems for allocating scarce resources. They are better thought of as systems for extracting and transforming natural resources, circulating them through more or less organized human societies, and dumping the waste. The difference between the two definitions represents a choice between heuristic boundaries. The latter definition sets the boundaries in such a way that our

Advances in Human Ecology, Volume 1, pages 149-176.
Copyright © 1992 by JAI Press Inc.
All rights of reproduction in any form reserved.
ISBN: 1-55938-091-8

continuity with natural processes, and our utter dependence on them, is emphasized. This makes it decisively better than the former. Economies become aspects of ecosystems, reminding us of our inescapable place within the biota of the earth.[1]

Consequently, while as a convenience we can speak of natural systems on the one hand, and social systems on the other, our investigation is located precisely at the edge where that dichotomy is particularly problematical. Most of the problems bedeviling extensions of the concept of entropy are located precisely at the intersection of human activity and its environment. Some of them concern the question of what entropy is a measure *of*. Is it a measure of anything, or an artifact of certain investigative practices? Others arise when informational conceptions of entropy are introduced. What is informational for us humans, as we examine systems of various sorts, may not be informational *for the investigated system*, and this issue will have to be treated very carefully.

The exploitation of an understanding of thermodynamics in economics inevitably focuses eventually on the concept of entropy. This has its good side and its bad. On the one hand, the exploration of entropy focuses us on the center of thermodynamics—where we ought to be. On the other hand, the concept of entropy has a dialectical history of extreme complexity, and has proved to be one of the most misusable concepts ever to emerge from serious science. Consequently, one of the most pressing items on the agenda as thermodynamic thinking is woven into economics is to try to set out reasonable ground rules for the extension of the concept of entropy into the new contexts. Concomitantly it will be possible to exhibit many of the potential benefits of the extension.

SOME NECESSARY HISTORICAL LORE

Thermodynamics began with the analysis of heat engines and refrigerators, an apparently very limited context. The subsequent development of the field consisted both of identifying a broader range of natural phenomena and human artifacts similar enough to heat engines to be analysed in the same terms, and of an elaboration of the analytic framework to make it more useful in the broader range. At the extremes of the extended range, simple heat engines and refrigerators seem far behind, but the first ground rule is ***never forget heat engines, and never forget that any extension of the concept of entropy must be traceable back to them by a rigorous route.***

Thus in the beginning there was Clausius, who spoke saying: "No process is possible whose sole result is the removal of heat from a reservoir at one temperature and the absorption of an equal quantity of heat by a reservoir at a higher temperature" (Sears 1950, 1953, p. 111). This is the "Clausius statement of the second law of thermodynamics." In a moment we will look at the more familiar statement of the second law in terms of entropy. But before we do, we must note some important features of the law even in the Clausius formulation. First and foremost it is in the form of *a prohibition*—a form it shares with, say, the Kelvin-Planck statement and, indeed, all other sound statements of the law. There are several useful ways of glossing the prohibition, from the popularizing "you can't get something for nothing" to the graphic "future possibilities are confined within firm boundaries" to the disciplinary "don't try to do what nature does not permit," and finally the discouraging "a perpetual motion machine of the second kind is impossible." Whatever their worth, each of these presses home the point that in its simplest form the second law of thermodynamics tells us nothing about what *will* happen, but only about what *cannot* happen.

Any claim that the second law helps us know what will happen must be scrutinized with great care. This is the second ground rule. Actually, we *will* get to the point where we can talk about what can be expected on the basis of second law considerations, but this talk will have to be very careful.

The basic character of the second law as a prohibition, statement of constraint, or limitation is a direct source of one of its major misuses. For we must remember the socioeconomic circumstances surrounding its formulation. The formulation of the second law was a clear sign that the industrial revolution was in full swing. Whatever the genesis of other scientific laws, the genesis of the second law was in a very practical context: the understanding of the capability of machines. It emerged directly out of the work of Carnot on efficiency, and was a major step in the linkage of technology and economy. But the context of its birth was also a religious context, as is the continuing context of its elaboration.

The hegemonic ethos of the cultures within which the industrial revolution took place was the ethos of optimistic confidence in God's bounty. We have only to recall Locke's assurance that capital accumulation need be bounded only by the spoilage limitation in order to be consistent with economic justice— the guaranteed availability of as much and as good for everyone. While, fifty years after Locke wrote, Hume was able to talk of moderate scarcity as the condition of a system of justice (in effect, an economic system), it was only with gloomy parson Malthus at the end of the century that religious optimism was challenged in a way that caught the attention of the religious public. The Godwin-Malthus debate was the context for the formulation of Malthus's principle of inevitable scarcity, that is, his principle of population, and this debate was precisely about the availability of an assumption of God's bounty as a premise for social policy. Now, while Malthus' principle of population may well be false, or at least very misleading, it is very closely analogous to the second law, especially insofar as it expresses a limitation on the conditions under which human life is led. A generation later, when the second law itself came to public notice, it seemed to make the Malthusian point in a more deeply cosmological way.

So true believers were led to fight over the religious significance of the fact that God had seemed to create a world in which scarcity was the human condition. The connection of the second law with the Protestant work ethic is obvious. The life of toil in God's vineyard seems to be a straightforward consequence of the second law in many of its glosses. To the Calvinist mind, the second law can even seem a (suitably ascetic) comfort. It is nearly inevitable in such a context that the second law is seen as a symbol of the godly injunction to diligence and toil. The sybaritic alternative smacks of temptation and sin.

Now, this conceptualization of the second law in the elaboration of a religious cosmology would be of only historical interest if it were simply a curiosity of the mid-nineteenth century, but as we proceed we will see that it has never ceased to generate cosmological profundities of a religious cast even in its most secular-looking scientific contexts. This infects many of its extensions both to economics and to evolutionary biology.

LOCATING SYSTEMS

A formulation of the second law more familiar than the Clausius formulation is "Processes in which the entropy of an isolated system would decrease do not occur, or, in every process taking place in an isolated system the entropy of the system either increases or remains constant" (Sears 1953, p. 12). A decrease in entropy is forbidden in isolated systems. The first thing we have to note here is the word "system" and its adjectives—here "isolated," but, very soon, "closed" or "open." Thermodynamics is the bedrock home of the word "system," which is defined, in the last analysis, in terms of interconnected processes *around which sound analytic boundaries can be drawn.* In thermodynamics these boundaries are drawn in terms of phase separations of various stringencies having to do with the passage of energy and matter. Of course the word "system" has gotten a much broader meaning, until now any interconnectedness tends to be enough for someone to start talking about a system. I don't suppose there's any real point to complaining about the extensions of the word system, but its ubiquitous use requires the imposition of the third ground rule: **If you want to talk about entropy, you must be able to talk about the thermodynamic boundaries of whatever it is for which you're measuring the entropy.** Failing this specification of normal thermodynamic boundaries, you must be able to provide a statement about boundaries that can be traced back in a rigorous way to the basic thermodynamic concept. The amount of cheating that goes on with respect to this requirement among otherwise intelligent people is truly colossal.

Obviously this third ground rule will be especially important if the concept of entropy is to be applied to economic "systems," and particularly if genuine quantitative results are sought. Economic systems are neither isolated nor closed, but rather open systems—a fact that will occupy us a great deal later. Here, though, what is in question is the justification for calling economic systems "systems" in the first place. This justification is all the more important since many people who have no deep first-hand experience with the techniques of thermodynamics have a lot of difficulty with the concept of an open system. After all, a *sine qua non* of systems identification is the specification of boundaries. Yet, by definition, the boundaries of an open system are constantly trespassed by both matter and energy. Does this not make the specification of boundaries, hence the identification of an open system intolerably loose? Does not the distinction between a system and its boundaries become hopelessly vague?

The difficulties in specifying the boundaries of open systems are no different from the parallel difficulties in establishing the boundaries of "an economy" for the purpose of Leontiev input-output analysis. Indeed, the Leontiev techniques are a species of the general techniques employed in any analysis of thermodynamic systems. That said, we can acknowledge legitimate concerns about systems boundaries, and realize that the question of systems boundaries is never closed once and for all. The investigation of complex systems is intrinsically dialectical in the precise sense that initial decisions necessary to fix the objects of investigation are themselves future objects of critical investigation. The "ontology" of systems is inextricably intertwined with the process of investigation itself. This echoes a more formal point about complex systems, namely that they can be defined as those systems whose analysis forbids the construction of an invariant phase space within which parameters are independent of the history of the system.

The consequences for economics of this "investigatory path dependence" of the analysis of complex systems may be quite significant. To put it grossly, the usual objects of economic investigation, such as nations, industries, firms, households, and the like, may be stable objects only under quite parochial lines of investigation, and not robust with respect to shifting investigative focus. Insistence on the categorizations demanded by these and only these objects may well be the source of serious illusion—"discrepancy" or "error." In fact, this point has been suggested quite frequently over the history of economic theorizing. For example, Jane Jacobs has advocated the adoption of import-replacing cities and their associated regions as a basic unit of economic analysis, and concomitantly attacked the utility of national accounting (Jacobs 1984).

From the point of view of meaningful thermodynamic closure and entropy accounts, the choice of a "nation" as the primary locus of system requires far more justification than it ever gets. Leontiev accounts are not thermodynamic accounts, and successful systems closure in terms of Leontiev accounts may unravel when new accounting categories come into play. The same can be said for each of the traditionally identified players of economic games: firms, households, and the like. In every case the motivation for identifying something as a system or subsystem has arisen historically in an investigative—and ideological—context, and for particular purposes. Dogmatic insistence on the perpetual usefulness of traditional systems identifications is a good way to court failure and the perpetuation of illusion. The point is not that nations, firms, and so forth *will* not serve as systems to be examined in terms of entropy accounts, but rather that if they are found to serve it will be as a result of dialectical probing to establish their robustness.

ISOLATING ENTROPY

Most of the work involved in making entropy a useful concept is done in the specification of systems and their closures. This has been true right from the first specification of the Carnot engine. It will remain true right to the end where black holes, species, and economies are specified. This is why the first ground rules are ground rules of careful systems identification. However, we can now allow ourselves to examine some basic features of entropy itself, if only to see additional background assumptions.

The last formulation of the second law we looked at stated that, in isolated systems, entropy can never decrease. Well, what is it that can never decrease? Can we look at it and watch it increase or remain the same? For an economist, the easiest way to see what's going on is to think about the concept of price, for in many (but not all) ways, entropy has a status in thermodynamic accounting very like that of price in economic accounting. Just as price is a number assigned to a system of transactions actual and potential, so entropy is a number assigned to a system of interactions and processes actual or potential. Just as price can be determined only in very specific contexts (call them markets), just so, entropy can only be determined in very specific contexts. Indeed, in their most primary uses, both price and entropy *must* be determined with respect to the approach of a system to an equilibrium of some sort. In the case of entropy, this can be appreciated in the way the concept must be very carefully constructed in the textbooks. The standard derivation of the expression for entropy requires that we be able to imagine adding heat to a system at various points in a reversible cycle so that it becomes meaningful to define the expression

$$\frac{dQ}{T} ,$$

the quantity of heat added at a point divided by the temperature at that point, in such a way that the expression is an exact integral. Then the expression for entropy is defined in terms of the integral over any path from a given state of the system to another, and "the change in entropy of a system between any two equilibrium states is found by taking the system along any reversible path connecting the states, dividing the heat added to the system at each point of the path by the temperature of the system, and summing the quotients thus obtained" (Sears 1953, p. 133). Notice how rigid the boundaries and method are here; and the specificity of the systems for which entropy is so far defined. Again in the words of Sears:

(a) The entropy of a system is defined for equilibrium states only. (b) Only *changes* in entropy or entropy *differences* can be computed [from the basic equation] . . . (c) The entropy of a system in an equilibrium state is a function of the state of the system only, and is independent of its past history. The entropy can therefore be expressed as a function of the thermodynamic coordinates of the system, such as the pressure and temperature or pressure and volume. (d) Changes in entropy can be computed [from the basic equations] for *reversible* processes only (p. 134).

Now there are very few systems, especially natural systems, that are in equilibrium or operating between equilibrium states. And there are really no reversible processes in nature.[2] In addition, of course, there are precious few isolated systems. What we have so far are the rigorous analytical roots of the concept of entropy without a useful way to apply the concept to real processes and real systems. Obviously, the next, and *vast preponderence* of successive development of the concept of entropy concerned the techniques of applicability. Little by little the concept was extended so that real processes could come under its scope. Each of these extensions from the theoretically precise case is justified very carefully in terms of appropriate closure, and appropriate analytical simplifications justified in rigorous ways. The success of thermodynamics over the last century is essentially the success of finding justified extensions. While there is no point in following these extensions and their justifications here, we must note the necessity for rigorous justifications for every extension, and demand as a fourth ground rule that any **new extension be as rigorously justified as the standard ones**. This can be a very tall order.

But now we have to step back and gain a bit of perspective on what we have gotten when we have defined entropy. First, we have a new way of expressing the second law, since under the classical conditions the expression

$$\frac{dQ}{T} = dS,$$

where S is entropy, is an exact differential and, thus, relates the old Clausius or Kelvin statements of the second law to a firm constraint on the way entropy can change in any process. Second, we know that the addition of heat to a system is merely one way in which energy can be added, so very quickly it becomes possible to relate entropy to the general energetics of systems. That is, we get very general information about how energy must be added to systems if any work is going to get done. Third, we get a precise picture of systems as "potentiated" (capable of work) or "run down" (no longer capable of work), and we know that potentiation is basically to be understood in terms of energy differentials—inhomogeneities such as temperature differences between heat reservoirs, electric potentials, economic gradients, and so forth. Thermodynamic equilibrium (most conspicuously in the real cases of irreversible processes) is uniformity.

These generalizations and extensions helped pave the way for the familiar Boltzmann formulation of the entropy of confined gasses. As before, the slow and careful way the formulation has to be set up is instructive for those interested in extending the concept of entropy. Just as Clausius-Kelvin entropies, Boltzmann entropies are defined in terms of a system of idealizations, then methods are developed to extend the results from the idealization to physically realistic cases. The soundness of Boltzmann's formulation depends on both a rigorous construction of the appropriate idealization *and* a rigorous path to the realistic cases. The construction of the idealization depends on specifying an ideal gas; justifying the assumptions (for analytic purposes) of perfectly elastic collisions, idealized containers whose inside surface is smooth rather than fractal, uniform gravitational conditions for all molecules at all times, reversibility of all internal processes, and so forth. In general, that is, an idealized system has to be specified for which the conditions of statistical "smoothness" or homogeneity are reasonable ones. In addition, a distinction will have to be set up between microstates, descriptions of the system in terms of the behavior of the gas molecules in terms of their positions and velocities, and macrostates, descriptions of the system in terms of the extensive state variables of the system—temperature, volume, pressure.[3]

Any pedagogically sound presentation of Boltzmann entropies will transparently exhibit the construction of the idealization, showing at every stage what simplifications, linearizations and so on are being employed. For, each of these simplifications and linearizations will have to be dialectically reexamined in the secondary task of extending the conceptualization from the ideal case to the realistic ones. This imposes a fifth ground rule, actually equivalent to earlier ones, but essential to emphasize here. **Any extension that we might want to make of the concept of entropy must be transparent to the idealizations necessary for its initial formulation**.

We can note here that the behavior of the ideal gas under the classic Boltzmannian conditions allows an apparent translation between the macroscopic thermodynamic state variables of the system and the microscopic state variables of the molecules of gas thought of as "Newtonian" particles. Some folks take this to be the sign that we can *reduce* thermodynamics to quantum mechanics via statistical mechanics; but this is a dangerous illusion.

For what we have actually found is a super-specific set of rigid boundary conditions under which a particular translation can take place. In particular, systems that are structureless and uniform, without any initial or emergent phase discontinuities, are candidates for the translation. Structured systems (and we will be very specific about that in a moment) are *not* candidates for the translation, and reduction attempts fail for them. A key point to remember in this regard is that the translation from thermodynamics to statistical mechanics requires a number of smoothness assumptions to allow averaging of, say, kinetic energies. Lumpy systems do not allow such averaging. It of course remains true that lumpy systems are subject to analysis both in terms of their thermodynamics and their kinetics, and the most interesting systems are those where we are obliged to employ both sorts of analyses. But the relationships between the kinetics and the thermodynamics of a complex system are themselves complex—not simply reductive.

HELLO INFORMATION

While in general there is no way to reduce thermodynamics to statistical dynamics, it is well worth setting up an expression for the entropy of classical Boltzmannian systems allowing the translation to go smoothly whenever possible. The entropy in a Boltzmann system is clearly best expressed in terms of the probability of finding the system in a particular macrostate. We furthermore know the shape that the entropy function ought to have, given the second law and other considerations. These and still other considerations eventually result in the particular Boltzmannian expression for entropy,

$$S = k\ln W,$$

where S is the Boltzmann entropy of a given macrostate, W is the number of microstates corresponding to the given macrostate, and k is the Boltzmann constant.

The classic extension of the Boltzmannian line of thought, harmless in its own bailiwick but gone beserk in some of its applications, is the Shannon expression for the "informational entropy" of a message transmitted down a noisy channel to a specifically tuned receiver. Shannon found that a very useful measure could be applied to such systems, allowing comparisons of the difficulty of decoding (receiving unambiguously) variously encoded messages under various conditions. The expression for this measure turned out to be, *mirabile dictu*, $H = p\ln p$ (Shannon and Weaver 1949), formally equivalent to the Boltzmann formulation. For reasons now legend, this led Shannon to talk of H as informational entropy. One would have thought that at this stage someone would immediately have begun to examine potential underlying *energetic* circumstances of the coincidence. Alas, this never happened. The reason it didn't runs as follows.

The Boltzmann formulation conceptualized entropy as a measure of relative disorder. From a surface mathematical point of view, this meant that an increase in entropy of a system could be associated with an increase in randomness. Correspondingly, of course, order is associated on this view with *non*randomness. So, from a mathematical point of view, the characterization of entropy seems to devolve upon a suitable characterization of randomness.

Such a characterization is a convenient quick inference from the Shannon conception of informational entropy. Shannon tells us how to compare two signal-channel-message-receiver systems with respect to the number of bits of information that would be required *by a particular well defined receiver* to disambiguate messages carried by a *particular* signal down a *particular* channel. Further assumptions about similarities between channels, messages, and receivers are used to license generalizations abstracted from all the particularities. Along these lines, the appropriate definition of randomness appears to have been found to justify talk of "entropy." How many bits of information would be required to disambiguate a message? The answer is an expression for the entropy of the message.

There are many serious reasons to worry about the slide from Boltzmannian to Shannon entropies. What Boltzmann found was a reliable symptom of entropy change in systems of a very specific sort. Similarly, in just the right circumstances, with just the right sorts of channels, signals, and receivers, Shannon measures can be a symptom of thermodynamic entropies, but they need not be. Indeed, it's possible to think of other entropy symptoms we might find useful. For example, if we were interested in leaves, then (with obvious exceptions that would be more illuminating than troubling) we could set up a color chart grading off from green to brown, and, comparing it with leaves, get a reading of their relative entropies. Indeed, such a method could well be employed with a high degree of precision. Yet we surely wouldn't conclude that entropy is brown. Similarly we should not conclude that entropy is randomness. Some occurences of brown are indicative of high entropy as are some occurences of randomness.

The Boltzmann entropies are defined in terms of microstates and macrostates of a system. Systems for which the Boltzmann entropies are appropriate allow a statement of the second law to the effect that a system will not move, by itself, from a more probable to a less probable configuration. The probabilities are defined in terms of the compatability of microstates with macrostates where these compatabilities are determined energetically. For, what we want to know of the system, in terms used earlier, is how much work we could still get out of it, how many inhomogeneities we can expect to remain in it, how close to equilibrium it is. All these are energetic considerations, and they are precisely what allow us to consider the Boltzmann probabilities as measures of entropy.

A contrast is instructive here, and can serve as a sort of demonstration of the point I am trying to make about energetically relevant and energetically irrelevant symptoms. Incidentally, the contrast is often blurred even in classic presentations of the Boltzmann apparatus (Sears 1950, p. 279). The difference between microstates and macrostates is often explicated in terms of the arrangements of a deck of cards. Thus it is pointed out to, say, the worldly wise bridge player that the chances of being dealt all thirteen spades is very low, while the chances of being dealt an anonymous collection of spots and faces of all four suits is very high. The enumerated microstate "Ace of spades, deuce of spades, trey of spades, . . . , King of spades" is consistent with only one macrostate. The quasi-enumerated collection "a few odd spades, a few odd diamonds, a few odd clubs, a few odd hearts" is consistent with many different exact enumerations thought of as microstates. Or, to put it another way, the bridge player's receipt of an "average hand" is much more probable than his receipt of a "very powerful hand." Now, these probabilities are under consideration every time a bridge hand is dealt, and the usefulness of knowing them is beyond dispute. Also beyond dispute is our ability to come up with macrodescriptions that lump together hands of varying microspecification. "Average hand" is a perfect case in point. But what is absolutely forbidden to us is the association of the probabilities thus arrived at with entropy of any sort. Even if we have ways (as we do) of talking sensibly about more ordered and less ordered hands (how could we play poker if we didn't?) we still cannot associate "ordered" and "disordered" arrays of cards with entropies. The reason for this is simple. Every array is energetically identical to every other. Specify an apparently disordered collection of cards, enumerated card by card. Then shuffle a deck and deal. It is precisely as unlikely that this apparently disordered collection will appear in a hand as that thirteen spades will appear in a hand.

Notice that nowhere have I denied that shuffling is an entropy producing activity. Nor have I foreclosed the possibility that the presence of spots on cards can in some contexts, under some boundary and closure conditions, have entropic and informational relevance. But as the situation is bounded and closed here, the spots are energetically irrelevant.

A more realistic, or at least nontrivial, situation is one often discussed since it seems paradoxical on the surface.[4] Take two nonreactive gases having parametric constants arbitrarily close to one another, and place each of them into isolation at the same temperature and pressure in containers side by side. Let them go to equilibrium. Then open the door between the two containers. Despite the fact that there will be an initial inhomogeneity that we can confidently expect to smooth out through a diffusive mixing process, there is never any entropy change in the system from the time the two separated gases reach equilibrium to the time when they are thoroughly mixed. Every accessible energy state of the system is the same as any other—just like in the deck of cards. A corollary of this observation is that the partitioning of a system into microstates necessarily requires careful attention to, for example, the size of the partitions with respect to the physically possible energetics.

We soon will have to confront theories that relate order and organization to entropy and the second law. Ecosystems and organisms, not to mention economic systems, will have to be evaluated with respect to their relative entropies. At that time we will scrupulously have to obey a seventh, nearly tautological, ground rule: **Any entropically relevant conception of order or organization must be an energetically relevant conception of order or organization.**

This is especially important since our ability to order and organize is nearly unlimited. Any set of objects we can imagine contains an innumerable array of similarities and differences any one or combination of which could be the basis of an ordering. Some of these similarities and differences, hence some of the orderings, will be energetically relevant—hence a ground upon which to assign entropies. But most of the similarities and differences will produce orderings with no energetic or entropic relevance at all.

Thus, not every difference in social organization, not even every difference in the division of labor, will be relevant to the entropic characteristics of an economy. Indeed, it will be possible to show that we can manage to find ways of evaluating social formations with respect to efficiencies of various sorts, and yet find these evaluations and efficiencies utterly irrelevant to the entropic accounts of the social systems involved. Pareto efficiencies are the most obvious instance. This has enormous consequences for the assessment of the ecological impact of all sorts of "economically" motivated activity.

LONG, LONG AGO IN A GALAXY FAR, FAR FROM EQUILIBRIUM

What about the role of equilibrium in our understanding of entropy? This long threatened to be a serious problem for the usefulness of the concept of entropy as a tool for examining natural systems, for very few natural systems of interest are in a state of equilibrium. Similarly, the concept of entropy has its most solid home in the context of isolated or closed systems, while nearly all interesting natural systems are open systems. A high priority task, then, is to extend our ability to work with entropies to open systems far from equilibrium. Much work has been done in this regard over the last fifty years—from the pioneering work of Onsager—and a lot of progress has been made. This is fortunate for anyone wanting to extend thinking about entropy to economics, for both human beings and their socioeconomic structures are open systems far from equilibrium.

Thermodynamic equilibrium is easily defined in terms of the usual state variables. Thus, "The final steady state of an isolated system is called a state of thermodynamic equilibrium and we postulate that in such a state the thermodynamic coordinates of a homogeneous system are the same at all points" (Sears 1953, p. 2). So the volume of the system does not change; anywhere you stick your thermometer you get the same temperature reading; and the same goes for the readings you get on your pressure gauge as you (quasi-statically) move it around. Equilibrium is a state of uniform boredom. Closed systems also can be stabilized in steady states, but these need not be equilibria. For example, if you put a quantity of water in a closed container that allows heat to go in and out, you can keep the water bubbling at almost exactly the boiling point by controlling the amount of heat you put in, and the amount of heat you let out. The extension of entropy considerations to such systems is not very difficult.

Open systems gain and maintain their stability by taking in matter and energy in a highly potentiated form, processing it, and discharging it to their environment at a lower potential. This last process is called dissipation, hence open systems stabilized far from equilibrium are called dissipative structures. We now have to pause to understand these structures as best we can, for they will concern us for the remainder of the paper.

It will help us to think in terms of phase spaces, representations of the quantitative behavior of systems. Phase spaces are entirely familiar to economists.[5] Commodity spaces are direct phase space analogues, as are production possibility spaces. Indeed, if appropriate functions can be defined for such spaces, they are not just analogues to phase spaces, but phase spaces proper. The phase spaces relevant to dissipative structures are defined in terms of energetics and possibilities of combination. Thus, for example, in the classic cases the phase spaces of multiple coupled chemical reactions are defined in terms of fluxes and concentrations. Many such reactions have been found in which, under the right initial conditions, the system stabilizes as an oscillating system in which the waves constitute a persistent structure. Less commonly, this wave structure can be made visible as an identifiable spatial structure, for example, the rings and whorls of the Belousov-Zabotinski reaction.[6] In the classical thermodynamics of the Boltzmann sort, we are used to thinking of a system as relatively homogenous, and, in the end, at equilibrium, really homogenous. Such systems come to occupy that region of phase space that contains all the points of minimum energy, proportional to the maximum entropy. The region of phase space that systems giving rise to dissipative structures come to occupy is quite different. To see what that region tends to be like we can draw on a simple analogy from classical microeconomics that we can progressively elaborate in illustrative ways.

If there are n traders in an m commodity market, then the state of the market at any moment can be expressed by n m-tuples associating each of the traders with the stock of each of the commodities that each possesses at the moment. The full "phase space" would, of course, be the space of all possible distributions of the m commodities between the n traders, and to ask what region of this phase space would tend to be occupied is to ask how commodities are initially distributed, how they would change hands, how their quantities change, and whether the number of traders would remain constant. To help us answer these questions we have the usual assumptions of neoclassical microeconomic theory to shape our hypothetical construction. We needn't worry here about the realism of the assumptions. We are deliberately constructing a fable.

So we begin by superimposing n indifference maps on the space, with the usual rationality assumptions giving us the family of permissible trajectories of the n individuals from all the various initial states. This is already enough, as is well known, for us to be able to say quite a lot about the regions of the phase space that will be explored by the system as the traders quasi-statically perform their hill-climbing bargaining act. And in terms of this hypersimplified picture we can discuss the approach of the system to stable configurations, suitable versions of Pareto surfaces. We can call the system "c/t."

However, we are trying to construct an analogue to a genuinely dynamical system, so we have to complicate the picture somewhat. We can begin the complications with the observation that, in general, the total quantities of the m commodities will not remain constant, but will vary, for two reasons. First, the traders have to eat to live, thus using up some of the commodities; and second, some of the commodities will spoil, and cease to be commodities. Fish close to equilibrium is not fish you can sell. These simple considerations introduce a genuine dynamics into the situation to go along with the quasi-statics of bargaining.

Let's look at the point on the Pareto surface reached in the quasi-static case, and ask about its stability with the dynamics added. We immediately note that the minute somebody eats something, or throws something rotten away, the system moves to a new point. If the used-up commodities are not replaced, then the system has contracted, in the straightforward sense that there are points in the original phase space that can no longer be accessed. This should tell us that we are getting closer to an analogue of a dissipative system, since it is a mark of such systems that their phase space contracts. But we are not there yet, since how the phase space contracts is also important. Of course, as various of the m commodities disappear from the market, the phase space correspondingly loses degrees of freedom. The phase space would also contract if any of the n traders were to die off, as would happen as the system ran out of resources. Perhaps we can imagine a penultimate phase in which the traders themselves reentered the phase space as commodities; but these lifeboat horror stories are really not to the point. For we can imagine the stock of commodities being kept up by replacement. Any reasonable scenario requires the introduction of a system of production. In this case, we can let production be an exogenous input, although eventually this strategy will outlive its usefulness.

With a system of production replacing used-up commodities, it begins to be clearer how we could hold the original system at a steady state. We have to notice right away, however, that the steady state is certainly not an equilibrium from a thermodynamic point of view, for we have opened the system to exogenous inputs precisely to prevent the trajectory of the system from going to thermodynamic equilibrium. To sharpen this point, we also want to notice that we are going to have to do something about the accumulation of waste in the system. Before very much time has gone by the accumulation of waste is sure to be destabilizing, perhaps altering the original indifference maps we used to find the original Pareto surface. So we have to think of the system as not just open to input, but open to throughput; and only under those conditions will it have a chance of being stable.

We can hope to make the initial Pareto point reached by the system of traders in the initial commodity space stable if we can adjust throughput so as not to disturb the behavioral assumptions that allowed us to find a potentially stable point in the first place. And at this point we have reached a schematic analogue of a dissipative structure. In turn, we can begin to see the regions of phase space that the system will tend to occupy.

The system will tend to occupy regions of the phase space defined by the Pareto surfaces. To say this is to say something about the internal structure of the system, a structure imposed precisely by the choice of normal neoclassical assumptions to define traders. We can well imagine other structure-determining assumptions that would lead the system to inhabit very different regions of the phase space.

ENTROPY AND OPEN SYSTEMS

The ease with which we can discuss a simple trading system—let alone a full bodied economy—in terms that are appropriate for dissipative structures suggests to some that such systems are dissipative structures. In order to see if this further step is justified, we would have to get clearer about the thermodynamics of such systems. If we were to do so we would automatically get what we have been looking for—a precise connection between entropy and economics.

Dissipative structures are far from thermodynamic equilibrium in a straightforward sense. That is, the distribution of accessible energy states of such systems is far different from their accessible energy states at equilibrium. Entropy, in other words, still measures distance from equilibrium. However, now the actual techniques of measurement become quite complex, and the normal methods of calculation of entropies have to be modified and supplemented. Indeed, it must be said that at the present time these methods of measurement and calculation are in the process of being devised. They are not firmly in place.[7]

This lack of reliable measurement and calculation methods is a problem at one level, and not at another. That is, at a level where precise numerical or analytic results are required there are serious difficulties. However, at a level where the identification of dissipative structures is in question, and where such qualitative identifications are sufficient to generate productive research even in the absence of precise numbers, the problems are far less acute.

This difference in investigative levels, and the room it gives us for theorizing, can be pulled free from a lot of the underlying epistemological tangle if we notice that the second law must hold for dissipative structures as it holds for everything else.[8] Confident that dissipative structures of all sorts must behave in straightforward conformity to the second law, we can inquire about their entropic circumstances, and especially the determination of boundary conditions needed for our confidence to be warranted. There are two basic facets to this. The first is the processing of throughput—low entropy input is processed yielding high entropy output. The classic example is the utilization of sunlight by the biota of the earth, and the resulting radiation of heat to deep space as a sink.[9] The second is the storage of incoming matter and energy to produce organized persistent wholes. The classic example of this is, again, a biota that captures input in chemical bonds with the eventual emergence of complex organic wholes. The entropy accounts must be kept in terms of the dissipation of heat and other wastes on the one hand, and the storage of matter and energy in system-building on the other.

Much is now becoming known about detailed processes from macromolecule formation to ecosystems development that conform to this pattern. We can try to apply some of it to c/t. We have already started to do so when we added a simple dynamics to the abstract quasi-static bargaining system. The step to a dynamic system in which things got used up or spoiled was, in fact, the step of insisting that the second law hold for this system as it does for others. Then, the concession that the system could remain stable only under a suitable throughput is a second step into thermodynamics. For it is the second law that requires renewing inputs of matter and energy, a source, and a way to get rid of wastes, a sink. The system is then a sort of engine (though not a machine) operating between the source and the sink.

Look first at the throughput. Since we made the production system an exogenous input, and the waste disposal facilities an exogenous sink (despite the obvious peril in doing so), the initial temptation is to treat the bargaining and consumption system itself as a sort of black box, and examine simply the relationship between input and output. It seems as if this would allow us to calculate "efficiencies," and rate of entropy production. And, indeed, within limits this is so. We would need to keep careful books on commodity entry and the escape of wastes; find a suitable model heat engine whose activity could be confined to converting just those commodities into work and waste; and compare the results with the input-waste figures of c/t. The finding and use of the model heat engine in this process is indispensible. Without it we have no way to assure ourselves that we are obeying any of the ground rules for the extension of the concept of entropy. With it we have some sort of measure of the "entropic needs" of the system, for remember, we have adjusted input to achieve stability in terms of the maintenance of a Pareto point. This should not sound like a simple task.

The "system" is stabilized far from equilibrium by the throughput. Given the way we have defined the throughput, the incoming energy and material must be of precisely the sort to replace what is used and what spoils. Thus the qualitative as well as the quantitative nature of the required incoming flux is determined by the internal structure of the system (the system of "preferences" of the n traders). This *particular* flux will be stabilizing only as long as the internal structure of the system remains unchanged. This is a general feature of all dissipative structures. A stably oscillating chemical reaction requires the input of the *right* chemicals, in the appropriate sense. Our ecosystem, based on the photosynthetic pigments, requires the impingement of photons of the *right* wave length. And so it goes. But it is easy to see that the stringency of qualitative requirements is crucially related to the "window of stability" of any dissipative structure. Thus the window of stability of c/t is extremely narrow. If a comparable system had arisen as the consequence, say, of biological evolution, we would tend to start talking about a species becoming cornered by its own evolved specialization. If the "right" qualitative flux were a limited nonrenewable resource, we might also have to start talking about a species eating itself out of house and home, and going extinct. Of course, to start talking of evolutionary cornering and limited resources is to start thinking ecologically about c/t.

The issue of stringency of *both* qualitative *and* quantitative requirements for stability has two facets: the ability of a system to control the quality and quantity of its input, and the ability of a system to change its internal structure in order to "match up" with the resources actually available. Dealing with the first of these two facets virtually compels us to alter the boundaries of c/t to include the production system as an internal subsystem rather than as an exogenous input. When we do so we end up with a newly bounded system that will undoubtedly look more sensible to most economists. However, there is a moral to the tale of our alteration of systems boundaries. On the line of thought we have been following, it is *utterly unreasonable* to examine a system of distribution cut off from its associated system of production. Put this way, the point may have a bite for some.

Because of the (artificially) stringent character of the flux requirements of c/t, the "entropy" calculations done for it are useless as they stand. We, in effect, have to get back closer to the source to find a meaningful systems boundary, hence the internalization of the production system. Now the production system looks to be a system of conversion—conversion of "naturally" occurring resources into qualitatively appropriate forms to enter the realm of commodities. But we can notice two things. First, each of the n initial traders was always involved in a conversion process—in order to live. Second, with the production system in view, many things can be seen to be both converters and things converted, and enter the system in both ways. This is the underlying truth in Sraffa's phrase "the production of commodities by means of commodities" (Sraffa 1960, 1963). Similarly, of course, the n traders will be both producers and consumers, embedded in the expanded c/t in both capacities. Systems membership and participation is hardly ever a simple one-dimensional matter whether we are talking about molecules, humans, or anything else. This again shows us that from a thermodynamic point of view even something like c/t is highly interactively structured, despite the possible surface appearance of independence of parts.

This structure, whatever it may be, is highly relevant to entropy considerations. For, in the absence of this structure the throughput of the system would be very different from what it is. Furthermore, as we saw briefly before, the establishment of this structure is what leads the system to occupy one region of phase space rather than another—what accounts, eventually, for its *failure* to access other regions of the phase space, even and especially those that are thermodynamically "downhill," that is, energetically lower states. In the language of nonlinear dynamics, the system has locked into an attractor, driven by the flux and constrained by the pathway of its structuring.[10] The particular attractor, in turn, is quite possibly one among many available to the system at an earlier time, but one into which the system was nudged into by a random fluctuation—noise. This is to say that the particular structure of a system may well be a matter of historical contingency, some would say "accident," and not, even in the case of human institutions, a matter of momentous events or decisions. But once a system is in an attractor, its capacity for other trajectories is very much diminished, at least for a considerable time, and at appropriate noise levels.

What these features of structure mean at a global level is that considerations of entropy—whether entropy can be measured precisely or not in the given case—are crucial in the account of how dissipative structures are generated, and their future behavior. Dissipative structures are committed structures and, as it were, "pay" for finding stable configurations by losing the ability to change in innumerable ways. The colossally obvious example of this is an organism, for example, a squirrel, an amoeba, or a redwood. Each is what it is from "birth" to "death." One will not transform into the other. If the world ceases to offer the flux conditions necessary for the continued far-from-equilibrium stability of any of them, it will lose its stability, and will proceed toward thermodynamic equilibrium. Indeed, part of the mystery of dissipative structures is dispelled if we realize that they are paths to equilibrium just as all other processes are. While they slow the march to equilibrium virtually to a halt in very local regions of the universe, this is, in a cosmological sense, temporary, and even, for some dissipative structures, ephemeral.

STRUCTURED RESTRUCTURING OF STRUCTURES

We have then, for rough analytical purposes, two terms to work with: external flux, and internal structure as it is relevant to the processing of that flux. These have to be matched to each other in establishing the stability conditions for far-from-equilibrium systems. We have talked about adjusting the flux qualitatively and quantitatively. We now have to talk of the potential internal restructuring of a system in order to bring it into line with an available flux that may not be qualitatively or quantitatively adequate to stabilize the originally structured system. We are considering, for example, altering a way of life to adapt it to the resources of its environment.

Natural systems do this all the time. Indeed, standard Darwinian phenomena must be looked at, from a systems point of view, as internal systems restructurings driven by ambient conditions. We need to take a quick look at these systems for clues to the possibility for human intervention in systems in order to restructure them. In passing, we can find a number of things to learn from the behavior of natural systems, and note a few cautionary tales.

Many natural systems are very well stabilized. They have persisted for a long time in a form that has changed little. Yet no natural system is immune to internal change resulting simply from its internal workings. We can hedge this by saying that internal changes must be caused by noise in the system; but then we have to remind ourselves that the second law guarantees that no system will be noise-free. Some of the internal changes of a system will be irrelevant to its stability, others will either improve stability or diminish it. To put this in a Darwinian way, for a moment, we can say that organisms are intrinsically subject to genetic mutations, and that there will be neutral, beneficial, and detrimental mutations. The *rate* at which mutations occur is, of course, a function of the stability of particular genomes, and particular *parts* of genomes. Now, the words "neutral," "beneficial," and "detrimental," in a Darwinian framework, are relativized to the survival of the organism in its environment. This is a choice of one sort of stability-relevant boundary to look at. There are, of course, others. Every dissipative structure is sensitive (to one degree or other) to its local environment. This means, among many other things, that a genetic mutation occurs within a genome internally sensitive to itself. It is a complex chemical environment with its own configurational requirements and limits. Furthermore, it occurs within a cell and in constant interaction with the other parts of the cell. The cell as a whole has its stability requirements and limits. And so it goes, through a series of reembeddings, recontextual-izations, and the imposition of new requirements. Each of the resulting levels of structuring must be taken into account in assessing the overall stability of the organism. Similarly, each level is the potential source of change. Organisms have evolved along trajectories sensitive to all these levels. Just as it is trivial to say that an organism is adapted to its environment in the sense of being adequated to it, but nontrivial to say *how* it is adapted, it is trivial to say that organisms have evolved in such a way that they are (relatively) stable at all levels, but nontrivial to say *how* these levels interact (or, sometimes, are prevented from interacting) in order to achieve overall stability. This means, among other things, that an internal change in an organism (or any other system) that temporarily improves its local stability at a certain level is very far from insuring improvement in its *overall* stability.

To provide an example here before we fly too far into generalities, it is quite possible that the conditions of internal stability for a country are incompatible with its stable fate in the international world. Or, it is quite possible that the internal stability conditions of a firm are incompatible, in some time frame, with the stability of the national economy of which it is a part. What is good for General Motors may be good for the country, but there is no guarantee of this, and quite possibly reasons to think that it aint so. Any judgment on these matters will require a careful examination of the internal dynamics of the firm, the country, and the world economy. Finally, to put the matter in terms of c/t, it may be that the maintenance of the Pareto surface is incompatible with the overall ability of the system to maintain its stability within its actual flux conditions.

The presence of structural levels in all sorts of systems of systems has led some people to talk about hierarchies, thus reifying the levels as hypostatized categories, rather than considering them as dialectically interactive structures in highly nonlinear dynamical systems. I have argued against this reification at length elsewhere (Dyke 1988). In this context only a few points need to be reemphasized. First, reification and totalization, as always, go hand in hand. A structure sealed off against interactions with its constituent structures would have complete hegemony over them in the sense that its stability conditions would be independent of events at the constitutent level. Every totalitarian government dreams of such a totalization. Every species would be fixed forever in such a situation—as long as its ambience supplied it with the conditions for its existence.

Of course this goes both ways. Structures sealed off from their constitutive structures are forever impotent to affect the conditions of their own existence. Certainly there are cases in which this is the way things are. Some structural constraints are very stringent. But evolutionary processes take place because in many cases constraints are *not* totalized. You don't have to be a Darwinian to believe this and, in fact, it helps if you're not a Darwinian. Organisms and environment are nonlinearly interactive, and it's very difficult to fit this with the canonical Darwinian view. Similarly, I would argue, participants in a market are nonlinearly interactive with the market structures that constrain their trading activity. They are neither hegemonic with respect to price, as the orthodox ideal would have it, nor are they immune to the restructuring of their behavior as a response to market constraints.

With these considerations in mind, let's look at c/t once again. We left it as a system of production, trading, and consumption in which all the participants of the system engaged in some way or other in all three activities. The overall activity of the system is to convert an input flux into an output flux while capturing and holding part of the incoming "basic resources" so as to keep the system and its participants from going to equilibrium. What can we expect of such a system? Well, first, if it is indeed comparable to natural systems with the same overall activity, we can expect it to be in constant structural change, but change within more or less stringent limits placed upon it by the history of the emergence of its structuring. That is, as the system moves through the phase space, it will be confined to relatively specific regions determined by the possible trajectories it has "left open for itself" as a consequence of prior structuring.

For *very* determinate structures such as organisms which are, as I said, highly committed, we can even have high hopes of understanding the entire process of constant restructuring that begins with conception (or the vegetable and protistic equivalents) and death. For a system such as c/t, however, we could expect less determinacy of future trajectory, far more plasticity in development. This expectation is, of course, based on the fact that c/t is a human system, and humans have shown a fair amount of creativity and variety in their institutions. We should not, however, let ourselves get carried away by human plasticity. Humans can't violate the second law any more than anything else can, and humans must act within windows of possibility just as everything else does. Human systems pursue trajectories in phase space and have their stability conditions as do all systems. So, while the kinetics of chemical systems and the kinetics of human systems may differ greatly, the thermodynamic phenomenology of the two are subject to many of the same sorts of analyses. No apology need be made for examining c/t as a potential dissipative structure. In particular, humans have only partial control over the stability conditions of the systems of which they are a part.

ANTICIPATABLE EXPECTATIONS

In most dissipative structures we can expect internal differentiation and specialization to occur. Complexification of this sort is ubiquitous in dissipative structures, and is virtually an identifying characteristic of them. In c/t this will express itself in a division of labor. No surprises here except, perhaps, for the realization that what looks like an intelligent response of humans to their world is in fact a conformity to the behavior of systems of all sorts. Beyond the expectation that a division of labor will develop, however, there are no further, more specific, expectations to be formed on the basis of the thermodynamic phenomenology alone. That is, how labor will be divided is subject to historical contingencies of all sorts including, of course, the historical contingencies of human knowledge. Sometimes the material conditions will provide a very narrow band of available trajectories in the system's phase space, whereupon the possibilities for human response are very limited, and the form the division of labor takes will be virtually predictable on the basis of those conditions. Less commonly, a broad range of alternatives will be available, in which case we would have to wait and see which one was adopted. In any case, we can expect that not all divisions of labor will be entropic alternatives relative to others, and that many factors will affect the establishment of particular divisions of labor.

Second, we can expect levels of organization or structure to develop. The exact pattern of this development is a matter of historical contingency, and here our sense of what is likely to happen depends on a judicious blend of historical knowledge and imagination. However, general considerations give us two points to ponder about multilevel complexity. One point is that for all the various reasons why systems move toward stable states as attractors, we have some reason to expect that the eventual structural patterns of human systems will fall into a relatively small range—occupy a rather small region of a phase space constituted by "imaginable" patterns. Many different initial conditions could lead to the same attractor. Whether or not this is a characteristic of human systems is, of course, a matter of real historical trajectories. We would have to make judgments about our own century, for example, where the material conditions set by world industrial capitalism seem to have led nations to a very narrow range of political and economic structures from what look to have been quite different starting points.

The other point is that if structural levels were to emerge in c/t, then each of these levels would have to be examined in any attempt to apply entropy considerations to the system. This is especially true for attempts to use informational or organizational entropies. Up to now, as I have emphasized before, *no one* has been able to provide fully adequate measurement and calculation methods for these "entropies," and there are many serious problems in the way of doing so. Each level constitutes a subsystem stabilized far from equilibrium. Measurements of entropies of systems far from equilbrium are as yet unavailable. Then, if we were fortunate enough to be able to measure organizational or informational entropies with respect to the various levels, the problem of the total entropy of the entire system would arise, and no one knows how to compute this either. Simple additivity is surely naive, since it implies a linearity in the structure of structures that is virtually guaranteed to be absent. Here economists trying to work with the concept of entropy will find themselves in the same tangles as evolutionary biologists.[11]

Third, we need to look at the *variety* of stable states that a system like c/t is likely to settle into. Traditionally, it has been assumed that economies will settle into an "equilibrium" that is quite static. But almost all systems bearing significant resemblance to c/t stabilize in limit cycles of various periods, or into strange attractors.[12] This scenario ought to be intriguing to economists for a number of reasons. First of all, it suggests some new ways of examining economic cycles of all sorts. There is more than ample evidence of many such cycles. There is, as yet, very little in the way of explanation for them. Nonlinear dynamics is at least a theory in which such cycles are an expected phenomenon rather than a disconcerting annoyance, so it has an initial promise.

One issue that will surely arise in this context is the economic role of governments. For a number of centuries (and maybe always), a major role of government has been to try to damp cycles and buffer their effects on individuals and institutions. This role has one meaning if economic cycles are aberrational. It has quite another meaning if the normal pattern of stability of economic systems is cyclical stability. In the latter case, attempts to damp cycles could well be destabilizing rather than stabilizing. Or, to put the matter another way, political stability and economic stability may be incompatible under some or many circumstances. This would depend in large part upon the criteria of political stability accepted at particular times and places. For Attila the Hun, political stability consisted in a strategy of continuous destabilization. Margaret Thatcher would like to have had other strategies available.

Fourth, we must talk about commitments to a policy of economic growth. This is one of the issues that can be dealt with fairly well on the basis of the qualitative considerations we have available about the throughput-structure matchup. While no one knows precisely what they are in particular cases, it is certain that economic systems have upper and lower thresholds on throughput. On the one hand, radical scarcity is obviously destabilizing, and there is enough historical evidence to make this observation virtually platitudinous. On the other hand there is the nest-fouling inevitably associated with higher levels of throughput than can be processed efficiently. The historical evidence is fast accumulating on this aspect of throughput, too. The production of enormous quantities of CO_2 is an inevitable consequence of a hydrocarbon-based industrial system. Other pressures lead to a deforestation that lessens the ability of the ecosystem to reconvert CO_2 to oxygen. The well known consequence of this situation, apparently already upon us, is the closing down of the heat sink of deep space, and an inevitable rise in the average temperature of the earth. This accelerates the movement of the biosphere to equilibrium.

Similarly, but perhaps not as inevitably, the modern industrial system has pumped huge quantities of hydro-flouro-chlorocarbons into the atmosphere resulting in the well publicized deterioration of the ozone layer. This is a sink problem that dialectically generates a source problem. As we have seen, the flux requirements of any open system stabilized far from equilibrium are qualitative as well as quantitative. Life on earth has evolved for millions of years in a qualitative flux from which ultraviolet radiation has been filtered. That filter is now breaking down. No one knows what will happen to the earth's biota under the new flux conditions and, it's fair to say, no one wants to have to find out.

Some of these source-sink problems are traceable to the strategies available within our present patterns of socioeconomic organization. For example, all modern western societies are structured on some conception of individual freedom. American society is simply an extreme in this regard. This individual freedom has been extended to the major actors in the industrial economy. Any proposed solution to the source-sink problems will involve restructuring that will reduce the degrees of freedom of these actors. But western industrial capitalism has a long history of resistance to any such restructuring, and an equally long history of dealing with problems like source-sink problems ("negative externalities" is the euphemism) by displacing them into *new* source-sink problems. The move to nuclear energy is simply one particularly visible case in point. Furthermore, western capitalism—and, increasingly, *all* modern economies—have dealt with the problem of internal political stability largely by Fordism, the attempted totalization of consumerism. So far these policies have staved off the "proletarian revolution" that seemed to threaten in the nineteenth century. But the price of the policy has been to convert all issues of political legitimacy into the issue of whether a particular system or regime can deliver the goods. Furthermore, this has been accomplished with the most minimal redistribution by, precisely, the policy of constant economic growth. It is far from clear whether the move to, say, zero growth economies would be a stable resting place overall for the societies of the world. Indeed, many, both conservative and liberal, are convinced that it would not be. It is clear, in any case, that the problems cannot be conceptualized simply in terms of the production of more or less entropy.

At the very least we can state another ground rule. **Systems far from equilibrium are differentially responsive to any given human action, strategy, or policy, depending on their time-dependent conditions of relative stability**. This ground rule is a banal consequence of the fact that systems far from equilibrium are differentially responsive to *everything* depending on their temporal state of relative stability. In fact, that's what allows us to talk about different states of relative stability in the first place. But notwithstanding the banality, these considerations are absolutely fundamental for any assessment of the possibility of change.

For example, these considerations bear directly on our understanding of "economies of scale." In pursuit of economies of scale firms, in effect, seek to modify their own flux conditions, usually quantitatively, but sometimes also qualitatively as when they farm out certain parts of their operation to other firms. In a similar way, national economies seek to expand, usually as a way of trying to promote internal well-being and stability. In both cases, the successful expansion of throughput *can be expected*, on the view presented here, to result in the internal complexification of the firm or nation, for increased structural complexity is required to process the increased throughput for these systems as it is for any other dissipative structure. The lament of the American Right for the good old days of small firms, small government, freedom from regulation, and so forth, can't be taken seriously for a single moment. Success depends on quantitative expansion, and that can't be had without increased structural complexity. The fact that this structural complexity has evolved even in the face of antithetical prevailing attitudes is something of a confirmation of the view I am presenting.

It should be noted that, in general, the view of change presented here is decidedly misanthropic, in that it emphasizes changes required by far-from-equilibrium systems, and downplays an intelligent human role in change. The message so far is that a great deal of human activity is a matter of making virtue out of necessity—thinking you create voluntarily that to which you in fact submit. But in general, thermodynamic requirements do not determine unique pathways, nor do they determine unique structurings. This by itself alllows space for human intervention. Add to this the almost dizzying plasticity of *Homo sapiens* with respect to the conditions of life, and considerable variety can be expected. However, thermodynamic considerations *do place boundaries on possibility*, and sometimes these boundaries can be very tight. To recall a point made earlier, it is possible to get locked deeply within an attractor offering few structural options, and judgment on whether this occurs in human affairs depends on the evaluation of phenomena such as we experience in our own time. It *appears* that a fundamentally capitalist world economy locks all nations into a very narrow range of internal structures. Hence the United States and the Soviet Union, for example, apparently having entered the attractor at very different points and on very different trajectories, ineluctably converge to very similar patterns of internal (especially bureaucratic) structure. Their histories within the attractor tend to be forgotten (by all but the most recalcitrant ideologues).

The problems of finding a place for intelligent action are roughly the same both for those who want things to stay the same, and for those who want them to change. Phase spaces can be specified in a "once-for-all" way for very few actually occurring complex processes. It is not forbidden by nonlinear dynamics for there to be determinable transients from one attractor to another—given the presence of fluctuations. Furthermore, life in one attractor can well determine the nature of future attractors. For example, while dissipative structures require a stabilizing flux for their emergence and continued existence, they often produce components that are stable independent of the flux. The shells of snails and bivalve molluscs are the most familiar case of this. They remain behind for us to collect when the dissipative structures that created them are kaput. The same may well be true of social structures. They create habitus and hexus, that is to say personality, that is all too likely to persist when the conditions of its viability are gone. In addition, social systems create their equivalent of shells: buildings, machines, and roadways, for example, that remain behind as potential organizers of a new life when the systems that built them have gone. The history of Rome is a lesson in this sort of thing.

In all this we should expect that the search for precise quantitative entropy accounts will be devilishly difficult to come by. But we should not thereby despair. We can learn much from a study of the qualitative aspects of dissipative systems. For example, we can tease out a number of very significant constraints on the *ways* in which the phase spaces of such systems can contract, hence we can come to understand the *kinds* of dissipative structures that will tend to emerge in such systems. Entropy does not cease to be relevant far from equilibrium. However we have to find new ways of respecting its importance. The techniques useful in the examination of systems near or at equilibrium may remain useful *locally* within systems far from equilibrium, but lose their power to be globally useful. Entropy considerations are always implied in any construction of a thermodynamic phenomenology, but the availability of balanced double-entry account books of entropy is not. We have to find other ways of respecting the relevance of entropy.

So in the end, my advice to economists seeking to utilize the concept of entropy is that the attempt to keep entropy books in the way that other account books are kept is probably a mistake. The most important entropy considerations for systems like economic systems is the entropy stored in structure and, quite frankly, nobody knows how to measure that entropy. Asking for the entropy accounts of, say, the automobile from ore and oil well to auto graveyard is a silly thing to do at the present time, and may well remain a silly thing to do even though issues of efficiency, pollution, style of life, and what have you are undeniably entropy-relevant. Robert Bruce Lindsay, one of the leading thermodynamicists of this century, once annunciated a maxim he called "the thermodynamic imperative": Act so as to create the minimum amount of entropy. Despite its Kantian charm, there is no reason to think that this maxim is sensible either globally or in any particular locality. For systems stabilized far from equilibrium the key question is not "How much entropy is being produced?" The key questions are "How is that entropy being produced," "What kind of entropy is it," and "How are these entropies related to the stability of this or that dissipative structure?" That is, in short, any useful extension of the concept of entropy to economics will have to be done in the context of nonlinear dynamics and nonequilibrium thermodynamics.

NOTES

1. Classic treatments of entropy and economy include: Georgescu-Roegen (1971), Boulding (1981), Adams (1982), Odum and Odum (1976), Allen (1985), Wicken (1987).

2. This may sound strong, and there are obviously many processes with reversible aspects to them, but it is, in the end, an important "truth," namely that time is directional.

3. See Wicken (1987) for an excellent discussion of this point.

4. What follows will be recognized as a version of Gibbs' paradox. I claim that the deck of cards offers another instance of the same "paradox."

5. Samuelson (1970) is the standard work treating economic systems as phase spaces.

6. The literature on dissipative structures is very large by now. Among the useful sources are Prigogine (1980), Vasiliev et. al. (1987), Ferracin et al. (1978), Atlan (1985), and the many references contained within each. Recent work can be represented by Cornell-Bell et al. (1989, pp. 470-473).

7. See, for example, Nicolis and Altares (1988).

8. If the second law were "known" with confidence to hold come hell or high water, this would change the attitude among physicists to this whole thing. But the question "Does the second law always hold?" is treated by them like "Is baryon number conserved?" where, of course, the possibility of a negative answer is a real one. As long as they do not know why the second law holds, that is, as long as they do not understand the second law, this lack of confidence will infect the epistemology of NET. The eventual understanding of the second law is getting closer to hand as the cosmology of the big bang becomes better understood. All dissipative structures are symmetry breakings of one sort or another in the sense that systems that are earlier indistinguishable under certain transformations later become distinguishable under those same transformations as a consequence of getting caught in an attractor that may but need not be in the dimensions defining the earlier symmetry. This is part, of course, of what it means to talk of emergent structure. Whenever conditions are right (such as in the insides of stars) there is always enough noise for auto-organization into dissipative structures to take place. Conditions are renewably right because of the active stretchiness of the post big bang universe.

9. This point is made most clearly by Wicken (1987).

10. Again, the literature here has gotten very extensive. Very useful are Serra and Zanarini (1986), Cvitanovic (1984), and Grebogi, Ott, and Yorke (1987).

11. Particular controversy has surrounded Brooks and Wiley (1986).

12. See, for example, Semmler (1986), and Gabisch and Lorenz (1987).

REFERENCES

Adams, R.E. 1982. *Paradoxical Harvest*. Cambridge: Cambridge University Press.

Allen, P. 1985. "Ecology, Thermodynamics, and Self-organization: Towards a New Understanding of Complexity." In *Ecosystem Theory for Biological Oceanography*, edited by R. Ulanowicz and T. Platt. Ottawa: Department of Fisheries and Oceans.

Atlan, H. 1985. "Information Theory and Self-organization in Ecosystems." In *Ecosystem Theory for Biological Oceanography*, edited by R. Ulanowicz and T Platt. Ottowa: Department of Fisheries and Oceans.

Boulding, K. 1981. *Evolutionary Economics*. Beverly Hills, CA: Sage Publications.

Brooks, D.R., and E.O. Wiley. 1986. *Evolution as Entropy*. Chicago and London: The University of Chicago Press.

Cornell-Bell, A.H., S.M. Finkbeiner, M.S. Cooper, and S.J. Smith. 1987. "Glutamate Induces Calcium Waves in Cultured Astrocytes: Long-range Glial Signaling." *Science* 247:470-473.

Cvitanovic, P., ed. 1984. *Universality in Chaos*. Bristol: Adam Hilger.

Dyke, C. 1988. *The Evolutionary Dynamics of Complex Systems: A Study in Biosocial Complexity*. New York: Oxford University Press.

Ferracin, A., E. Panchelli, M. Benassi, A. DiNallo, and C. Steindler. 1978. "Self-organizing Ability and Living Systems." *Biosystems* 10:307-317.

Gabisch, G., and H-W. Lorenz. 1987. *Business Cycle Theory*. Berlin, Heidelberg, New York, Springer Verlag.

Georgescu-Roegen, N. 1971. *The Entropy Law and the Economic Process*. Cambridge, MA: Harvard University Press.

Grebogi, C., E. Ott, J. Yorke. 1987. "Chaos, Strange Attractors, and Fractal Basin Boundaries in Nonlinear Dynamics." *Science* 238.

Jacobs, J. 1984. *Cities and the Wealth of Nations*. New York: Random House.

Nicolis, G., and V. Altares. 1988. "Physics of Nonequilibrium Systems." Pp. 299-328 in *Synergetics and Dynamic Instabilities*, edited by G. Caglioti, H. Haken, and L. Lugiato. Amsterdam: North Holland.

Odum, H., and E. Odum. 1976. *Energy Basis for Man and Nature*. New York: McGraw Hill.

Prigogine, I. 1980. *From Being to Becoming*. New York: W.H. Freeman.

Samuelson, P.A. 1970. *Foundations of Economic Analysis*. New York: Atheneum.

Sears, F.W. 1950 1953. *Thermodynamics, The Kinetic Theory of Gases, and Statistical Mechanics*. Reading, MA: Addison-Wesley.

Semmler, W., ed. 1986. *Competition, Instability, and Nonlinear Cycles*. Berlin, Heidelberg, New York: Springer Verlag.

Serra R., and G. Zanarini. 1986. *Tra Ordine e Caos* Bologna: Editrice CLUB.

Shannon, C.E., and W. Weaver. 1949. *The Mathematical Theory of Information*. Urbana, Illinois Press.

Sraffa, P. 1960 1963. *Production of Commodities by Means of Commodities*. Cambridge: Cambridge University Press.

Vasiliev, V.A., Yu.M. Romanovskii, D.S. Chernavskii, and V.G. Yakhno. 1987. *Autowaves Processes in Kinetic Systems*. Dordrecht: D. Reidel Publishing Company.

Wicken, J. 1987. *Evolution Thermodynamics, and Information*. New York: Oxford University Press.

THE ETHICAL FOUNDATIONS OF
SUSTAINABLE ECONOMIC
DEVELOPMENT

R. Kerry Turner and David W. Pearce

ABSTRACT

The concept of sustainable economic development is used as a means of exploring the interface between environmental economics, human ecology and ethics. The conventional economic paradigm, illustrated by utilitarian benefit-cost analysis, is modified to allow for the concept of intergenerational equity. A 'constant natural assets' rule is introduced into the benefit-cost calculus, in order to establish the sustainability paradigm. Both efficiency and equity concerns can be encompassed by this modified paradigm. Although the sustainability analysis allows for non-utilitarian values, it is still anthropocentric in its focus. Our conception of the sustainability paradigm does not make allowance for intrinsic values in nature. Such values are part of what we call the bioethics paradigm. This paradigm we criticize on three grounds—it inhibits development and therefore may well be socially costly; it is potentially regressive in its impacts especially in the developing economy context; and it is redundant, since the modified sustainability approach can yield an acceptable level of environmental quality for current and future generations.

Advances in Human Ecology, Volume 1, pages 177-195.
Copyright © 1992 by JAI Press Inc.
ISBN: 1-55938-091-8

ALTERNATIVE PARADIGMS FOR CHOOSING BETWEEN CONSERVATION AND DEVELOPMENT

"Sustainable development" has become a catch-all phrase for forms of economic development which stress the importance of environmental quality and the conservation of Nature's assets (World Commission on Environment and Development 1987; Pearce et al. 1989; Turner 1988). Definitions of sustainable development abound (see the list given by Pearce et al. 1989), but our interest in the concept lies in its catalytic role as a means of exploring the interface between environmental economics, human ecology, and ethics. In this paper we establish the conventional economic paradigm for the evaluation of policies, programs and projects. We take the conventional paradigm to be illustrated by *benefit-cost analysis* in which efforts are made to compare gains and losses in utilitarian terms. A subsidiary requirement of benefit-cost procedures is that any given target for policy should be achieved at *minimum cost*. In turn, the minimum cost requirement favors the use of certain *economic* instruments which act primarily on *prices* in the economy.

We then relate the utilitarian benefit-cost paradigm to allow for a concept of intergenerational equity. We argue that true sustainable development involves compensating the future for damage being done now, and damage done in the past. Conspicuous examples include the storage of radioactive waste, damage to the ozone layer and the prospect of global warming. Compensation requires the passing-on to future generations of a stock of natural assets no smaller than the stock in the possession of current generations. This "constant natural assets" requirement produces modifications to the cost-benefit paradigm, notably by raising the implicit value of environmental impacts relative to "development." In this way, we suggest that a modified benefit-cost rule is capable of accommodating both the traditional *efficiency* concerns of economists and the intergenerational equity concerns of economists and noneconomists.

The economic paradigm, unmodified by the constant natural assets requirement, relates solely to values *of* human beings. It is utilitarian and *anthropocentric*. The *modified* paradigm, allowing for a constraint on the functioning of the economic system set by the requirement to maintain natural assets, relaxes the utilitarian bias. Constant natural assets reflects a moral imperative to care for the next generation, and this imperative is not readily interpreted in terms of utilitarian gains and losses. As a clear example, maintaining natural assets is wholly consistent with current generations bearing a cost, say X, which generates benefits for future generations of, say, 0.5X. The utilitarian rule would reject this "trade" because future benefits are less than the current sacrifice. The "constant natural assets" (CNA) rule could, however, be entirely consistent with the trade taking place. That is, current generations may have to bear higher costs than future gains in order to maintain constant natural assets. The modified paradigm, which we call the *sustainability paradigm*, thus allows for nonutilitarian values but remains anthropocentric: The "fairness" in question is fairness between people.

To relax the economic paradigm further involves making allowance for what ethicists would call "intrinsic" values in nature. These are *noninstrumental* values—that is, they do not necessarily provide any function or service to humans in order to be valuable. The values are "essential," that is, are *in* the assets in question rather than *of* human beings. Expanding the range of relevant values to intrinsic values results in what we call the *bioethics paradigm*. The economist's difficulty with intrinsic values is that due allowance for them in practical decision-making produces stultifying rules of behavior. Evaluating developments, for example, a proposal to drain a wetland for agricultural use, ceases to be an issue of comparing benefits and costs (the unmodified paradigm), or of debiting the development with the costs of creating alternative environmental assets of equal value (the modified paradigm). Rather it becomes one of maximizing the sum of instrumental and intrinsic values, or some variant of this rule. One such variant would be to "elevate" intrinsic value above instrumental value so that human society has to operate with technologies and products which use only the minimum of resources in order not to deplete intrinsic value more than is absolutely necessary. Such minimum intrinsic depletion rules risk wholly inequitable "trades," such as conserving intrinsic values now at the expense of social justice, and even survival if the context is that of poor developing countries.

The essential contrast, then, is between a modified economic paradigm, the sustainability paradigm, which allows for sustainability in the sense of intergenerational equity, and the bioethics paradigm which expands the objective function to be maximized to instrumental plus intrinsic values. Endless variations of these paradigms occur. The most notable is the "strong" bioethics view, or "deep ecology," which appears to raise the "worth" of intrinsic values above that of instrumental values (Naess 1973). In our view there is no prospect of relaxing the modified economics paradigm to embrace wholly the bioethics paradigm. However, we argue that by employing a CNA rule the *incidental* effect is to protect the very values that are of concern to the bioethicists. By protecting habitats, ozone layers, water quality and so forth, we protect the values that the bioethicists believe are in nature. Conservation of species, for example, entails conservation of habitats which in turn entails the avoidance of biogeographical "islands."

Deep ecologists will find this stance unacceptable since the moral ground, in their view, rests with those who intend to behave morally, not with those who happen to secure moral outcomes because they pursue other rules of behavior. We reject this claim to the moral high ground because of our belief that bioethics is consistent with the sacrifice of basic human values, including fundamental rights to exist at an acceptable standard of living. In short, we argue for the modified economic paradigm as a means of integrating economic efficiency and intergenerational equity. Our further belief is that the resulting "constant natural assets" rule has two incidental effects: (a) It protects the environments of the poorest communities in the world who depend directly on those environments for fuel, water and food; and (b) it protects the environments of sentient nonhumans and nonsentient things.

BENEFIT-COST PARADIGM

Within the central core of the sustainable development notion is the fact that economic systems are dependent on ecological foundations and ultimately on the maintenance of the global waste assimilation and life-support systems. The way humans manage their economies impacts on the environment and, in the reverse direction, environmental quality impacts on the working of the economy. Neither market-based economies nor planned economies are systems with in-built features that would guarantee sustainability. *A vital sustainable economics principle is that natural resources and environments are multifunctional and represent vast storehouses of economic value.* To treat some of these functions and services as if they had zero value (free goods) is seriously to risk over-use and destruction of the whole capital asset. It is therefore vitally important that the environment is valued correctly and that these values are integrated into economic policy.

Three environmental value relationships seem to underlie the policy and ethics adopted in industrialized economies: values expressed via individual preferences; public preference value; and functional physical ecosystem value (see Figure 1). At a fundamental level economic systems are dependent on ecological foundations and ultimately on the maintenance of the global waste assimilation and life-support systems. The long-run survival of human society depends on these functional requirements that are met by a set of social norms. Over time, if sustainability is the accepted policy goal, such norms must be consistent with the natural laws governing ecosystem maintenance.

The individuals in such economic systems are assumed to operate according to their own preferences within the context of physical requirements and social norms. Some analysts claim that there is a need to emphasize the intuitive environmental ethic which is present in society but which has remained largely dormant. A growing philosophical literature has sought to give rational and theoretical support to this intuitive ethic, as well as attempting to determine the content of the ethic. On the other hand, according to conventional economic theory, the value of all environmental assets is measured by the preferences of individuals for the conservation of those assets.

Figure 1.   Environmental Values

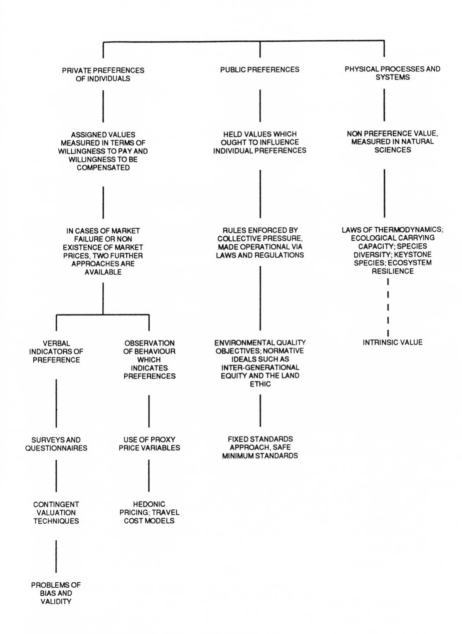

Source: Pearce and Turner (1990).

TOTAL ECONOMIC VALUE

Environmental economists have gone a considerable way toward a taxonomy of economic values as they relate to natural environments (Pearce and Turner 1990). The terminology is still not fully agreed, but the approach is based on the traditional explanation of how value occurs, that is, it is based on the interaction between a human subject (the valuer) and objects (things to be valued). Individuals have a number of held values which in turn result in objects being given various assigned values.

In order to arrive at a measure of total economic value, economists begin by distinguishing user values from intrinsic values. In a straight forward sense, user values derive from the actual use of the environment. Slightly more complex are values expressed through options to use the environment (option values). They are essentially expressions of preference (willingness to pay) for the preservation of an environment against some probability that the individual will make use of it at a later date. Provided the uncertainty concerning future use is an uncertainty relating to the "supply" of the environment, economic theory indicates that this option value is likely to be positive. A related form of value is bequest value, a willingness to pay to preserve the environment for the benefit of one's children and grandchildren.

Intrinsic values present more problems. They suggest values which are in the real nature of the thing but unassociated with actual use, or even the option to use the thing. Instead such values are taken to be entities that reflect people's preferences, but include concern for, sympathy with, and respect for the rights or welfare of nonhuman beings. Individuals may value the very existence of certain species or whole ecosystems. Total economic value is then made up of actual use value plus option value plus existence value. The contexts in which analysts are seeking to determine total economic values often contain the features of irreversibility, uncertainty (particularly in terms of ecosystem functions), and uniqueness. Economic theory indicates a precautionary or safety margin approach in such circumstances. Preservation or conservation of the natural assets will be relatively more favored in comparison to development.

A certain amount of progress has been made by economists attempting to determine empirical (monetary) measures of both environmental use values and nonuse values. None of the techniques that have been utilized are problem free but enough empirical work has been undertaken to indicate that humans do value the environment positively. Interestingly, nonuse values appear to be significantly positive. While the estimates made so far are subject to quite wide error margins, no one can doubt that the values uncovered are real and important.

THE BENEFIT-COST RULE

Consider the choice between developing, say, a wetlands area or preserving it: often a discrete choice problem because many commercial uses of the wetlands would destroy its preservation benefits (Turner 1991). Then, writing $PV(B_D)$ as the present value[1] of development benefits, $PV(B_p)$ as the present value of preservation benefits, $PV(C_D)$ as the development costs and $PV(C_p)$ as the direct costs of preservation (e.g., policing, maintenance and monitoring costs), the rule we have been using would indicate that we should develop the wetland if:

$$\{PV(B_D) - PV(C_D)\} > \{PV(B_p) - PV(C_p)\}$$

or

$$\{PV(B_D) - PV(C_D) + PV(C_p)\} > 0.$$

Dropping the PV notation for convenience, we know that we can also write:

$$B_p = TEV + OP + EXV$$
$$= AUV + OV + EXV,$$

where TEV is total economic value, OP is option price, EXV is existence value, AUV is the expected actual use value of the wetlands in its preserved form, and OV is the option value preservation. Option price is simply the sum of actual use value and option value.

Thus our rule for deciding on development becomes:

$$(B_D - C_D - C_p) > (OP + EXV).$$

In terms of measurability, it will be clear that development benefits, development costs and preservation costs are likely to be the subject of well-defined monetary estimates. This raises two immediate cautions. First, since OP and EXV are difficult to measure (difficult, not impossible), there is a danger of "misplaced concreteness." The things that can be measured might appear to be somehow more important than those which cannot be measured. This is a wise deduction, for the economic values embodied in nonmarket preferences are just as important as those embodied in market preferences. Second, because something is easy to measure it does not mean that the estimate is correct. It always pays to scrutinize the alleged development benefits. Ex post evaluations of development projects frequently show that development benefits are exaggerated at the time of the proposal: There is an in-built benefit "optimism" on part of the planners and developers. This bias, for example, has been present in energy planning with respect to nuclear power, and in the building of large hydroelectric dams. Another reason for bias is the underestimation of technological progress: As technology advances it tends to displace the technology that is generating the development benefit.

On the conventional economic model, then, values are anthropocentric and utilitarian. However, the logical inclusion of existence values raises the real possibility that the motivation for existence values is nonutilitarian. Thus, if existence values reflect concerns on behalf of nature, they may well be capturing part at least of what the bioethicist is calling intrinsic values. The current state of the art in economic valuation offers no real way of testing this proposition. One major authoritative review has argued that, while valuation techniques can secure reliable estimates of *TEV*, they cannot separate out the components of *TEV* (Mitchell and Carson 1989). For the moment, we simply speculate that existence values may encompass nonutilitarian values through the normal mode of revealed preference (Brookshire, Eubanks, and Sorg 1986).

THE MODIFIED ECONOMIC PARADIGM: SUSTAINABLE DEVELOPMENT DEFINING SUSTAINABLE DEVELOPMENT

Since "development" is a value word, implying change that is *desirable*, there is no consensus on its meaning. What constitutes development depends on what social goals are being advocated by the development agency, government, analyst or advisor (Pearce et al. 1989, 1990a, 1990b). We take development to be a *vector* of desirable social objectives, which might include increases in real income per capita, improvements in health and nutritional status, education achievement, access to resources, a "fairer" distribution of income, and increases in basic freedoms. The vector components are also readily expanded to include the "rights" of sentient nonhuman species.

Correlation between the vector elements, or an agreed system of weights to be applied to the elements, might permit development to be represented by a single "proxy" indicator, but this is not an issue pursued here.

Sustainable development is then a situation in which the development vector, D, increases monotonically over time, that is,

$$dD/dt > 0.$$

However, such a simple definition is not problem-free. For example, use of the term tends to imply the adoption of an infinite time horizon, whereas practical decision making requires adoption of some finite horizon. Nor does it tell us if dD/dt must be positive for each and every time period (which we might term *strong sustainability*), or whether only the trend of dD/dt must be positive (*weak sustainability*). For current purposes, sustainable development is better interpreted in its weak form as saying that dD/dt is *generally* positive over some selected time horizon.

Subject to the above caveats, we suggest that sustainability be defined as the general requirement that a vector of development characteristics be monotonically increasing over time, where the elements to be included in the vector are open to ethical debate, and where the relevant time horizon for *practical* decision making is similarly indeterminate outside of agreement on intergenerational objectives. This level of generality may seem unsatisfactory, but the essential point is that *what* constitutes development, and the *time horizon* to be adopted, are both ethically determined. Such an ethical debate can be illuminated by discussion of the alternative views on both issues, but it cannot be resolved other than by ethical consensus.

THE CONDITIONS FOR SUSTAINABILITY

Much of the sustainable development literature has confused definitions of sustainable development with the conditions for achieving sustainability. The preceding discussion suggests that the definition, the meaning, of sustainable development, is evident from the phrase itself. We now consider the necessary conditions for achieving sustainable development. These conditions, elaborated below, are not sufficient, however. A sufficient set of conditions is likely to include, for example, institutional requirements for implementing sustainable development policy, and may even require systematic changes in social values (O'Riordan 1988).

We summarize the necessary conditions as "constancy of the natural capital stock." More strictly, the requirement is for nonnegative change in the stock of natural resources such as soil and soil quality, ground and surface water and their quality, land biomass, water biomass, and the waste assimilation capacity of receiving environments.

The presumption that sustainability has something to do with nondepreciation of the natural capital stock is explicit in the Brundtland Report of 1987. Thus, "If needs are to be met on a sustainable basis the Earth's natural resource base must be conserved and enhanced" (World Commission on Environment and Development 1987, p. 57).

It is somewhat more vaguely embraced in the World Conservation Strategy in terms of maintaining "essential ecological processes and life support systems," "preserving genetic diversity," ensuring "sustainable utilisation of species and ecosystems" (IUCN 1980, Section I). Both sources offer rationales for conserving natural capital in terms of moral obligation and the alleged mutual interdependency of development and natural capital conservation. We offer our own rationale but before doing so we need to ask why the *existing* capital stock should be preserved, and what conserving the natural capital stock might mean.

EXISTING AND OPTIMAL CAPITAL STOCKS

Conserving the natural capital stock is consistent with several situations. The stock in question might be that which exists at the point of time that decisions are being taken—the *existing* stock—or it might be the stock that *should exist*. The latter is clearly correct in terms of the application of neoclassical economic principles to resource issues. The optimal steady state stock will be one for which any small increase in the stock will yield benefits just equal to the discounted costs of achieving the increase. Relevant to the cost calculation in this respect is the use to which the land or water resource might be put if it was not used to supply environmental capital. That is, to establish the optimal stock of natural assets it is necessary to engage in a cost-benefit analysis of changes in the stock of assets.

Two observations are in order on the use of optimal rather than existing capital stocks. First, existing stocks would generally be regarded as being below optimal stocks in many developing countries. For some Sahelian countries they are significantly below the optimum in that desertification actually threatens livelihoods (Falloux and Mukendi 1988). To some extent, therefore, deliberations about what precisely constitutes an optimum are redundant. Requiring that the existing natural capital stock be constant or increasing is consistent with the idea that one should move to an optimal capital stock, and has particular significance for poorer countries.

The second observation relates to the meaning of "optimum" in this context. To say that capital stocks "should" be optimal is tautologous. The interesting feature of optimality is how the benefits of augmenting natural capital are calculated. The critical factor here is, as we noted earlier, that the *multifunctionality* of natural resources needs to be recognized, including their role as integrated life support systems. Thus, a cost-benefit analysis that compares the "value" of, say, afforestation with the opportunity cost of land in terms of foregone development values, needs more careful execution than might otherwise appear to be the case. How far life-support functions such as contributions to geochemical cycles can be captured by cost-benefit analysis is open to question. In the face of uncertainty and irreversibility, conserving what there is could be sound risk-averse strategy.

There is a powerful case in analytical economics for thinking in terms of maintaining optimal rather than existing natural capital stocks as the basic condition for sustainability. In practice, and for poor countries dependent upon the natural resource base, optimal stocks will in any event be above the existing stock. In other cases there are rationales in terms of incomplete information (the failure to appreciate and measure multifunctionality), uncertainty and irreversibility for conserving the existing stock.

Conserving the natural capital stock serves goals which would command wide, though maybe not universal, assent. Sustainable development based on this notion is consistent with justice in respect of the socially disadvantaged, justice between generations, justice to Nature, and aversion to risk arising from our ignorance about the nature of interactions between environment, economy and society, and from the social and economic damage arising from low margins of resilience to external "shocks" such as drought and plagues, or to "stresses" such as soil erosion and agro-chemical residues.

INTRAGENERATION EQUITY

A constant or rising natural capital stock is likely to serve the goal of intragenerational fairness, that is, justice to the socially disadvantaged both within any one country and between countries at a given point in time. The clearest evidence for this exists for poor developing economies in which direct dependence on natural resources is paramount. Examples include reliance on biomass fuels such as fuelwood, crop residues, and animal waste; reliance on untreated water supplies; dependence on natural fertilizers (organic materials) to maintain soil quality; fodder from natural vegetation for livestock and wildlife meat for protein.

The equity function of natural capital is less obvious for developed economies. Indeed, the contrary view, that the demand for environmental assets is biased toward the rich, tends to define the conventional wisdom. However, the evidence for supposing that there is a higher income responsiveness of demand for environmental goods is distinctly unpersuasive (for a review see Pearce 1980). Additionally, the *physical* incidence of pollution—that is, exposure to air and water pollutants, solid waste and noise—appears inversely correlated with income (Berry 1977).

The general result, therefore, is that, as far as developing countries are concerned, environmental improvement is likely to be consistent with the goal of intragenerational equity, and very much so in the poorest agriculture-dependent economies. In the latter case the "environment-poverty trap" prevails: As poverty increases, natural environments are degraded to obtain immediate food supplies. As environments degrade so the prospects for future livelihoods decrease: Environmental degradation generates more poverty, thus accelerating the cycle. The provision of natural capital offers one way of breaking into the cycle.

INTERGENERATIONAL EQUITY

Although not intended for the purpose, Rawls' theory of justice offers a moral basis for arguing that the next generation should have access to at least the same resource base as the previous generation (Rawls 1972; Page 1977). Rawls' "maximum" strategy suggests that justice is to be equated with a bias in resource allocation to the least advantaged in society. Such a rule could emerge from a constitution drawn up by individuals brought together under a "veil of ignorance" about where in society they would be allocated. Risk aversion dictates that the constitution-makers would avoid disadvantaging certain groups for fear that they themselves would be allocated to these groups. The intergenerational variant of the Rawls outcome simply extends the veil of ignorance to the intertemporal context in which each generation is ignorant of the time period to which it will be allocated.

Interpreted this way there would appear to be no particular reason for focusing on *natural* capital as the instrument for achieving intergenerational equity. It might apply more to man-made capital or to some composite of both types of capital. There are some reasons for supposing that natural capital is more important, however. First, natural capital may qualify as a Rawlsian "primary good"—a good with the characteristic that any rational being would always prefer more of it to less. The life support functions of the natural environment would seem to fit this category since less of them would remove the very capability of choosing and having preferences. The ability to make a choice would, on this argument, have a higher ethical status than the rights and wrongs of making a particular choice. Moreover, natural capital differs from man-made capital in a crucial respect. Man-made capital is virtually always capable of symmetric variation—it can be increased or decreased at will. Natural capital is subject to *irreversibilities* in that it can be decreased but often not increased if previous decrements lead to extinction. The primary good and irreversibility features of natural capital thus suggest that natural and man-made capital are substitutes only to a limited extent.

SUSTAINABLE DEVELOPMENT AND THE BENEFIT-COST PARADIGM

We are now in a position to consider how the idea of sustainability can be incorporated into cost-benefit analysis. Benefit-cost analysis (BCA) embodies intuitive utilitarian rationality in that any course of action is judged acceptable if it confers a net advantage, that is, if "benefits" outweigh "costs." What constitutes a gain or loss depends on the objective function chosen. Most BCA operates with a function based on economic efficiency, that is, on the basis that a benefit is anything whereby more is preferred to less, and a cost is anything whereby less is preferred to more. But this is only *one* objective function. It is widely used because economic efficiency is embodied in the very structure of the welfare economics developed over the last century. In principle, however, any other objective function can be chosen, or, more profitably, a *set* of objectives can be chosen. Common parlance has it that BCA using more than one objective is termed "extended" BCA. Such terminology is neutral if the idea is to compare multi-objective CBA with the "norm," that is, CBA based on economic efficiency alone. It is misleading terminology if it is meant to imply that the basic structure of BCA is somehow overturned by the inclusion of other objectives. Indeed, integrating the sustainability objective into BCA can be shown to leave the basic structure of BCA intact, but the resulting modifications to the basic theorems are of interest, and, we suggest, of importance.

Sustainability can be introduced into the benefit-cost models through the idea of *compensating offsets*. Since the aim is to maintain a constant natural environment, any set of policies, projects or programs which damages the environment needs to be offset by a specific investment which restores natural or other environments to an equal value. The requirement is not that each project or activity should be obliged to restore the environment to its original state—that would be stultifying. Instead, by analysing an overall *portfolio* of investments it should be possible to detect the cumulative environmental impact and then identify offsetting environmental improvements. This use of offsetting projects defines the modified benefit-cost approach. Notice that the modified benefit cost rule becomes the instrument for achieving constant environmental assets. In turn, constant environmental assets afford protection for future generations, the poor of current generations who depend directly on natural assets, *and* the inhabitants of the spatial areas containing the natural capital. Moreover, the benefits relevant to this rule include the existence values earlier identified as the means whereby individuals reveal their concern for intrinsic values in the sense of the bioethicists. By these means, we argue, the modified benefit-cost rule achieves: (a) a comprehensive capture of anthropocentric values, and (b) the potential for capturing part at least of the intrinsic values identified by bioethicists.

Figure 2 summarizes the main ideas of sustainable development and their linkages to different value systems.

BIOETHICAL VALUES

The debate about the need for and content of a new environmental ethic highlighted supplementary and alternative measures of value (Turner 1988). It has been claimed that individuals have public preferences as well as private preferences and related assigned values. Public preferences are said to involve opinions and beliefs about what ought to be the case rather than individual desires or wants. They are the basis of social norms and legislation. It is still argued that all value is found in human loci, but it is not restricted to satisfactions of felt preferences of human individuals. Individuals may also hold "considered preferences" related to the public, group or community interest. For example, they may believe that the current generation has a generalized

Figure 2.   Sustainability Paradigm

SUSTAINABILITY PARADIGM	INTERDISCIPLINARY LINKING CONCEPTS AND THEMES
SUSTAINABLE ECONOMIC DEVELOPMENT PERSPECTIVE; BALANCE TO BE STRUCK BETWEEN RESOURCE CONSERVATION, SUSTAINABLE UTILISATION AND ECONOMIC DEVELOPMENT	ENVIRONMENTAL IDEOLOGIES: (ecocentrism versus technocentrism).
EFFICIENCY AND EQUITY WITHIN AND BETWEEN GENERATIONS; EFFICIENCY AND EQUITY OBJECTIVES ARE SECURED BY ACTUAL COMPENSATION; REJECTION OF POTENTIAL WELFARE CONCEPT.	ECONOMICS AND ETHICS: PARETO WELFARE, UTILITARIANISM, INTRAGENERATIONAL EQUITY, CONTRACTUALISM, INTERGENERATIONAL EQUITY, BIO-ETHICS.
ACTUAL COMPENSATION IS OPERATIONALIZED VIA THREE TYPES OF CAPITAL TRANSFER IN ORDER TO PASS ON A PORTFOLIO OF PRODUCTIVE OPPORTUNITIES OF EQUAL OR GREATER VALUE TO THE NEXT GENERATION:	ENVIRONMENTAL SCIENCE, CIRCULAR ECONOMY THERMODYNAMICS AND ENTROPY;

'CRITICAL' NATURAL CAPITAL   +   OTHER NATURAL CAPITAL   +   MAN-MADE CAPITAL

$$K_N^C < \text{VERY LIMITED SUBSTITUTION} > K_N < \text{GREATER SUBSTITUTION} > K_M$$

	ECOSYSTEM RESILIENCE AND THE LACK OF AN "EXISTENCE THEOREM" IN ECONOMICS: CRITICAL ECOSYSTEMS AND BIOSPHERE FUNCTIONS.

$K_N^C + K_N + K_M = $ TOTAL CAPITAL STOCK

GNP $- \Delta K_N = $ SUSTAINABLE INCOME FLOW

	NATIONAL INCOME AND NATIONAL RESOURCE ACCOUNTING.
BENEFIT-COST APPROACH (MODIFIED) VALUATION OF THE CAPITAL STOCK: TOTAL ECONOMIC VALUE = USE + OPTION + EXISTENCE; CONSUMER SURPLUS, EQUIVALENT AND COMPENSATING VARIATIONS, WILLINGNESS-TO-PAY AND WILLINGNESS-TO-ACCEPT COMPENSATION; VALUATION METHODS AND TECHNIQUES; TRAVEL COST, HEDONIC PRICING, CONTINGENT VALUATION ETC.	ENVIRONMENTAL VALUE RELATIONSHIPS: INSTRUMENTAL VERSUS INTRINSIC VALUE; UNCERTAINTY, IRREVERSIBILITY AND SUSTAINABILITY CONSTRAINTS, SAFE MINIMUM STANDARDS; SHADOW PROJECT APPROACH (COMPENSATING OFFSETS).
MANAGEMENT OF THE MULTIFUNCTIONAL NATURAL CAPITAL STOCK TO ENSURE SUSTAINABLE FLOW OF INCOME.	

obligation to maintain a stable flow of resources into the future (an inheritance of environmental and conventional goods and services) in order to ensure continuing human life, rather than just being concerned with meeting individual requirements.

More radically, some environmentalists believe that nature has inherent value which exists whether or not humans are around to sense and experience it. The "new naturalistic" ethical positions encompass this notion of inherent value in nature and go on to extend the moral reference class to nonhuman nature both animate and inanimate (see Figure 3).

An on-going debate has evolved among philosophers and environmentalists about the theoretical basis for "new naturalistic" ethics, as well as the content of the ethics. The extension of the moral reference class beyond human beings in the current generation opens up a multitude of complex questions. Our responsibilities toward future humans are difficult to discern because of, among other factors, the uncertainty surrounding the likely future consequences of economic activities undertaken in the present. Thus global warming may or may not be occurring and may or may not turn out to involve significant environmental and economic dislocation impacts. At the very least it would seem that the current generation has a duty to reduce uncertainty where feasible, by funding scientific monitoring and modelling resarch.

Assuming that it is possible to differentiate "critical natural capital" from other assets, the current generation has a duty under the sustainability paradigm, to try to ensure that the basic life-support systems of the planet and other high value environmental assets are not destroyed. But the degree and extent of future capital substitution possibilities are uncertain and will be determined by the rate of technical progress. The "constant natural assets" rule will involve trade-offs and so improved functional assessments and valuations of ecosystems will be required.

Future human preferences are also unknown but it seems likely that a grossly despoiled environmental quality would not be welcomed by our descendants. A balance is required between ignoring the future and allowing current wants and needs to be completely offset by the requirement to promote the well-being of those in the future. From the sustainability perspective the current generation's responsibility to future people extends indefinitely into the future, but the further it extends, the smaller is the present's share of that responsibility. The present has a duty to hand on to its immediate successors a set of assets sufficient to guarantee them a similar level of well-being and the capacity to discharge their obligation to all their successors (the "constant natural assets" rule).

Once the moral reference class has been opened up, however, it is difficult to know exactly where to logically stop the process. Figure 3 summarizes some of the positions that have received some support in the literature. The notion of environmental value (particularly the distinction between instrumental and

Figure 3.   Environmental Ethics

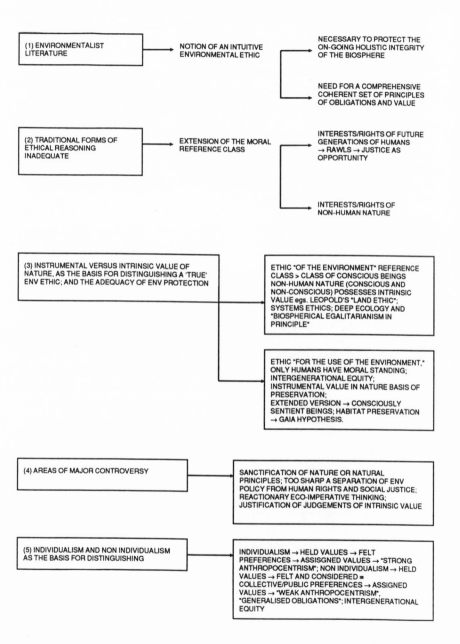

intrinsic value in nature) has become one focal point in the wider debate. The more radical ethical positions (ethics "of the environment") involve an acceptance of the idea that nonhuman nature (both conscious and nonconscious) be capable of being inherently valuable (that is, both possess intrinsic value (Regan 1981).

We have argued that an ethic "for the use of the environment," which restricts rights to humans and recognizes primarily only instrumental value in nature, can in any case offer sufficient environmental safeguards. More progress may be made if analysts turned their attention to the individualist basis of utilitarianism and conventional economics. Adopting a more collectivist approach would allow the recognition of "generalised obligations" (Norton 1987), obligations of the current generation to maintain a set of opportunities (our CNA rule) into the indefinite future, in order to ensure an adequate standard of human welfare, rather than just meeting individual requirements.

CONCLUSION

The issue of development versus conservation poses some of the most complex problems for modern environmental ethics. In this paper we have contrasted three broad paradigms for the decision-making process. The benefit-cost approach, rooted in utilitarianism, is an approach which evaluates the problem from the standpoint of economic efficiency. It does not, in its basic form anyway, consider other social objectives such as equity, duty or moral obligation. The benefit-cost approach is deliberately anthropocentric, but it does not exclude judgements on behalf of other species, the "stewardship" motive. The phenomenon of "existence value" identified and measured by environmental economists may well capture such values. The second paradigm identified was the modified benefit-cost approach which is derived from the concept of sustainable development. Sustainability requires, we argue, a commitment to the conservation of natural capital stocks. Benefit-cost analysis is modified through the idea of offsetting or compensating investments designed to compensate for cumulative damage done by investments which pass the orthodox benefit-cost test. In the current context, our interest in this rule lies in its role as a means of securing nonutilitarian values, including intergenerational equity, concern for the disadvantaged in current society, sentient nonhumans and nonsentient things. The protective nature of the rule is an incidental effect of its primary purpose—economic efficiency and intergenerational equity. Thirdly, the bioethical standpoint argues either for some broad equality between anthropocentric values and "intrinsic" values, or for "higher moral ground" for intrinsic values. Intrinsic values in this context are "in" beings and objects rather than "of" human beings. We argue against the bioethical standpoint on three grounds. It is stultifying of development and therefore has high social costs in terms of development benefits forgone. It is conducive to social injustice by defying development benefits to the poorest members of the community, now and in the future. It is redundant in that the modified sustainability approach generates many of the benefits alleged to accrue from the concern for intrinsic values.

NOTE

1. The "present value" refers to a single-valued estimate of the stream of net benefits over time. The means of "collapsing" the stream of values is through *discounting*.

REFERENCES

Berry, R.J. 1977. *The Social Burdens of Environmental Pollution*. Cambridge, MA: Ballinger.

Brookshire, D., L. Eubanks, and C. Sorg. 1986. "Existence Values and Normative Economics: Implications for Valuing Water Resources." *Water Resources Research* 22(11):1509-1518.

Falloux, F., and A. Mukendi, eds. 1988. *Desertification Control and Renewable Resource Management in the Sahelian and Sudanian Zones of West Africa."* World Bank Technical Paper No. 70. Washington DC: World Bank.

International Union for the Conservation of Nature (IUCN). 1980. *World Conservation Strategy*. Gland, Switzerland: IUCN.

Mitchell, R.C., and R.T. Carson. 1989. *Using Surveys to Value Public Goods: The Contingent Valuation Method*. Washington, DC: Resources for the Future.

Naess, A. 1973. "The Shallow and the Deep, Long-Range Ecology Movement: A Summary." *Inquiry* 16(1):95-100.

Norton, B.G. 1987. *Why Preserve Natural Variety?* Princeton, NJ: Princeton University Press.

O'Riordan, T. 1988. "The Politics of Sustainability." In *Sustainable Environmental Management: Principles and Practice*, edited by R.K. Turner. London: Belhaven Press, and Boulder, CO: Westview.

Page, T. 1977. *Conservation and Economic Efficiency*. Baltimore: Johns Hopkins University Press.

Pearce, D.W. 1980. "The Social Incidence of Environmental Costs and Benefits." In *Progress in Resource Management and Environmental Planning*, Vol. 2, edited by T. O'Riordan and R.K. Turner. Chichester: Wiley.

Pearce, D.W., E. Barbier, and A. Markandya. 1990a. *Sustainable Development*. Aldershot: Edward Elgar.

Pearce, D.W., A. Markandya, and E. Barbier. 1990b. "Environmental Sustainability and Cost Benefit Analysis." *Environment and Planning* A22: 1259-1266.

Pearce, D.W., A. Markandya, and E. Barbier. 1989. *Blueprint for a Green Economy*. London: Earthscan.

Pearce, D.W., and R.K. Turner. 1990. *Economics of Natural Resources and the Environment*. Hemel Hempstead: Harvester Wheatsheaf, and Baltimore: Johns Hopkins University Press.

Rawls, J. 1972. *A Theory of Justice*. Oxford: Oxford University Press.

Regan, T. 1981. "The Nature and Possibility of An Environmental Ethic." *Environmental Ethics* 3:19-34.

Turner, R.K., ed. 1988. *Sustainable Environmental Management: Principles and Practice*. London: Belhaven Press, and Boulder: Westview.

_____. 1988. "Wetland Conservation: Economics and Ethics." In *Economics, Growth and Sustainable Environments*, edited by D. Collard, D.W. Pearce, and D. Ulph. London: Macmillan.

_____. 1991. "Economics of Wetland Conservation." *Ambio* 20: 59-63.

THE ENERGY CONSUMPTION TURNAROUND AND SOCIOECONOMIC WELL-BEING IN INDUSTRIAL SOCIETIES IN THE 1980s

Marvin E. Olsen

ABSTRACT

Sociophysical energy flows constitute the dynamic linkage between basic ecological factors and the political economy of a society, and the "energetic theory of society" argues that energy use influences all aspects of social organization. Historically, energy use has been highly related to economic productivity and societal well-being. However, this "energy and society coupling thesis" has been challenged by recent studies which have discovered a fair amount of uncoupling among the industrialized nations. The research reported here examines that process among all the industrialized societies in the l980s, distinguishing between nations that have undergone an energy turnaround and now have decreasing rates of energy use and those that still have increasing rates. Three measures of energy use—per capita consumption, percentage rate of change in consumption, and energy intensity—are related to economic productivity and 20 indicators of social

Advances in Human Ecology, Volume 1, pages 197-234.
Copyright © 1992 by JAI Press Inc.
All rights of reproduction in any form reserved.
ISBN: 1-55938-091-8

well-being. Overall, energy consumption per capita is still moderately coupled with many forms of social well-being. Rates of change in energy use are becoming uncoupled, however, and high energy intensity is now totally uncoupled from societal well-being. Those patterns occur among both energy-decreasing and energy-increasing societies. These findings have theoretical implications for the "energetic theory of society" and policy implications for all industrial nations.

THEORETICAL CONTEXT

Energy Theorists

Although energy use has been studied extensively by environmental sociologists since the early 1970s, this topic has not received much attention from sociological ecologists. Duncan and Schnore's (1959) classical POET ecological model—Organization = f(Environment, Technology, Population)—does not include energy, and it is only briefly mentioned in Amos Hawley's (1986, pp. 111-112) most recent theoretical treatise on human ecology. Fred Cottrell has been the only sociological ecologist to give serious theoretical attention to the argument that "the energy available to man limits what he *can* do and influences what he *will* do" (italics in original; 1955, p. 2). Several ecological theorists in other fields have been concerned about the role of energy in society, however.

Anthropologist Leslie White (1949) attempted to formulate a general theory of societal evolution in which the amount of energy per capita available to a society and the technological efficiency of its use directly influence the level of development in that society.

Economist Nicholas Georgescu-Roegen (1971, 1976) has dealt primarily with the consequences of finite energy resources for modern economic systems. Attacking orthodox assumptions of continual economic growth, he has argued that economic production (and hence also energy consumption) depends ultimately on energy availability.

Biologist Howard Odum (1971, 1976) has based his work on the assumption that "any and every process and activity on earth is an energy manifestation measurable in energy units" (Odum 1971, p. 34). He has used an ecological system model to demonstrate the ways in which the activities of all living organisms, including humans, depend on energy flows from the natural environment.

Anthropologist Richard Adams (1975, 1988) takes energy as the fundamental factor in human life: "Everything in the environment of man is composed of energy forms and process and can be measured in terms of the energy that is potentially available for conversion or is being converted" (1975, p. 12). He views all forms of social organization as "dissipative structures" because they continually dissipate energy into the environment, and hence require a continual inflow of energy to maintain their existence.

Energy Theory

Theoretical Perspective

The principal theme running throughout all of these theoretical writings has been termed "the energetic theory of society" by Rosa and Machlis (1983). When applied to social change and development, that theme might be called "the energetic theory of societal evolution." It asserts that the broad process of societal development—the movement of societies through the ecological-economic stages of foraging, horticulture, agriculture, and industrialization—has been highly dependent on humanity's slowly increasing ability to generate and utilize inanimate energy. This theoretical perspective has been extensively reviewed and critiqued in four recent publications (Nader and Beckerman 1978; Olsen and Harris n.d.; Rosa and Machlis 1983; Rosa, Machlis, and Keating 1988).

The question remains, however, of how energy flows fit into basic social ecological processes. Rosa, Machlis, and Keating (1988, p. 155) offer a starting point with their observation that: "energy plays a crucial role, perhaps *the* crucial role, in the link between societies and their biophysical environments."

That argument was recently carried one step further by Olsen (1991, p. 111) in a model of the process of ecological evolution in which "sociophysical energy flows" (which always include social as well as physical components) constitute the dynamic linkage between the ecological factors of environment, technology, and population and the economy (or more broadly, the political economy) of a society. The interplay of those ecological factors generates flows of sociophysical energy—in such forms as natural resources, fuels, environmental knowledge, and human effort—that are transformed by the economy to provide or produce the goods and services used in a society.

From this theoretical perspective, "commercial energy" (Adams 1988)—which is the concern of this paper—is only one of several forms of energy flows within societies. This form of energy—obtained from oil, gas, coal, nuclear, water, and other sources—is nevertheless crucial for the functioning of the economy, for societal growth and development, and for the overall process of social organization. This "energetic perspective" has generated two arguments concerning the role of energy in societal development and well-being that have often been assumed to be antithetical, but which may not be. Since the purpose of this paper is to investigate these arguments and suggest that they are complementary, each of them is discussed at some length in the following sections.

The Coupling Thesis

This initial argument, which can be called the "coupling thesis of energy and societal development," asserts that societal modernization and subsequent well-being are tightly linked to the availability and use of energy. It can be expressed more explicitly as two causal propositions: (1) National economic productivity and growth requires a continually expanding supply of commercial energy. (2) Economic development is a necessary (but not sufficient) requirement for improving the socioeconomic well-being of a society. From these two propositions, the conclusion is drawn that continual energy expansion is essential for improving societal well-being.

The first proposition has long been viewed by many economists as virtually an axiom of economic development (Allen 1979; Schurr and Netscheret 1960). This generalization is strongly supported by the often-documented observation that the two variables of national energy use and Gross National Product (measured on either a total or per capita basis) are consistently correlated at about .95 across all nations. The second proposition has been supported by numerous studies of societal development that have discovered moderately strong correlations between GNP per capita and many diverse measures of national well-being (Isaac 1982; Jackman 1975; Olsen 1982), and also with a Quality of Life Index based on nearly sixty variables (Liu and Anderson 1979). In combination, these two propositions can be diagrammed as a linear process:

$$\text{Energy use} \rightarrow \text{Economic growth} \rightarrow \text{Societal well-being.}$$

The substantial empirical support that exists for both of these propositions has led some writers (e.g., Simon 1981) to make sweeping generalizations about the imperative necessity of constantly increasing our energy supply to ensure continual economic and social development throughout the world. As expressed by Ulf Lantzke, Executive Director of the International Energy Agency: "Energy is an essential component of the economic development and social progress of all nations" (International Energy Agency 1979).

The Uncoupling Thesis

This second argument, which can be called "the uncoupling thesis of energy and societal well-being," maintains that when societies become highly industrialized they no longer require constantly increasing energy consumption to improve the economic and social well-being of their citizens. In other words, energy consumption becomes "uncoupled" from socioeconomic well-being in these societies. This thesis thus challenges the applicability of both the propositions constituting the "coupling" argument in regard to highly industrialized societies, although its principal emphasis is on the overall linkage between energy use and societal well-being. The uncoupling thesis rejects the linear model of the coupling thesis in regard to highly industrialized nations, and implies a more complicated model in which several factors affect the level of social well-being, which might take either of the two forms as shown in Figure 1.

The uncoupling argument was implicit in several studies which found numerous similarities in levels of well-being among industrial societies despite great differences in their rates of energy use per capita (Darmstadter et al. 1977; Makhijani and Lichtenberg 1972; Schipper and Lichtenberg 1976). A number of other studies have specifically investigated this uncoupling thesis.

Previous Uncoupling Studies

Allan Mazur and Eugene Rosa (1974) examined the relationships between energy consumption per capita and a wide variety of economic, health, education, and other indicators of well-being in 19 highly industrialized nations with market economies, as well as across all nations. For the world as a whole, there were—as expected—fairly strong correlations (.40 or higher) between energy consumption and 26 of their 28 well-being indicators. When they focused on only the highly industrialized societies, the correlations for four of their five "economic" indicators were still quite strong. However, among all the other 23 well-being indicators, only seven were related to energy consumption at .40 or higher. They tentatively concluded that: "Of the life-style indicators examined here, only the economic indicators show a consistently high association with energy consumption" (1974, p. 609). In a later paper, Rosa et al. (1988, pp. 158-59) observed that:

> This counterintuitive finding, embarrassing to the conventional wisdom of the time, contained a key strategic and planning implication; so long as their consumption did not drop below that of other industrial societies, high energy consuming societies like the United States could reduce [their] energy demand[s] without serious deterioration to [their] general well-being.

Frederick Buttel (1978, 1979) repeated the Mazur and Rosa study, but with several methodological modifications. He (1) included 25 countries with "developed market economies"; (2) used "energy intensity" rather than energy consumption as the indicator of national energy use (which is the amount of energy used per U.S. dollar of GNP); (3) examined a larger set of 50 indicators of what he called "social welfare," as well as several measures of national socioeconomic development; (4) collected data for three points in time (1955, 1965, and 1970); (5) analyzed the relationships of both energy intensity and GNP with social welfare, both separately and jointly in multiple regressions; and (6) calculated those relationships for the three points in time and for their rates of change between 1955 and 1970.

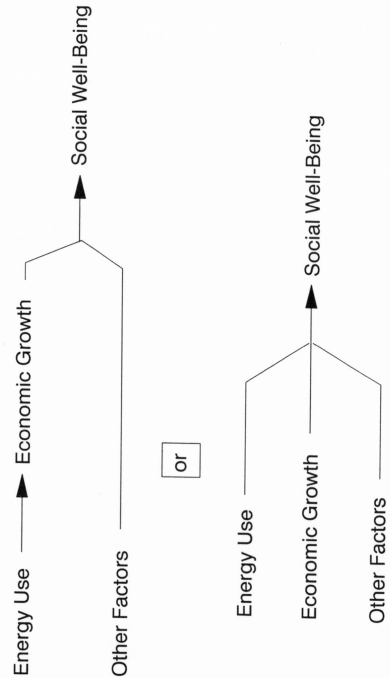

Figure 1. Two Models for the Uncoupling Thesis

The first proposition of the coupling thesis—that economic productivity depends on energy use—was not substantiated for these societies in regard to energy intensity, since that correlation was not significant (although it was .68 for a more inclusive set of 118 nations at all levels of economic development). Energy intensity was also unrelated to the degree of urbanization in the developed societies. The second proposition of that thesis—that societal well-being depends on economic productivity—was only modestly substantiated. For instance, GNP per capita was significantly correlated with only 10 of the 50 indicators of social welfare in 1970, and with just 3 of 27 rates of change in the GNP.

In regard to the overall linkage between energy intensity and social welfare, Buttel found that only 8 of the 50 possible correlations for 1970 were statistically significant, and only 7 of the 27 possible correlations for rates of change between 1955 and 1970 achieved significance. Five of those relationships—for both 1970 and change between 1955-1979—were with measures of health and health care. And all of those relationships were inverse, indicating that health and health care tended to improve as energy intensity decreased. (Of the ten indicators of social and economic inequity included in that study, none was significantly correlated with energy intensity.)

When each of the social welfare measures was regressed on both energy intensity and GNP per capita simultaneously, the betas for energy intensity in 1970 (holding constant the effects of GNP) were significant for 10 of the 50 social welfare measures. Four of those continued to be inverse relationships with health and health care measures. The others were direct positive relationships with educational expenditures as a percentage of GNP, newspaper circulation per capita, and televisions per capita; and direct negative relationships with suicides per capita, homicides per capita, and frequency of internal war. The betas for rate of change in energy intensity were significant for just four of those 27 measures: telephones per capita, and manufacturing work hours per week (positive), and divorces per capita and homicides per capita (negative).

On the basis of these findings, Buttel (1979, p. 315) concluded that:

> The link between energy use—conceptualized and measured in terms of energy intensity—and quality of life is less pronounced than often assumed by many observers of the advanced industrial societies. More specifically, both cross-sectional and longitudinal data indicate that reduced aggregate energy intensities of production and consumption need not result in a massive deterioration of the quality of life. Indeed, industrial societies with low energy intensities frequently exhibit more favorable social welfare conditions than those with higher energy intensities.

Eugene Rosa, Allen Radzik, and Kenneth Keating (1980) and Rosa, Keating, and Clifford Staples (1981) conducted a relatively similar study, examining 25 industrial countries with market economies and using 36 indicators of societal well-being. The unique feature of this research was that it collected longitudinal data for a 25-year period (1950, 1955, 1960, 1965, 1970, and 1975). Their measure of energy use was consumption per capita, not energy intensity.

One of the most interesting findings to emerge from this study was that the correlation between energy consumption and GNP per capita remained quite high (between .75 and .82) from 1950 to 1970 but was only .53 in 1975, suggesting that economic production was starting to become uncoupled from energy use in the industrial countries at that time. Of the 36 well-being indicators, only 8 displayed consistently significant correlations with energy consumption across that 25-year period: one health measure, three nutrition measures, newspaper circulation, radios, telephones, televisions (beginning in 1960), and divorces. The study did not include any regression analyses. Rosa, Radzik, and Keating (1980, p. 19) concluded that: "There appears to be little relationship between levels of energy consumption in the advanced industrial societies and a wide range of indicators of societal well-being. What is more, this lack of relationship is generally consistent for the twenty-five year period of our study."

Unresolved Concerns

These previous studies leave two methodological questions and two theoretical issues unresolved.

Methodological Questions

First question. Since none of them included measures of both energy consumption per capita and energy intensity, how are these two different energy use measures differentially related to economic production and societal well-being? To answer that question, the research reported here included both of those energy measures.

Second question. Since all of the previous studies were limited to highly industrialized nations with market economies, what happens to the relationships between energy use and economic productivity and with various social well-being indicators when industrialized nations with socialist economies are included in the study? That could be done in the research reported here because data from those countries (except Albania) are now available for many economic and social variables, although in some cases these are essentially informed estimates.

Theoretical Issues

First issue. What happens to all of these possible linkages when societies begin to reduce their energy use? All of the previous studies were conducted prior to 1980, during a time when all industrial nations were still increasing their energy use every year. Since 1980, however, a number of industrial societies—most notably the United States and Canada—have undergone an "energy consumption turnaround" that has (at least temporarily) halted the long-established pattern of continual expansion in energy use.

Consequently, *the principal objective of the study reported here is to discover what happened to the linkages between energy use and both economic productivity and social well-being in the highly industrialized nations during the 1980s, with particular attention to those countries that have experienced declining rates of energy use.* Have economic productivity and social well-being become even further uncoupled from energy use among all highly industrialized societies in recent years, or are new patterns of "coupling" beginning to emerge? And do those patterns differ between energy-decreasing and energy-increasing nations?

Second issue. This issue concerns the apparent contradiction between the coupling and uncoupling theses. The inference that can be drawn from the results of the previous studies is that the coupling thesis—which tends to be supported by data for all nations across all levels of economic development—pertains essentially to the change from an agricultural to an industrial type of economy. Because the process of societal industrialization involves a massive increase in energy use, when both developing and industrialized nations are included in the sample energy consumption is fairly highly correlated with many measures of societal well-being that are associated with a rising Gross National Product. As expressed by Rosa, Radzik, and Keating (1980): "It may be that high energy inputs are essential to becoming an industrial society, and this is why strong correlations [between energy consumption and social well-being] occur in samples that include both nonindustrial and industrial nations" (1980, p. 11).

If that inference is correct, the uncoupling thesis may apply to the highly industrialized societies without contradicting the coupling thesis. The uncoupling thesis would instead be a narrower specification of the broader coupling thesis. This possibility was implied by Rosa, Machlis, and Keating (1988, p. 159) in these words: "While a threshold level of high energy consumption is probably necessary for a society to achieve industrialization and modernity, once achieved, there is wide latitude in the amount of energy needed to sustain a high standard of living."

The study reported here does not directly address this inference concerning the applicability of the coupling and uncoupling theses, although its findings are compatible with that inference. Further research now being conducted will directly address this issue.

Organization of the Paper

As background for the investigation of the uncoupling thesis among all highly industrialized nations that is reported in this paper, the next section contains a detailed examination of the situation in the United States during the 1980s. There are two reasons for this initial focus on the United States: (1) Because this country consumes 32% of the world's energy supply (despite containing less than 5% of the world's population) its energy use has much greater effects on world energy patterns than any other single country. (2) It was the first country to undergo a significant energy turnaround.

The following section presents a comparative analysis of the relationships during the same period between energy use (both energy consumption and energy intensity) and (1) economic productivity, and (2) socioeconomic well-being among 30 highly industrialized societies. It includes separate analyses of energy-decreasing and energy-increasing nations.

The final section of the paper discusses some theoretical and policy implications of the research findings.

THE UNITED STATES

Energy Use

Historically, energy use in the United States increased constantly throughout the nineteenth century and during much of the twentieth century. The nation experienced a turnaround in its energy intensity rate in 1971, however, and a turnaround in both its total and per capita consumption rates in 1980. Although its total energy consumption has recently been rising again, both the energy intensity and per capita consumption rates presently remain considerably lower than in their peak years of 1970 and 1979.

Table 1 reports total energy consumption (in quadrillion BTUs), per capita energy consumption (in million BTUs), and energy intensity (in thousand BTUs per dollar of GNP in constant 1987 dollars) in the United States between 1960 and 1987 (the last year for which data are presently available).[1] Total energy consumption declined to a low point of 70.5 quadrillion BTUs in 1983, but since then has slowly risen back up to its 1980 level of 76.0 quads. At this time, therefore, we cannot tell whether future amounts of energy use in the United States will remain below the 1979 peak or whether they will resume their historical pattern of annual increases. Per capita energy consumption was also lowest in 1983 and has since gone back up slightly, but in 1987 it was still considerably below the 1979 peak. The energy intensity rate, however, continued to decline steadily, and in 1987 was lower than ever before.

Table 1. United States Energy Consumption between 1960 and 1978; Total, Per Capita, and Per Dollar of GNP in 1987 Dollars

	Energy Consumption		
Year	Total Quad. BTUs	Per Capita Mil. BTUs	Per $1 GNP Thous. BTUs
1960	43.8	243	30.8
1965	52.7	272	29.5
1970	66.4	326	32.2 (High)
1975	70.5	327	30.7
1979	78.9 (High)	351 (High)	28.9
1980	76.0	335	27.8
1981	74.0	322	26.7
1982	70.8	305	26.0
1983	70.5 (Low)	301 (Low)	25.2
1984	74.1	313	24.8
1985	74.0	310	24.0
1986	74.3	308	23.4
1987	76.0	312	23.3 (Low)
Change 1980-87	0.0%	−4.3%	−16.2%

Economic Productivity and Social Well-Being

Table 2 presents data for a wide variety of economic productivity and social well-being indicators for the United States in 1980 and 1987, to show what happened in the country during this period of declining per capita and energy intensity use.[2] We see in this table that the Gross National Product—both total and per capita—increased more than 16% during that seven-year period. Because of this economic growth, the energy intensity rate (energy used per dollar of GNP) declined steadily despite small increases in total national energy use.

Among the demographic factors, small declines occurred in both the crude birth and crude death rates, and the infant mortality rate dropped by over 17%. Life expectancy at birth increased by 1.6 years, but the suicide rate rose more than 11%.

Expenditures for health care increased by a huge 33% in real dollars, but it is not obvious whether this was an increase or decrease in well-being. The availability of hospital beds declined, but so did the average number of days that an individual was confined to bed. The situation with education presents a paradox. On the one hand, expenditures per capita in real dollars fell by more than 29%. On the other hand, the amount of education received by the population rose dramatically—in terms of median years of schooling, percentage of high school graduates, and percentage of college graduates. The explanation for this situation may lie in a fairly rapid dying off of poorly educated older people, rather than any drastic increase in school enrollments

Table 2.   Indicators of Economic Productivity and Social Well-Being in
the United States in 1980 and 1987

Indicator	1980	1987	% Change
Gross National Product in million 1987 $	3,884	4,529	+16.6
GNP per capita in thousand 1987 $	16.0	18.6	+16.3
Crude birth rate per 1000 population	15.9	15.7	−1.2
Total fertility rate (children per woman)	1.84	1.84	0.0
Crude death rate per 1000 population	8.8	8.7	−1.1
Infant mortality rate per 1000 live births	12.6	10.4	−17.5
Life expectancy at birth	73.7	74.9	+1.6
Suicide rate per 1000 population	11.9	12.8	+11.2
Percent of population in metropolitan areas	76.1	76.9	+1.0
Health expenditures per capita in 1986 $	1,381	1,837	+33.0*
Hospital beds per 1000 population	59.9	52.6	−12.2
Bed disability days per capita per year	7.0	6.5	−7.1
Educational expenditures per capita in 1987 $	1,000	706	−29.4
Median years of school completed	12.5	12.7	+1.6
Percent of people high school graduates	66.5	75.6	+13.7
Percent of people college graduates	16.2	19.9	+22.8
Unemployment rate (percent of labor force)	7.0	6.1	−12.9
Social welfare expenditures per capita in 1986 $	2,834	3.189	+12.5*
Personal income per capita in thousand 1987 $	13.7	15.5	+13.2
Disposable income per capita in thousand 1987 $	11.6	13.2	+13.2
Median family income in thousand 1987 $	29.0	30.9	+6.6
Median household income in thousand 1987 $	24.4	26.0	+6.6
Percent of families with median income over $50,000 in 1987 $	17.5	22.9	+30.9
Percent of total family income received by those in the bottom quintile	5.1	4.6	−9.8
Percent of individuals below poverty line	13.0	13.5	+3.8
Number of automobile per 1000 population	273	257	−5.9
Total research and development expenditures per capita in 1987 $	377	483	+28.1

Note: * Figures are for 1986.

and completions. The unemployment rate dropped slightly, while total expenditures for social welfare programs increased somewhat.

Aggregate income figures (derived from the GNP) increased more than 13%, reflecting the growth of the economy during this period. Median family and household incomes also increased, but only by 6.6%. The proportion of families receiving more than $50,000 annual income (in 1987 dollars), expanded more than 30%. At the same time, the proportion of people below the official poverty line increased nearly 4%, and the proportion of all income received by the lowest income quintile declined by nearly 10%. In other words, while many people were somewhat better off financially in 1987 than in 1980, the income distribution became more bifurcated.

The number of cars per capita increased slightly, but travel by commercial airlines nearly doubled during that time span. The number of telephones per capita rose somewhat, while newspaper circulation per capita declined slightly.

Finally, total expenditures for all research and development activities grew by 28% during those seven years.

With a few glaring exceptions—such as the rising suicide rate and the drop in educational expenditures—the economic productivity and social well-being of American society (as measured by the indicators in this study) did not deteriorate during the 1980s, despite declining per capita energy consumption and energy intensity. And in many realms the national well-being appears to have improved at least moderately during that period. We can therefore conclude that *the United States has largely uncoupled both economic productivity and social well-being from energy consumption*—although there is no guarantee that this will continue during the 1990s and beyond.

THE INDUSTRIAL NATIONS

Procedures

The United States has been able to uncouple energy consumption from most aspects of social life, but to what extent has this also occurred in other industrialized societies? To answer that question, this section reports the results of an analysis of all the highly industrialized nations. The designation of "highly industrialized" is made by the United Nations on the basis of the proportion of the GNP originating in industry and the GNP per capita. At the present time, 35 nations are included in that category. However, the four countries with populations of less than one million—Cyprus, Iceland, Luxembourg, and Malta—were omitted from this analysis, and Albania had to be eliminated because of extensive missing data.

Otherwise, all of the Eastern European nations that had socialist economies are included. The N for this study is therefore 30 nations. GNP data were obtained for all of them, but data were missing for some countries on several of the well-being indicators. When data were missing for a specific variable, those countries were deleted from that correlation and the reduced *N*'s are noted below.

Energy Measures

The energy measures used in this analysis are the following: (1) total energy consumption in 1980 and 1987, expressed in million metric tons of coal equivalent; (2) energy consumption per capita in 1980 and 1987, expressed in kilograms of coal equivalent; (3) percent change in per capita energy consumption between 1980 and 1987; and (4) energy intensity in 1980 and 1987, expressed in metric tons of coal equivalent per million current U.S. dollars of GNP.[3] (Data for percent change in energy intensity between 1980 and 1987 are presently being calculated by the World Bank but are not yet available, and could not be determined from other existing data because the U.S. inflation rate cannot be applied to other currencies to convert 1980 GNP figures into equivalent 1987 figures.)

Economic Measures

The economic productivity measures used are: (1) total Gross National Product (GNP) in 1980 and 1987, expressed in billion 1987 U.S. dollars; (2) average annual percentage change in real GNP between 1980 and 1987; (3) GNP per capita in 1980 and 1987, expressed in 1987 U.S. dollars; (4) average annual percentage change in real GNP per capita between 1980 and 1987; and (5) percent change in industrial production between 1980 and 1987.[4]

Well-Being Measures

Twenty different measures of societal well-being are used in the analysis, covering most of the areas examined in previous studies. These particular measures were selected because of their substantive importance for industrial nations and because relatively recent data were available for them. (Unfortunately, no current data are available for any measures of socioeconomic inequality.) The data used were the most current available, which is generally for 1985, 1986, or 1987. These measures, arranged by categories, are the following:[5]

Demographic measures:
Crude birth rate per 1000 population
Total fertility rate, or mean number of children per woman
Crude death rate per 1000 population
Infant mortality rate per 1000 live births
Life expectancy at birth
Suicide rate per 1000 population ($N = 23$)

Urbanization measure:
Percent of the population living in urban places, as defined by each country

Health measures:
Expenditures per capita for health care in US dollars ($N = 21$)
Hospital beds per 1000 population
Percent of private expenditures on items other than food ($N = 25$)
Calories consumed per person per day ($N = 29$)

Education measures:
Public expenditures for education as a proportion of the GNP
Percent of the population age 25 or older with some amount of post-secondary schooling ($N = 26$)
Students enrolled in third-level schools per 1000 population

Communications measures:
Telephones per 1000 population
Television sets per 1000 population
Newspaper circulation per 1000 population

Transportation measure:
Automobiles per 1000 population

Other governmental spending measures:
Expenditures for all nonmilitary purposes, as a proportion of the GNP ($N = 28$)
Expenditures on all research and development activities as a proportion of the GNP ($N = 26$)

The statistics used throughout the analysis are ordinary least-squares correlation and multiple regression. For the bivariate correlations, tests of statistical significance are not strictly applicable, since the correlations are for populations of industrial nations, not samples. However, because of the small Ns in this study, statistical significance at the .05 level (one-tailed) is reported. Since a coefficient must be at least .40 to .50 to attain significance in most of those relationships, statistical significance can serve as a rough indicator of correlations that are strong enough to be considered substantively important. The beta coefficients obtained in multiple regressions are considered statistically significant if their unstandardized B coefficient is at least twice as large as their standard error.

National Energy Use

The 30 highly industrialized countries included in this study are listed in Table 3, together with their population in 1987 in millions, energy consumption per capita in both 1980 and 1987 in 100 kilograms of coal equivalent, percent change in energy consumption between 1980 and 1987, GNP per capita in 1987 in U.S. dollars, and energy intensity in 1987 in metric tons of coal equivalent per million 1987 U.S. dollars.

For all 30 countries, the mean growth in per capita energy consumption from 1980 to 1987 was 4.5%. However, 10 countries reduced their consumption and hence experienced an energy turnaround: Austria, Belgium, Canada, Czechoslovakia, France, West Germany, Poland, Spain, Sweden, and the United States. The other 20 countries increased their energy consumption per

Table 3. Highly Industrialized Nations Included in the Study, with their 1987 Population, Energy Consumption Per Capita in 1980 and 1987, Percent Change in Energy Consumption Per Capita between 1980 and 1987, Gross National Product Per Capita in 1987, and Energy Intensity in 1987

Country	Population in Millions 1987	Energy Consumption Per Capita in 1000 Kg of Coal Equivalent			GNP Per Capita in U.S. Dollars 1987	Energy Intensity in Tons of Coal Equivalent Per U.S. Dollar 1987
		1980	1987	% Change		
Australia	16.2	6.2	6.9	+10.5	11.2	608
Austria	7.6	4.1	4.0	−1.0	12.0	331
Belgium	9.9	6.0	5.6	−7.3	11.5	488
Bulgaria	9.0	5.3	5.9	+12.6	6.7	885
Canada	25.9	10.6	9.9	−5.9	15.1	658
Czechoslovakia	15.6	6.4	6.3	−0.1	9.0	701
Denmark	5.1	5.3	5.4	+1.9	14.9	360
Finalnd	4.9	5.5	5.7	+3.3	14.7	391
France	55.6	4.4	3.7	−15.6	12.9	288
Germany, East	16.7	7.3	7.9	+8.4	10.9	721
Germany, West	61.0	5.8	5.6	−3.6	14.4	387
Greece	10.0	2.1	2.5	+17.2	4.0	613
Hungary	10.6	3.8	3.8	+0.8	2.2	1688
Ireland	3.5	3.3	3.4	+5.8	6.3	568

Israel	4.4	2.3	2.8	+22.9	10.4	381
Italy	57.4	3.1	3.6	+14.8	10.4	342
Japan	122.2	3.7	3.7	+0.3	15.8	236
Netherlands	14.6	6.5	7.2	+11.0	11.8	613
New Zealand	3.3	3.2	3.9	+22.2	7.9	488
Norway	4.2	6.4	6.8	+5.6	17.5	388
Poland	37.8	4.9	4.8	−2.6	1.9	2593
Portugal	10.3	1.1	1.3	+15.7	2.9	469
Romania	22.9	4.5	4.6	+2.4	5.7	815
Spain	39.0	2.4	2.1	−10.6	6.0	352
Switzerland	6.6	3.6	3.9	+4.1	21.3	178
USSR	284.0	5.5	6.6	+19.4	8.4	783
United Kingdom	56.8	4.9	5.1	+5.4	10.5	485
United States	243.8	10.4	9.5	−8.2	18.6	513
Yugoslavia	23.4	2.1	2.4	+13.5	2.5	978
All 30 countries	1,191	4.87	5.00	+4.5	7.9	621

capita. For some of the analyses, the countries are divided into two sets: Set I = 10 energy-decreasing nations, and Set II = 20 energy-increasing nations. This enables us to determine if those countries that have undergone an energy turnaround differ in economic productivity and social well-being from those that have not.

Energy intensity figures vary enormously among these 30 countries, from 178 metric tons of coal equivalent per dollar of GNP for Switzerland to 2593 for Poland, with a mean of 621. In general, the Eastern European nations have much greater energy intensities than the other industrialized nations.

Energy Use and Economic Productivity

Eight types of relationships between various energy use and economic productivity measures were examined. In addition, for the 1987 and percent energy change measures, separate correlations were calculated for the energy-decreasing and energy-increasing nations. All of those correlations are reported in Table 4, with statistically significant correlations indicated by an asterisk.

These findings tell us—across all 30 highly industrialized countries—that total energy use was still tightly linked with total GNP in both 1980 and 1987, with r's of .95. Moreover, in 1987 that correlation was even higher among the energy-decreasing nations (.99) than among the energy-increasing nations (.89). However, energy consumption per capita has become partly uncoupled from GNP per capita, since those r's are only .49 in both years. (Rosa et al. [1980] had previously discovered that this uncoupling began in 1975, when the corresponding correlation was .53, whereas in 1970 it had been .82.) Surprisingly, that uncoupling is more pronounced among the energy-increasing countries (.42) than among the energy-decreasing countries (.58). This may partly be due to the fact that the United States and Canada—with their very high energy consumption rates and relatively high GNPs—are both in the energy-decreasing category. Although through time they have both moved in the direction of uncoupling economic productivity from energy consumption, at any specific point in time (e.g., 1980 or 1987) their high rates on both those measures have disproportional effects on cross-national correlations.

The relationship between the percentage change in energy consumption per capita and the average annual percentage growth in real GNP per capita between 1980 and 1987 is different for energy-decreasing and energy-increasing nations. Among the energy-decreasing countries, the negative correlation (−.33) indicates that the greater their rate of decrease in energy consumption, the less their rate of GNP growth. Although this coefficient is not large enough to be statistically significant, it suggests that energy consumption and economic productivity are still somewhat linked in these countries. Among the energy-decreasing countries, meanwhile, the significant negative correlation (−.54) indicates that the greater the rate of increase in energy consumption, the less

Table 4. Correlations between Energy Use and Economic Productivity Among All 30 Highly Industrialized Nations and Among Energy-Decreasing and Energy-Increasing Nations

Measures	All Industrial Nations	Energy- Decreasing Nations	Energy- Increasing Nations
Total energy use and total GNP in 1980	.95*	—	—
Total energy use and total GNP in 1987	.95*	.99*	.89*
Energy use per capita and GNP per capita in 1980	.49*	—	—
Energy use per capita and GNP per capita in 1987	.49*	.58*	.42*
Percent change in energy use per capita and percent change in GNP per capita 1980-1987	—	−.35	−.54*
Percent change in energy use per capita and percent change in industrial productivity 1980-1987	—	−.23	−.39
Energy intensity and GNP per capita in 1980	−.55*	—	—
Energy intensity and GNP per capita in 1987	−.61*	−.68*	−.69*

Note: * Statistically significant at .05 one-tailed.

the economic growth. In these countries, economic productivity is no longer linked with increasing energy use. Instead, increasing energy consumption rates are apparently hurting their economies.

That same pattern also occurs between the percentage change in energy consumption per capita and the percentage change in the rate of industrial productivity, although these correlations are weaker and not significant for either set of nations. (Correlations between changes in energy consumption and GNP would not be meaningful across all 30 countries, since for some of them that change was positive while for others it was negative, and the coefficients would ignore that critical distinction.)

Finally, energy use intensity was significantly but inversely related to GNP per capita in both 1980 and 1987 at about the same strength (−.55 and −.61, respectively). And in 1987 that inverse relationship occurred among both sets of countries. In other words, the smaller the amount of energy use associated with each dollar of GNP, the larger the GNP per capita, which appears logical. It should be noted, however, that Buttel (1979) found that in 1965 this relationship was direct although trivial (.09) for 25 industrial nations with market economies. The inverse relationship observed here may be due at least partly to the inclusion of the Eastern European countries in the sample, which generally have high energy intensities and low GNP's per capita.

Economic Productivity and Social Well-Being

On the basis of previous research, we would expect that Gross National Product per capita should be significantly related to most of our measures of

Table 5.   Correlations between Gross National Product Per Capita and Social
Well-Being Indicators among all 30 Highly Industrialized Nations

Social Well-Being Indicators	Correlation Coefficients
Crude birth rate	−.27
Total fertility rate	−.45
Crude death rate	−.15
Infant mortality rate	−.68
Life expectancy	.69
Suicide rate	.02
Urban residents	.43
Health care expenditures	.81
Hospital beds	.36
Nonfood expenditures	.81
Calories consumed	−.28
Educational expenditures	.46
Postsecondary education	.31
Third-level enrollment	.59
Telephone ownership	.84
Television ownership	.63
Newspaper circulation	.61
Automobile ownership	.70
Nonmilitary expenditures	.30
R&D expenditures	.36

social well-being. Those correlations for all 30 countries in 1987 are given in
Table 5.

All of these relationships are in the expected direction, with two exceptions:
(a) the suicide rate, for which there is essentially no correlation; and (b) the
number of calories consumed per person per day, which is weakly but inversely
related to GNP per capita. (In all these societies, the average calories consumed
is quite sufficient [between 2900 and 3800 per person per day], but in several
societies with relatively high GNPs [e.g., Japan, Norway, Sweden] the average
calorie consumption is somewhat less than in other societies with lower GNPs
[e.g., East Germany, Greece, Yugoslavia]. The United States is rather
anomalous in having both a high GNP and high calorie consumption.)

The most interesting finding here is that several of these correlations are
weaker than might have been expected. In addition to the two measures
mentioned above, six other indicators of social well-being have correlations
below .40 that are not statistically significant: the crude birth rate, the crude
death rate, hospital beds per person, postsecondary educational attainment,
nonmilitary public expenditures, and research and development expenditures.
In general, nevertheless, we can conclude that Gross National Product per
capita is associated in the expected direction with most measures of social well-
being in the highly industrialized societies.

Energy Consumption and Social Well-Being: Bivariate Relationships

Findings

We now turn to our primary concern with the relationships between energy consumption and various indicators of societal well-being. We first examine those relationships for all 30 highly industrialized nations, as reported in Table 6. It gives data for both energy consumption per capita and energy intensity, for 1980 (since there may be a time lag between energy use and some well-being factors) and for 1987.

The first thing to note about these findings is that—with one possible exception—there are no important differences between the 1980 and 1987 correlations for either energy measure. (The possible exception is for energy intensity with health care expenditures, which shifts from a positive to a negative correlation, but neither of those figures are large enough to be statistically significant.) For convenience, consequently, the following discussion deals only with the 1987 figures for both energy measures.

For per capita energy consumption in 1987, seven of the well-being indicators have statistically significant correlations of .52 or higher: health care expenditures, nonfood expenditures, educational expenditures, postsecondary education, third-level school enrollment, television ownership, and research and development expenditures. In addition, the four measures of urban residency, hospital beds per person, newspaper circulation, and automobile ownership have moderate correlations between .35 and .39 that do not quite attain statistical significance. In short, since 11 of these 20 measures had noteworthy relationships in 1987, we must conclude that there is still a considerable amount of coupling between energy consumption per capita and social well-being across all the highly industrialized nations. That coupling has been essentially broken with the demographic measures considered here, however, since all six of those relationships are extremely weak.

Intensity of energy use in 1987 shows an entirely different pattern of relationships. Five indicators of well-being have statistically significant—but inverse—correlations of .47 or higher with this energy measure: infant mortality, life expectancy, nonfood expenditures, telephone ownership, and automobile ownership.

The relationships for all the other indicators are relatively weak. The critical point, however, is that (with two minor exceptions) all of the well-being indicators—regardless of their strength—show an uncoupling from high energy intensity. Instead, as energy intensity decreases, virtually all indicators of social well-being improve. (The two exceptions are calorie consumption, which has a very small positive relationship, and R&D expenditures, which has no relationship.) In contrast, Buttel (1978, 1979) had discovered several direct correlations between high energy intensity and various social well-being

Table 6.   Correlations between Energy Use and Social Well-Being Indicators
among All 30 Highly Industrialized Nations

Social Well-Being Indicators	Energy Consumption Per Capita		Energy Intensity	
	1980	*1987*	*1980*	*1987*
Crude birth rate	.00	.05	.35	.30
Total fertility rate	−.24	−.18	.34	.32
Crude death rate	.13	.15	.27	.25
Infant mortality rate	−.22	−.17	.51*	.57*
Life expectancy	.14	.10	−.62*	−.63*
Suicide rate	−.04	−.08	.22	.19
Urban residents	.34	.35	−.26	−.32
Health care expenditures	.84*	.79*	.36	−.09
Hospital beds	.28	.35	−.26	−.32
Nonfood expenditures	.58*	.55*	−.59*	−.68
Calories consumed	.15	.16	.20	.21
Educational expenditures	.53*	.53*	−.02	−.15
Postsecondary education	.54*	.54*	−.01	−.11
Third-level enrollment	.64*	.59*	−.25	−.36
Telephone ownershi	.35	.30	−.55*	−.59*
Television ownership	.69*	.65*	−.07	−.21
Newspaper circulation	.33	.39	−.17	−.23
Automobile ownership	.45*	.39	−.44*	−.47*
Nonmilitary expenditures	−.05	−.03	−.30	−.23
R&D expenditures	.48*	.52*	.17	.00

Note: * Statistically significant at .05 one-tailed.

indicators in 1970. This discrepancy between the two studies may reflect the inclusion of the energy intensive but relatively poor socialist nations in the present research, although this is only an inference since separate analyses were not performed on socialist and capitalist nations.

Provisional Conclusions

Four provisional conclusions can be drawn from the findings in Table 6 in regard to all highly industrialized nations:

1. Energy consumption per capita is essentially unrelated to all of the standard demographic variables. This should not be surprising, since several of those measures have absolute limits (i.e., there will be births, and everyone eventually dies) that the industrial nations may now be approaching.

2. Energy consumption per capita is still closely coupled with many nondemographic indicators of social well-being in a positive direction.

3. High energy intensity is not positively associated with any indicators of social well-being. Instead, this measure of energy use appears to be inversely

related to a number of them, so that as the intensity of energy use decreases, social well-being improves. In other words, a coupling may still exist with this energy measure, but in the opposite direction from what the coupling thesis predicts.

4.   The overall relationship between energy use and social well-being appears to be influenced by two methodological factors: (a) whether energy use is measured as per capita consumption or as energy intensity; and (b) whether or not the socialist industrial nations are included in the analysis.

Let us now examine the relationships between energy use and social well-being within the two sets of energy-decreasing versus energy-increasing nations, as reported in Table 7. Three measures of energy use are given for each set: energy consumption per capita in 1987; percent change in energy consumption per capita between 1980 and 1987; and energy intensity in 1987.

Energy-Decreasing Nations

For energy consumption per capita, eight indicators of social well-being display relatively strong positive correlations of .51 or higher that are statistically significant: health care expenditures, calories consumed, educational expenditures, postsecondary education, enrollment in third-level schools, television ownership, automobile ownership, and R&D expenditures. Nonfood expenditures are nearly as strongly related, although the correlation is not quite significant. With all of these relationships, the higher the per capita energy consumption, the greater the social well-being. In other words, this measure of energy consumption is still tightly coupled with many measures of social well-being in these nations despite their declining energy consumption per capita since 1980. (None of the six demographic variables have very large correlations, however, and the birth rate rises with energy consumption.)

For percent energy change between 1980 and 1987, a positive correlation indicates a direct relationship with the amount of energy reduction in these countries. Only three of the well-being indicators have statistically significant relationships with this measure of declining energy use: infant mortality, life expectancy, and hospital beds. The first two of these demonstrate an uncoupling from energy use, however. Four other indicators—the crude death rate, urban residency, postsecondary education, and newspaper circulation— have moderately strong but not significant relationships, although all but the last of these represent an uncoupling from energy use. Thus only two well-being indicators show a coupling with this measure of energy use, while five show an uncoupling.

For energy intensity in 1987, eight of the social well-being indicators have relatively strong inverse correlations of .54 or higher that are statistically significant. In addition, three other indicators have moderate correlations of

Table 7. Correlations between Energy Use and Social Well-Being Indicators among Energy-Decreasing and Energy-Increasing Nations

Social Well-Being Indicators	Energy-Decreasing Nations			Energy-Increasing Nations		
	Energy Consumption Per Capita 1987	Percent Change Energy Consumption Per Capita 1980-87	Energy Intensity 1987	Energy Consumption Per Capita 1987	Percent Change Energy Consumption Per Capita 1980-87	Energy Intensity 1987
Crude birth rate	.34	-.04	.72*	.07	.46	.08
Total fertility rate	-.01	-.09	.72*	-.21	.43	.17
Crude death rate	-.32	-.48	-.08	.39	-.25	.57*
Infant mortality rate	-.12	-.52*	-.62*	.09	-.23	-.77*
Suicide rate	-.11	-.24	-.20	-.06	-.50	.57*
Urban residents	-.07	.45	-.46	-.52*	.01	-.33
Health expenditures	.85*	-.05	.49	.69*	-.52	-.51*
Hospital beds	-.02	-.59*	-.16	.71*	-.41	-.06
Nonfood expenditures	.48*	.29	-.84*	.57*	-.42	-.59*
Calories consumed	.56*	-.13	-.13	.05	.11	.48
Educational expenditures	.68*	.05	-.25	.47	.01	-.09
Postsecondary education	.85*	.41	-.12	.24	.36	-.13
Third-level enrollment	.72*	.29	-.34	.39	.19	-.53*
Telephone ownership	.41	.34	-.63*	.16	-.25	-.68*
Television ownership	.70*	.15	-.34	.60*	-.40	-.16
Newspaper circulation	.14	-.41	-.22	.61*	-.43	-.27
Automobile ownership	.51*	.37	-.64*	.25	-.12	-.49
Nonmilitary expenditures	-.30	-.08	-.54*	-.01	-.74*	-.18
R&D expenditures	.77*	.11	-.17	.39	-.22	.14

Note: * Statistically significant at .05 one-tailed.

220

.34 or higher that do not reach significance. The crucial point about all but one of these correlations—as we saw when we examined energy intensity across all 30 countries—is that they are not associated with high energy intensity. Instead, the lower the energy intensity, the better the social well-being on 10 of these well-being measures. The lone exception is infant mortality, which increases sharply with lower energy intensity.

Energy-Increasing Nations

For energy consumption per capita, six of the social well-being indicators have relatively strong positive correlations of .52 or higher that are statistically significant and represent couplings with this measure of energy use: urban residency, health care expenditures, hospital beds, nonfood expenditures, television ownership, and newspaper circulation. In addition, the correlations for four other indicators—the crude death rate, educational expenditures, third-level school enrollment, and R&D expenditures—are moderately strong between .39 and .47, although they are not quite significant. (The correlation for the death rate represents an uncoupling from energy consumption, however.) Thus nine well-being indicators show noteworthy couplings with per capita energy consumption in these countries that are still increasing their energy use—which is the same number of moderate to strong relationships observed among the energy-declining countries. (Six of those nine indicators are the same in both sets of nations.)

For percent of energy change between 1980 and 1987, a positive correlation for these countries indicates a direct relationship with increasing energy consumption. Only one indicator of well-being—nonmilitary public spending—is strongly and significantly correlated at $-.74$ with this energy use measure, and this represents an uncoupling from energy use. Nine other indicators have moderately strong relationships between .36 and .52, although they are not significant. However, all but two of those correlations—for the suicide rate and postsecondary education—represent an uncoupling from energy use; the greater the increase in energy use, the poorer the well-being on those other eight indicators.

Finally, energy intensity displays eight rather strong but inverse correlations of .51 or higher that are statistically significant, plus three others that are moderately strong between .33 and .48 which are not quite significant. Once again, all 11 of these relationships represent an apparent inverse coupling with this measure of energy use, so that lower energy intensity is associated greater social well-being.

Conclusions

At this point, we can reexamine the four provisional conclusions presented earlier to see if they are substantiated by these separate analyses of energy-decreasing and energy-increasing nations.

1.   The generalization that energy consumption has become almost entirely uncoupled from the six demographic indicators of well-being is substantiated. None of the relationships for these six indicators are significant with per capita energy consumption in either set of nations. And although the other two energy measures are strongly or moderately related to some demographic variables in both sets of nations, all of those relationships demonstrate an uncoupling from energy use.

2.   The generalization that energy consumption per capita is still fairly tightly coupled with many nondemographic indicators of social well-being is substantiated in both sets of countries. Among both energy-decreasing and energy-increasing nations, 9 of the 14 nondemographic indicators of social well-being have strong or moderate correlations with per capita energy consumption. It thus appears that amount of energy consumed per capita is closely coupled with many nondemographic indicators of social well-being in all industrial nations regardless of whether or not they have experienced an energy turnaround.

3.   The rate at which countries have been increasing or decreasing their energy consumption shows the opposite pattern, however. Most of the well-being indicators that are related to that energy change measure demonstrate an uncoupling from energy use. Among the energy-decreasing countries, the greater the decrease, the higher the well-being on several indicators. Among the energy-increasing countries, the slower the increase, the higher the well-being on several indicators.

4.   The generalization that high energy intensity is not directly related to any social well-being measures is true for both sets of nations. More critical, however, is the fact that almost all of those relationships show an apparent inverse coupling, so that the lower the intensity of energy use, the greater the social well-being among both sets of countries.

5.   The generalization that the results of these studies of linkages between energy use and social well-being appear to be influenced by the measures of energy use employed and the inclusion of socialist societies is further supported. Energy use per capita still tends to support the coupling thesis that societal well-being increases with higher energy use, whereas the other two energy measures generally negate that thesis. And with the socialist nations included in these analyses, energy intensity appears to have a noteworthy inverse relationship with social well-being.

Energy Consumption and Social Well-Being:
Multivariate Analyses

The final step in this analysis of the linkages between energy consumption and social well-being in industrial nations is to determine what happens to the bivariate correlations between both energy consumption per capita and energy intensity in 1987 and the various well-being indicators when Gross National Product per capita in 1987 is held constant. Are the direct couplings that were discovered for energy consumption per capita, as well as the inverse couplings that were discovered for energy intensity, all transmitted through the intervening variable of GNP as previous writers have often assumed? Or do either of those energy measures have direct effects on social well-being that are not mediated by GNP? These questions can be answered by regressing the well-being indicators on each of those two energy use measures, as well as GNP per capita.

These regression analyses were done on all 30 industrialized, but not on the separate sets of energy-decreasing and energy-increasing, countries. The reason for this was that partial beta coefficients become rather unstable—and hence not reliable—with small N's (especially with only ten cases, as in Set I). To compensate for that limitation, the regressions were rerun with a dummy variable representing the two sets of nations (1 = energy-decreasing and 0 = energy-increasing). The beta for that variable tells us whether or not the direction of recent energy changes significantly affects the linkages between energy use and social well-being.

Because none of the bivariate correlations with energy consumption per capita in 1987 were anywhere near significant for the six demographic variables, those relationships were not examined here. Two of the bivariate correlations with energy intensity—for infant mortality and life expectancy—were significant, however, in an inverse direction. Consequently, multiple regressions were conducted on those two demographic variables. The beta for infant mortality becomes nonsignificant under these conditions, but the beta for life expectancy remains barely significant at −.34 (still in an inverse direction). (The beta for GNP is significant in each of those equations, at −.52 and .48, respectively.)

Partial beta coefficients for each of the 14 nondemographic well-being indicators with each of the two energy use measures are given in Table 8, together with the betas for GNP in those regression equations. Because the statistical significance of the betas is a relevant concern in multiple regressions, even though the 30 nations are a population rather than a sample, only those betas that achieve significance (having an unstandardized B at least twice the size of its standard error) are reported in the table.

Energy Consumption Per Capita and GNP

In the A set of regressions involving energy consumption per capita, six of these nondemographic well-being indicators retain significant partial relationships when GNP per capita is held constant: health care expenditures, educational expenditures, postsecondary educational attainment, enrollment in third-level schools, television ownership, and research and development

Table 8. Multiple Regresions of Social Well-Being Indicators on Two
Different Energy Use Measures and Gross National Product
Per Capita in 1987 among all 30 Highly Industrialized Nations

Social Well-Being Indicators	Regression A Betas		Regression B Betas	
	Energy Consumption Per Capita	GNP Per Capita	Energy Intensity	GNP Per Capita
Urban residents	NS	NS	NS	NS
Health expenditures	.45	.56	.33	.98
Hospital beds	NS	NS	NS	.46
Nonfood expenditures	NS	.72	NS	.62
Calories consumed	NS	−.48	NS	NS
Educational expenditures	.41	NS	NS	.59
Postsecondary education	.52	NS	NS	NS
Third-level enrollment	.40	.40	NS	.59
Telephone ownership	NS	.92	NS	.77
Television ownership	.45	.41	NS	.80
Newspaper circulation	NS	.54	NS	.77
Automobile ownership	NS	.67	NS	.66
Nonmilitary expenditures	NS	NS	NS	NS
R&D expenditures	.45	NS	NS	.58

Note: NS = Not statistically significant.

expenditures. Only one indicator that had a significant zero-order correlation—nonfood expenditures—becomes nonsignificant under these controlled conditions.

Particularly interesting is the observation that all three of the educational indicators retain significant relationships with energy consumption, while for two of them (educational expenditures and postsecondary educational attainment) GNP is not significant. This suggests that energy consumption is more important than economic productivity in promoting education in industrial nations. In addition, R&D expenditures—which are often associated with higher education—are also significantly related to energy consumption but not to GNP. (With the other two significant indicators of health care expenditures and television ownership, GNP per capita also has a significant partial relationship.)

At the same time, GNP per capita has significant relationships with 5 of these 14 nondemographic indicators whose betas for energy consumption are not significant: nonfood expenditures, calorie consumption (in an inverse direction), telephone ownership, newspaper circulation, and automobile ownership. Thus both energy consumption and GNP per capita have several direct linkages with various well-being indicators.

Energy Intensity and GNP

In the *B* set of regressions involving energy intensity, only one of the well-being indicators—health care expenditures—displays a significant partial relationship with energy intensity under these controlled conditions. (And its beta with energy intensity is much lower than its beta with GNP per capita.) From this we can conclude that, in addition to the lack of relationships between high energy intensity and social well-being, the apparent inverse linkages between low energy intensity and well-being that were observed earlier were probably due to the effects of GNP on social well-being. In short, energy intensity presently has no direct effects on measures of social well-being in either direction.

Moreover, holding constant the effects of energy intensity raises, above their zero-order correlations, the strength of the betas for GNP with five well-being indicators: health care expenditures, hospital beds per person, educational expenditures, newspaper circulation, and R and D. This finding again indicates the importance of economic productivity for those forms of well-being, regardless of the level of energy intensity.

Dummy Variable Analyses

When a dummy variable for energy decreasing or increasing status was included in all of the above regressions, it had virtually no effects on any of the outcomes. In only one case did a previously nonsignificant beta for a well-being indicator become significant with this additional control; nonfood expenditures now has a beta of $-.35$, which is small and inverse in direction. No previously significant betas were markedly affected at all by the inclusion of this dummy variable. Moreover, only two of the betas for the dummy variable are significant: health care expenditures with per capita energy consumption (beta for dummy variable $= .25$), and newspaper circulation with energy intensity (beta for dummy variable $= -.32$). Because this dummy variable has virtually no effects on these regression equations, the results from this last series of regressions are not reported here.

Conclusions

From these regression analyses, we can draw three conclusions:

1. Energy consumption per capita has direct linkages with several measures of well-being in highly industrialized societies that are not totally mediated through the intervening factor of GNP per capita. This is especially noticeable in regard to education. Consequently, the commonly assumed linear-effects model of

$$\text{Energy use} \rightarrow \text{GNP} \rightarrow \text{Social well-being}$$

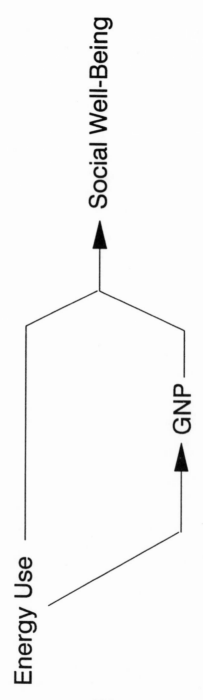

Figure 2. Compound Effects Model

must be supplemented with a compound-effects model of the kind shown in Figure 2.

2.   Many nondemographic indicators of social well-being are still closely coupled with energy consumption per capita even when GNP per capita is held constant.

3.   Energy intensity is unrelated to virtually all nondemographic well-being indicators when GNP per capita is held constant. The previously observed inverse relationships between energy intensity and many of these well-being indicators were spurious consequences of the intervening factor of Gross National Product (except in the one case of health care expenditures).

THEORETICAL AND POLICY IMPLICATIONS

Theoretical Implications

The results of this research suggest several theoretical implications for the energy and society coupling and uncoupling theses, and also for the underlying energetic theory of society.

Energy Consumption Per Capita

The principal empirical conclusion that emerges from this study is that the amount of energy consumed per capita among all of the highly industrialized nations is still rather tightly coupled with many (9 out of 14) nondemographic dimensions of social well-being. Moreover, these linkages are relatively independent of the intervening factor of Gross National Product per capita, especially in regard to higher education. In addition, these linkages occur among both energy-decreasing and energy-increasing nations.

Theoretically, these findings appear to substantiate the basic coupling thesis, but with a major modification. Whereas that thesis has usually been depicted as a simple linear process from energy consumption through GNP per capita to social well-being, we have discovered that it requires a somewhat more complex model that includes a number of direct effects from energy consumption per capita to social well-being that are not mediated through economic productivity. Nevertheless, with this measure of energy use the uncoupling thesis does not appear to be valid for many societal well-being measures.

A rather different picture emerges, however, when we use either of two alternative energy use measures.

Percentage Change in Energy Consumption

When the percentage change in energy consumption per capita between 1980 and 1987 is used as the energy measure, we find that: (1) Among the energy-decreasing nations, only two well-being measures are reduced with a declining rate of energy consumption, while five measures improve as energy consumption declines. (2) Among the energy-increasing nations, just two well-being measures improve with an increasing rate of energy consumption, while eight measures are reduced when that rate rises.

Theoretically, these findings appear to support the uncoupling thesis much more than the coupling thesis. How can the apparent contradiction between these two sets of findings be reconciled? The explanation lies in the difference between a static energy measure taken at one point in time (consumption per capita in 1987) and a dynamic energy measure (percentage change in per capita consumption between 1980 and 1987) taken through time.

At a given point in time (the present), the higher-energy-consuming countries—most notably the United States—score higher on many social well-being measures than do the lower-energy-consuming countries, which supports the coupling thesis. These relationships reflect several interrelated historical trends, especially the very strong associations that have existed in the past between energy consumption and GNP and between GNP and societal well-being in most industrial societies.

When we examine energy consumption changes through time, however, we are ignoring the absolute levels of energy use in all countries and are focusing instead on their recent relative shifts (either downward or upward) in per capita energy consumption. This focus thus enables us to put aside the historical coupling between energy consumption and social well-being, and ask whether the shifts that have occurred during the 1980s have had any effects of their own on well-being. Our findings, as we have seen, are that a declining rate of energy consumption tends to be associated with improvements in several well-being measures, while a continued increasing rate of energy consumption depresses several of those measures.

In short, the modified coupling thesis is still relatively valid across all industrial nations (and among both energy-decreasing and energy-increasing nations) at the present time because of long-established historical relationships, but the uncoupling thesis does apply to recent change trends among both sets of countries. In other words, energy consumption and societal well-being are still coupled, but are tending to become less so through time.

Energy Intensity

When the energy intensity rate in 1987 is used as the energy measure, a still different pattern emerges. Buttel's earlier (1978, 1979) finding of numerous direct relationships between energy intensity and many measures of well-being is no longer valid. Instead, energy intensity is now inversely related to many well-being measures, in both energy-decreasing and energy-increasing nations. Improvements in well-being now tend to be associated with lower rates of energy intensity. A similar inverse relationship occurs between energy intensity and GNP per capita. However, energy intensity has no direct effects on any well-being measures (with two minor exceptions); all of those inverse relationships appear to be transmitted through the intervening variable of GNP.

Theoretically, these findings tend to support the uncoupling thesis: high energy intensity is no longer associated with high levels of societal well-being. One might, however, make the opposite argument that energy intensity is now inversely linked with social well-being among all industrial countries, using the simple linear model with GNP as an intervening variable. Whether or not that theoretical argument is valid depends on how one interprets the role of GNP in the linear model. If GNP is seen as a necessary linkage between declining energy intensity and improvements in social well-being, then the argument may be valid—although perhaps rather trivial, since GNP is more immediately relevant than energy intensity in this process. On the other hand, if the observed inverse correlation between energy intensity and GNP is merely a spurious consequence of other causal factors, then only GNP need be included in the model and energy intensity is irrelevant. That matter cannot be resolved from the findings of this study, but in either case energy intensity has no direct inverse effects on social well-being and any indirect effects it may have are not terribly critical.

Industrial versus Developing Nations

Across all the highly industrialized nations, energy consumption per capita is still partially linked with social well-being—both directly and indirectly—because energy use is an integral part of the fundamental historical process of industrialization and economic development. However, economic productivity is slowly becoming less dependent on energy use in these nations, and many well-being measures are beginning to become uncoupled from per capita energy consumption. In addition, energy intensity no longer has positive effects on societal well-being.

These conclusions have theoretical implications for the distinction between industrial and developing nations that was mentioned at the beginning of the paper. The energy and societal development coupling thesis may very likely apply to most or all developing societies, as they attempt to industrialize. After societies reach a relatively high level of industrial development, however, the energy and society uncoupling thesis apparently begins to apply. They may then start to uncouple energy use from economic productivity and social well-being, and over time this uncoupling may in fact enhance their development. In the ten industrial nations that have reduced their energy consumption since 1980, this reduction is associated with improvements in several indicators of social well-being.

Energetic Theory of Society

If highly industrialized societies do manage to uncouple their economic productivity and social well-being from use of commercial energy, what implications would this have for the underlying energetic theory of society? Although that situation would certainly necessitate some modifications or elaborations of the basic theory, it would not negate it for two reasons.

First, this theory was formulated to explain the broad process of ecological-economic-social evolution across all societies through long periods of time. In particular, it was meant to explain the fundamental transformation from an agricultural to industrial type of society. As suggested above, increasing energy use undoubtedly remains crucial for that transformation, so that the energetic theory of society would still apply to the historical process of societal evolution.

Second, this theory is not limited to the use of commercial energy, as mentioned earlier. Richard Adams makes this point quite emphatically in his most recent (1988) book. He argues, in fact, that information is much more crucial than commercial energy in the overall process of social organization. Consequently, as the highly industrialized nations gradually shift their primary economic base from manufacturing to information processing, that form of energy flow will likely come to dominate their patterns of social organization. As that occurs, the broad energetic theory of society will continue to apply to them—perhaps to an even greater extent than when they were extremely dependent on the use of commercial energy. We thus need to expand and elaborate the basic energetic theory of society, not discard it.

Policy Implications

Economic Productivity

National economic and political policy makers have long assumed, almost as a matter of economic faith, that continued economic growth in the highly industrialized societies depended on constantly increasing the use of commercial energy. As that linkage has begun to loosen in recent years, some policy makers have started to ask if we might eventually totally uncouple economic productivity from energy use. However, it is generally assumed that this will not happen for some time, since there is still a moderately strong correlation (.49) between energy use and GNP per capita across all of the industrial nations. In addition, among the ten energy-decreasing nations, the greater the decline in energy use since 1980, the slower the rate of economic growth ($-.39$).

Total uncoupling of economic growth from energy consumption may become reality much sooner than expected by most policy makers, however. In the United States, the energy turnaround occurred in 1980, but since then the GNP has increased by an average of about 2.4% per year. Although this has not been spectacular economic growth, it nevertheless demonstrates that in this country economic productivity is no longer dependent on increasing energy use. And across all the industrial nations, the correlation between energy use and GNP declined from .82 in 1970 to .49 in 1987, which was a fairly rapid rate of uncoupling. Finally, the 20 industrial nations that have not yet undergone an energy turnaround have suffered economically since 1980, as indicated by the inverse correlation of $-.54$ between their rate of energy increase and the rate of GNP growth.

The rather obvious policy implication of these trends is that postindustrial societies can undoubtedly develop highly productive economies that require much less energy than consumed by economies based on manufacturing. As an example, consider Switzerland, which has the world's highest per capita GNP ($21,300 in 1987) but a rather low rate of energy use per capita, which gives it the world's lowest energy intensity rate. Moreover, postindustrial societies may likely discover that economic growth in the future will depend on reducing rather than increasing their energy use, as commercial energy becomes increasingly more scarce and hence expensive.

Social Well-Being

The extent to which various forms of social well-being can and should be unlinked from energy use is a more complicated matter. In the first place, this clearly depends on which dimensions of well-being one is considering. All six of the demographic measures examined in this study have become entirely uncoupled from energy consumption in the industrial nations. Moreover, among the energy-decreasing countries, the infant mortality rate tends to decline and life expectancy to increase with a decline in energy use and lower energy intensity of the economy. Among the energy-increasing countries, meanwhile, infant mortality rises and life expectancy declines with an increase in energy use. Quite clearly, therefore, future improvements in these demographic dimensions of societal well-being will not depend on increased energy use, and may in fact by adversely affected by it.

The 14 nondemographic measures of social well-being examined in this study present a somewhat more ambiguous picture. Many of them are still moderately linked with level of energy consumption per capita, regardless of whether or not societies have undergone an energy turnaround. However, as we have seen, the rate at which energy use is being reduced in the energy-decreasing nations is associated with improvements on several of those measures. And the rate of increase in energy use in the energy-increasing nations is associated with reductions on several well-being measures. Moreover, declining energy intensity is associated with improvements on many of these measures in both sets of countries. Finally, a great many indicators of well-being have risen in the United States since it experienced an energy turnaround in 1980.

These findings suggest that in the future it may very likely be possible for all industrial nations to uncouple most dimensions of social well-being from energy use. Policy decisions about future energy use will of course involve many considerations besides the consequences of energy consumption for social well-being. At the very least, however, it appears that a national policy decision to reduce energy use can be made without the concern that it will harm most dimensions of societal well-being. In the long run, moreover, it may likely turn out that decreasing use of commercial energy will have beneficial consequences for many forms of well-being.

One final question remains to be addressed. This study discovered that energy consumption per capita has direct linkages with six measures of social-well being that are partially independent of the intervening factor of GNP per capita. These are health care expenditures, educational expenditures, postsecondary educational attainment, third-level educational enrollments, television ownership, and R&D expenditures. While those statistical associations are real, we cannot tell from this study whether or not they are necessary. Is the rate of energy consumption really affecting them directly, or are other causal or intervening factors involved in this process? The answer to that question will require further research, and will have important implications for future national energy use policies in the industrial nations.

ACKNOWLEDGMENTS

An earlier version of this paper was presented at the 1990 World Congress of Sociology. I am deeply indebted to Fayyaz Hussain for performing all of the data analyses for this study. And I want to thank Lee Freese and Eugene Rosa most sincerely for their numerous very helpful comments on the earlier version of the paper. Their suggestions assisted me in improving the paper immensely.

NOTES

1. These data were all taken from the U.S. Bureau of the Census' *Statistical Abstract of the United States, 1987*, Tables 926 and 928.

2. These data were all taken from the U.S. Bureau of the Census' *Statistical Abstract of the United States, 1987*, Tables 32, 83, 87, 106, 115, 125, 135, 158, 175, 200, 210, 211, 565, 620, 689, 712, 720, 721, 722, 735, 902, 914, 926, 928, 970, 1011, and 1044.

3. These energy data were taken primarily from the United Nation's *Energy Statistics Yearbook* for 1980 and 1987, but some came from the U.S. Bureau of the Census's *Statistical Abstract of the United States 1989*, and the Population Reference Bureau's "World Population Data Sheet" for 1982 and 1989.

4. Data for the first four of these economic productivity measures were taken from *The World Bank Atlas 1989*. Data for the last measure were taken from the U.S. Bureau of the Census' *Statistical Abstract of the United States 1989*. Gross National Product figures for other nations are not an ideal measure of economic productivity, since they are based on official exchange rates with the U.S. dollar, and do not take into account the purchasing power of local currencies in their own countries. A more precise measure is Purchasing Power Parities (PPP), which are based on the purchasing power of local currencies. PPP figures are now available for the OECD countries, but not for other industrial countries, and hence could not be used in this study.

5. Data for these social well-being measures were taken from a variety of sources, often involving two or more sources for each variable. Those sources were Mueller 1988; the Population Reference Bureau's "World Population Data Sheet" for 1982 1987, and 1989; the U.S. Bureau of the Census' *Statistical Abstract of the United States 1989*; the United Nations' *National Accounts Statistics*; UNESCO's *Statistical Yearbook 1989*; and *The World Bank Atlas 1989*.

REFERENCES

Adams, R.N. 1975. *Energy and Structure: A Theory of Social Power*. Austin: University of Texas Press.
_____. 1988. *The Eighth Day: Social Evolution as the Self-Organization of Energy*. Austin: University of Texas Press.
Allen, E. 1979. *Energy and Econmic Growth in the United States*. Cambridge, MA: MIT Press.
Buttel, F. H. 1978. "Social Structure and Energy Efficiency: A Preliminary Cross-National Analysis." *Human Ecology* 6:145-164.
_____. 1979. "Social Welfare and Energy Intensity: A Comparative Analysis of Developed Market Economies." Pp. 297-327 in *Sociopolitical Effects of Energy Use and Policy*, edited by Charles T. Unseld et al. Washington, DC: National Academy of Sciences.
Cottrell, F. 1955. *Energy and Society*. New York: McGraw-Hill.
Darmstadter, J., J. Dunkerly, and J. Alterman. 1977. *How Industrial Societies Use Energy: A Comparative Analysis*. Baltimore: The Johns Hopkins University Press.
Duncan, O. D., and L.F. Schnore. 1959. "Cultural, Behavioral, and Ecological Perspectives in the Study of Social Organization." *American Journal of Sociology* 65:132-146.
Georgescu-Roegen, N. 1971. *The Entropy Law and the Economic Process*. Cambridge, MA: Harvard University Press.
_____. 1976. *Energy and Economic Myths*. New York: Pergamon.
Hawley, A. 1986. *Human Ecology: A Theoretical Essay*. Chicago: University of Chicago Press.
International Energy Agency. 1979. The International Energy Association. Paris: IEA.
Isaac, L. 1982. "Comparative Economic Inequality." Pp. 62-85 in *Comparative Sociological Research in the 1960s and 1970s*, edited by J. M. Armer and R. M. Marsh. Leiden: E. J. Brill.
Jackman, R. W. 1975. *Political and Social Equality: A Comparative Analysis*. New York: Wiley.
Liu, B.-C., and C.F. Anderson. 1979. "Income, Energy Requirements, and the Quality of Life Indicators: An International Comparison 1975." Report by the Midwest Research Institute, Boulder, CO.
Makhijani, A. B., and A. J. Lichtenbert. 1972. "Energy and Well-Being." *Environment* 14:10-18.
Mazur, A., and E. Rosa. 1974. "Energy and Lifestyle: A Cross-National Comparison of Energy Consumption and Quality of Life Indicators." *Science* 186:607-610.
Mueller, G. P. 1988. *Comparative World Data: A Statistical Handbook for Social Science*. Baltimore: The Johns Hopkins University Press.

Nader, L., and S. Beckerman. 1978. "Energy as It Relates to the Quality and Style of Life." *Annual Review of Energy* 3:1-28.

Odum, H. T. 1971. *Environment, Power, and Society.* New York: Wiley.

Odum, H.T., and E. C. Odum. 1976. *Energy Basis for Man and Nature.* New York: McGraw-Hill.

Olsen, M. E. 1982. "Linkages Between Socioeconomic Modernization and National Political Development." *Journal of Political and Military Sociology* 10:41-69.

————. 1991. *Societal Dynamics: Exploring Macrosociology.* Englewood Cliffs, NJ: Prentice-Hall.

Olsen, M. E., and C. Harris. n.d. "Energy and Society." Forthcoming in *Handbook of Environmental Sociology,* edited by R.E. Dunlap and W. Michelson.

Population Reference Bureau, Inc. 1982 1987, and 1989. "World Population Data Sheet." Washington, DC: Population Reference Bureau.

Rosa, E., and K. M. Keating. 1988. "Energy and Society." *Annual Review of Sociology* 14:149-72.

Rosa, E., K.H. Keating, and C. Staples. 1981. "Energy, Economic Growth, and Quality of Life: A Cross-National Trend Analysis." Pp. 258-64 in *Proceedings of the International Congress of Applied Systems Research on Cybernetics.* New York: Pergamon Press.

Rosa, E., and G. E. Machlis. 1983. "Energetic Theories of Society: An Evaluative Review." *Sociological Inquiry* 53:152-78.

Rosa, E., G.E. Machlis, and K.H. Keating. 1988. "Energy." *Annual Review of Energy* 14:149-72.

Rosa, E., A.E. Radzik, and K. M. Keating. 1980. "Energy, Economic Growth, and Societal Well-Being: A Cross-Sectional Trend Analysis." Paper presented at the annual meeting of the American Sociological Association.

Schipper, L., and A. J. Lichtenberg. 1976. "Efficient Energy Use and Well-Being: The Swedish Example." *Science* 194:100-13.

Schurr, S.H., and B. C. Netscheret. 1960. *Energy in the American Economy 1850-1975.* Baltimore: The Johns Hopkins University Press.

Simon, J. 1981. *The Ultimate Resource.* Princeton: Princeton University Press.

United Nations. 1980 and 1987. *Energy Statistics Yearbook.* New York: United Nations.

————. 1985. *National Accounts Statistics: Analysis of Main Aggregates.* New York: United Nations.

UNESCO. 1988. *Statistical Yearbook.* Paris: United Nations Educational, Scientific, and Cultural Organization.

U.S. Bureau of the Census. 1989. *Statistical Abstract of the United States.* Washington, DC: U.S. Government Printing Office.

White, L. 1949. *The Science of Culture.* New York: Fairer, Straus, and Girioux.

World Bank. 1989. *The World Bank Atlas.* Washington, DC: The World Bank.

Research in the Sociology of Organizations

Edited by **Samuel B. Bacharach,** *New York State School of Industrial and Labor Relations, Cornell University*

Associate Editors: **Richard Magjuka,** *University of Indiana,* **Pamala Tolbert,** *Cornell University* and **David Torres,** *University of Arizona*

Volume 9, I991, 358 pp. $63.50
ISBN 1-55938-398-4

CONTENTS: Toward a Theoretical Distinction Between the Stress Components of the Job Insecurity and Job Loss Experiences, *Dan Jacobson, Tel-Aviv University.* **Information Technology and the Redefinition of Organizational Roles,** *Debra C. Gash, Cornell University.* **Organizations as Parties in a System: A Concept and Its Practical Relevance,** *William F.G. Mastenbroek, Holland Consulting Group in Amsterdam.* **The Determinants of Organizational Harm,** *Michael Masuch, University of Amsterdam.* **Cooperation or Competition? Disbanding Rates in a Population of Marketing Cooperatives,** *Udo Staber, Cornell University and Barry Boothman, University of New Brunswick, Canada.* **Whistle-Blowing as an Organizational Process,** *Marcia P. Miceli, Ohio State University, Columbus and Janet P. Near, Indiana University, Bloomington.* **OD Applications in Developmental Settings: Four Perspectives on Action Research in an Important Locus,** *Robert T. Golembiewski, University of Georgia.* **Reinventing Innovation,** *Peter Bamberger, Bar Ilan University.* **Organizations and Types of Occupational Communities: Grid-Group Analysis in the Linkage of Organizational and Occupational Thory,** *William J. Sonnenstuhl and Harrison M. Trice, Cornell University.* **Strategic Decision Making: An Integrative Explanation,** *Michael I. Harrison and Bruce Phillips, Bar Ilan University.* **Biographical Sketches of the Contributors.**

Also Available:
Volumes 1-8 (I982-I991) $63.50 each

JAI PRESS INC.
55 Old Post Road - No. 2
P.O. Box 1678
Greenwich, Connecticut 06836-1678
Tel: 203-661-7602

Advances in Group Processes

Edited by **Edward J. Lawler, Barry Markovsky, Cecilia Ridgeway, and Henry A. Walker** *The University of Iowa*

Volume 8, 1991, 257 pp. $63.50
ISBN 1-55938-382-8

Also Available:
Volumes 1-7 (I984-I990) $63.50 each

JAI PRESS INC.
55 Old Post Road - No. 2
P.O. Box 1678
Greenwich, Connecticut 06836-1678
Tel: 203-661-7602